*To Rosie, Elinor,
Miranda and Catriona, my daughters.*

*I hope you will always live as Leonora did:
on your own terms.*

THE SURREAL LIFE OF

CARRINGTON

BRYN BARNARD

THE SURREAL LIFE OF

Leonora

CARRINGTON

Joanna Moorhead

virago

VIRAGO

First published in Great Britain in 2017 by Virago Press

1 3 5 7 9 10 8 6 4 2

A CIP catalogue record for this book
is available from the British Library.

ISBN 978-0-349-00877-6

Typeset in Bembo by M Rules
Printed and bound in Great Britain by
Clays Ltd, St Ives plc

Papers used by Virago are from well-managed forests
and other responsible sources.

Virago Press
— An imprint of
Little, Brown Book Group
Carmelite House
50 Victoria Embankment
London EC4Y 0DZ

An Hachette UK Company
www.hachette.co.uk

www.virago.co.uk

Contents

Prologue

Her name was Prim, and she left our family on an autumn day in 1937 when she was only twenty years old.

She had been an impossible creature: a wild child, an unfathomable puzzle of a girl; a young woman who refused to be tamed and who eventually, when she had wreaked more havoc than any family could reasonably be expected to bear, had simply flounced off into the sunset.

Prim's story was never much expanded on in my hearing; neither my Great Aunt Maurie, who was her mother, or my grandmother Miriam, who was her aunt, ever told it to me. Nor did her brother Gerard, who was my father's best friend as well as his cousin. But there were occasional snatches: a hushed phone call where the word 'Mexico' was just audible; a whispered conversation on the sofa after Sunday lunch between Maurie and Miriam. There were guffaws occasionally from Gerard and my father: 'And then she painted a creature with three breasts!'

She had run off, my grandmother told me, with an artist,

1

to become his model. She had been a girl with everything: the golden creature of a family that was affluent, advantaged and close-knit. And she gave it all up for – what? A shady half-life with a crowd of degenerates, first in Europe and then in Mexico.

No-one sitting round the table during those long Sunday lunches in the 1970s in Lancashire believed any of us would see Prim again. Maurie, who was by then in her eighties, had not seen her daughter for many years; Gerard had barely seen her since she left in 1937, and my father, who had been five at the time of her disappearance, had only met her a handful of times. In my generation, hardly anyone had ever had contact with her.

It was a random meeting that changed all that; although for a Surrealist like Prim, as I later discovered, nothing in the world is ever truly random. She believed that events that seem to be chance are actually preordained by the subconscious; the people and objects we encounter are embodiments of our inner desires, waiting to be discovered. The secret lies in daring to grasp opportunities, however they present themselves. So had I always wanted to meet her, somewhere inside? Looking back, I think I had.

Despite having heard about her vaguely in my teens, I had all but forgotten her: until a day in the spring of 2006. I was standing in a neighbour's garden at a drinks party: most of the guests were my friends, but then I found myself talking to someone new – a dark-haired woman in her fifties whose hair was pulled back in a ponytail from her carefully made-up, handsome face. I told her I lived round the corner and had children at the same school as our hosts. She told me that she lived in Mexico and was an art historian.

As we sipped our wine I scraped together a few questions about the only Mexican artist I knew anything about – Frida Kahlo; in turn, the woman asked some polite questions about my children and my work as a journalist. And then, just as I was about to turn away to talk to someone else, I suddenly remembered Prim.

'I'm sure you won't know anything about her,' I said, 'but I wonder whether by any remote chance you might have heard of my father's cousin? She ran away – I don't know the whole story – and she was connected with art and artists. I think eventually she went to live in Mexico. She might even be dead by now, it was all a long time ago. Her name was . . . '

Here I faltered. I knew her surname well enough: but on the rare occasions when she was mentioned, it was always using her family nickname. What was her actual name?

'Leonora,' I said at last. 'That's what she was called. Leonora Carrington.'

The art historian opened her eyes wide and stared at me. 'Leonora?' she said. 'Leonora Carrington?' And for the first time I heard Prim's surname pronounced not in the flat Lancashire way I was used to hearing it, but with a new enunciation that was somehow exciting, exotic and entirely different, with the 'r's rolled out richly and the final syllable heavily emphasised.

'Are you telling me,' the art historian was saying, 'that Leonora Carrington is a member of your family, and you don't know who she is? For heaven's sake . . . She's probably the most famous artist alive in Mexico today. Her paint-ings are extraordinary. Of course we Mexicans know she was originally from England; but she's been in our country for so long we consider her to be one of us now. She's a national treasure.'

The fizzle of amazement around her now transferred itself to me. Back home I Googled her name, and found photographs of a beautiful woman whose paintings drew me into a strange, Hieronymus Bosch-style world filled with horse-like creatures who floated, danced and curled their way across alien landscapes. There were birds too, plenty of them: elegant, long-necked geese, ducks and swallows captured on the canvases mid-flight, so they swooped dramatically into the paintings and then took off just as energetically out of them again. Some of her pictures depicted unfamiliar and sinister-looking worlds: one showed a country with a red sky and amber hills across which traipsed a procession of people wearing white robes. More figures, wearing black, huddled around a huge eunuch-like creature, while an outsize turquoise snake unfurled itself dramatically in mid-air. There seemed to be various elements competing to be the centre of the action in that painting: a globe, a God-like effigy and a cathedral all nestled beneath a rainbow. And the story, whatever it was, didn't end there because across the bottom of the canvas Prim had painted an underworld in which more people (dead, presumably) seemed to have been trans-formed into animals with pointy black heads. They were crawling, or trying to crawl; and their efforts were being watched, ominously, by a sharp-toothed, one-eyed tiger.

I hadn't the faintest idea what any of it was about or what it meant. But then I clicked again and pictures with more familiar elements appeared on the screen. They seemed to connect with the world Prim had left, the world I knew. One, *Green Tea*, showed a beautifully tended garden with an avenue of shaped fir trees leading to a fountain: it could have been Lancashire on a sunny day, in the middle of the rolling English countryside.

As well as a painter, it seemed Prim was a writer too. There was a novel, and several collections of short stories. And there seemed to be photographs of sculptures too, and even tapestries she had designed, as well as stage sets she had created. Prim seemed to have a prolific output, and across many fronts. Our family's black sheep was starting to seem like its secret Renaissance woman; why had I not heard anything about her art until now?

The following morning I phoned my father with questions about Prim. He was vague; the only time he remembered meeting her was at her mother's funeral in 1978. 'We all had to wait until she arrived by ship, because she refuses to fly anywhere,' said my father. After the funeral there had been a big row between her and her three brothers. 'She ended up walking out of the wake and her parting shot was that she was never going to set foot on the same continent as any of them again.'

The family story was that Prim was so-called because a friend of her father's, visiting her in her nursery when she was a small child, had watched her playing carefully with her toys and remarked: 'She looks a bit prim.' Perhaps it was the inherent irony of that observation that made her parents latch on to it as her nickname; perhaps they already knew that nothing she would ever do would be demure, or proper, or prudish.

My father seemed surprised, though, when he heard what the art historian had said. His cousin, Prim's brother Gerard, had spoken about her, but he had never given my father the impression her work was much good. 'She was sent to the best schools and then to finishing schools abroad, and I think she was expelled from every one of them,' said my father. After that she had been a debutante and was presented at court: her parents had thrown a ball for her at the Ritz. The scandal, and elopement, came not long after. 'She disappeared off to Europe,' said my father. 'Got into all sorts of trouble there, and was a huge worry to everyone.'

The only person who had had any recent contact with Prim was her nephew Rupert who had called in to see her a few years earlier while travelling through Mexico. I phoned him. 'I wouldn't exactly describe her as friendly,' he said. 'I got the impression she felt she'd gone a long way to leave us behind and didn't relish that someone had caught up with her.'

Five months later I was looking out of a plane window at a vast network of streets lined with colourful houses in different shades of yellow, red and blue. This was Mexico City, and in my pocket was a piece of paper on which was written a phone number. I had made contact with the gallery that sold Prim's work, and a message had come back that if I was visiting Mexico City she would try to make time to meet me. As the plane bumped down on to the runway I was nervous: what if she wouldn't see me after all? What if Rupert was right, and I'd come all this way only to be turned back at her door?

The taxi lurched through noisy, fume-filled, crowded streets; horns blared, street vendors shouted, neon lights flashed in every direction. At some points on the journey we were on a double-decker highway with the noisy sounds of the brakes and beeping of the unseen cars and trucks beneath us. On the pavements, children in shorts and T-shirts were selling bracelets, pots and toys on table-cloths laid out on the ground; behind them, women in grubby aprons were cooking on griddles in kitchens that opened on to the street.

As we neared the centre of town the low-rise buildings of the suburbs gave way to grander structures, and the three-lane highway became tree-lined and more reminiscent of a European city. At the lights children darted perilously into the traffic to clean windscreens and to try to sell tiny packets of sweets through car windows. We swung through a vast square – the Zócalo, explained my driver, the heart of the ancient Aztec settlement of Tenochtitlan. An enormous red, white and green flag was draped across the front of one huge building, while outside the railings of the cathedral men wearing sand-coloured uniforms stood playing accordions and held out their hats for coins. The noise of their instruments, and of other music, filled the air. There were men in black trousers and white shirts playing guitars – the mariachi – and women in brightly coloured headscarves standing behind stalls piled with even more brightly coloured fruit: watermelons, papaya, pineapples and mangoes.

My hotel was cheap but clean, and the receptionists were polite and helpful. They pointed along the main road in the direction of the street I needed, where Prim's house was. And then, because the gallery had suggested I should call her after 10am the following morning, there was nothing to do but sit in the bar and try my first tequila, served with a separate shot of freshly squeezed tomato juice. Outside the window, market stall-holders were shutting up for the day in the warm evening sunshine. I sipped my drink to the tinny music blaring out from the loudspeakers, and the sounds of Spanish voices in the air; and I wondered again how Prim had ended up in a place that was five thousand miles and light years away from the Lancashire in which we had both grown up.

The next morning I paced my bedroom floor until a minute after 10am, and then dialled her number. After just one ring the phone was answered.

'Hello,' said a deep voice; it might have belonged to a man, but it was unmistakably English, and I knew it was Prim.

'It's your cousin from England,' I said. 'I'm here in Mexico City.'

'Well. It's nice to hear from you. I've been waiting for you to call.'

There was a pause. 'So when do I see you?' she said.

A few minutes later I was walking quickly and nervously along the *avenida*, another wide, leafy road: and although it wasn't as busy as the huge highways the taxi had taken the previous day, it was certainly lively, and music seemed to be spilling out of every doorway. Along the middle of the street was a central reservation that was in effect a long square with benches, statues, fountains and market stalls. Many of the cars speeding past were green and white Volkswagen Beetles, which I now knew were taxis: they ducked and wove their way through the traffic, as likely to undertake as overtake. I hurried past street stalls selling fruit and tortillas, and in the spring-like sun people were breakfasting at pavement cafés.

Colonia Roma had clearly been a smart neighbourhood once; ornate mansions laced with shuttered French windows and intricate little balconies faced on to the street. There were grand front doors and locked gates, behind which I glimpsed courtyards with fountains, open-air staircases and wrought-iron balustrades. But today the paintwork on many of the mansions was peeling, and several were boarded up and sprayed with graffiti.

Prim's street was much quieter than the main thoroughfare. On the corner two women in grubby overalls were cooking meat and vegetables for tortillas, and a boy sitting on a red plastic chair outside a tiny tabac was selling cigarettes, sweets and Mexico's newspapers, *La Jornada* and *El Universal*. Outside my cousin's house were two large trees so abundantly in leaf that they almost obscured the windows of the upper floors. There were no windows on the ground floor, just garage doors and a heavy wooden front door. I took a deep breath and pressed the doorbell. A loud ringing echoed around the hall within.

For a few seconds nothing happened. Then came the

sound of footsteps, and a voice called out: '*Quien es? Que quieres?*' (Who's there? What do you want?). Almost immediately I could hear another voice, quieter, saying something else; and then the door swung open and a plump woman in a white overall stood looking out at me. Behind her was cave-like darkness from which a tiny figure was emerging. As she neared the light I saw she was dressed almost entirely in black. Black trousers, a dark grey jumper, black cardigan. Across her chest was the strap of a small handbag which, I would shortly discover, held her most important possessions: her packet of Marlboro Lights and her plastic cigarette lighter. Grey hair was pulled back from her forehead, and she had round, piercing eyes just like my father's; and though her face was lined with many years of life, it was still handsome. When she reached the door she smiled, and her whole face lit up, so that for a few seconds she was genuinely beautiful. 'Well,' she said, looking me over. 'It's good to meet you.'

'Prim?'

The smile disappeared. 'It's not Prim,' she said, and her voice was a tiny bit sharper. 'I left Prim behind a long time ago. It's Leonora now.' Her tone softened. 'Well, come in. Let's go into the kitchen. Would you like tea?'

She turned back into the corridor, and I followed her across the threshold into a different country, Leonora's country, a surreal country I so nearly never knew existed if it hadn't been for her. The housekeeper shut the door behind us, resealing the border. I was about to discover that in Leonora's world it was always twilight on a cold, quiet winter's day. At the end of the shadowy, flagstoned passageway I could make out a staircase; off to the right was a room with a low, beamed ceiling and a huge, disused range. Sculptures reared up out of gloom: a tall figure peering out of a long face; a small woman, forearms pressed together, hands open. Cupped, hopeful.

Through another door was what I would come to know as the inner sanctum, Leonora's kitchen, tabernacle-like at the centre of her fortified island. It seemed the coldest, darkest place yet: a smallish, square room with a window that faced not outside, but on to a narrow, high-walled courtyard dominated by a huge tree whose canopy of leaves prevented even the tiniest glimmer of light from sneaking through.

Here I remained ensconced with Leonora for the next five days, drinking sometimes tea and sometimes tequila, listening to an unfolding story that brought together magic and madness, love and disappointment, bravery and single-mindedness.

She was a mesmerising character, and she had me hooked from that first morning. I was dazzled, just as Max Ernst and the Surrealists had been back in the 1930s, captivated by a presence that was immediate, and yet somehow just out of reach. The ghosts of her past seemed to swirl around us in that kitchen; she was a tantalising link to the greatest moment of twentieth-century art – a world centred in the cafés and boulevards of pre-war Paris, peopled by characters such as Pablo Picasso and Marcel Duchamp, Salvador Dalí and Man Ray, Joan Miró and Francis Picabia, and of course, her lover, Max Ernst. Leonora had been at the centre of that world: this was where she had bolted to from

Lancashire. Her art had been formed there, in that artistic whirlwind, and now she was the only one left. She had been a young woman barely into her twenties then, on the cusp of her career; they had been men in their forties and fifties, in their prime. Most had gone on to be household names, while she had ended up (outside of Mexico anyway) as not much more than a footnote in art history. And yet here she was, seven decades on, still producing art and still championing Surrealism: the focus of the art world had shifted, but Leonora had simply carried on regardless.

She set great store by her appearance, even now aged eighty-nine. Her usual outfit was trousers and a sweater, and her usual colour was black, although occasionally she wore a cardigan or jumper of grey or cream. Her hair, still long, also grey, tended to be piled up on her head, and with her favourite drop pearl earrings in, there was an air about her of the Edwardian lady her mother had been. Her voice, clear and with clearly-enunciated vowels, was strongly and unmistakably English, with a hint still of her upper-class roots and no trace whatsoever of any influence of the language of the country she had inhabited for the last seventy years. When she spoke Spanish to Yolanda, the housekeeper, she seemed to almost delight in pronouncing her words in as English a way as possible. The only undertones were of a Lancashire accent, and she had a matter-of-fact manner.

Leonora had clearly never sought, or needed, fame or attention. She was the complete antithesis of artists who fawn to the world of gallerists and collectors, academics and journalists; she had ignored the existence of all of them, shut herself away in this cold, dark house in Mexico, and painted. She had never been a people-pleaser; she had no time for it, and it seemed to her to detract from the important business of life, which was being true to her curiosity about ideas and art.

By the time I knew her, Leonora was in her late eighties, and she was living an isolated and lonely life. On my first visit her husband Chiki was still alive: he was in his nineties and infirm. He inhabited two rooms on the first floor, and Leonora did not spend much time with him. They had not had a difficult marriage, but Leonora had always kept her independence within it: there had been years when she lived apart from him in the US, and there had been other lovers. They felt like a couple whose relationship had run out on them, rather than a couple who should never have been together. The centre of Leonora's life in Mexico was her boys, Gabriel and Pablo; in the time I knew her, the most important events in her life were her weekly lunch with Gabriel, a professor of comparative literature at the University, and her frequent phone calls to Pablo, a pathologist in Richmond, Virginia. Her house, now dark and quiet, had known a noisier and brighter past: it had been the home where the boys were raised, and it had been the epicentre of the group of European artists of which Leonora was the driving force.

There was no softness round the edges with Leonora: she had taken a hard path, suffered a great deal as a result, and she wore her toughness like a badge of honour she had earned from herself. It was far more of an honour than the certificate Blu-Tacked to her cupboard door, the honour the Mexican government had given her; it was certainly more of an honour than the OBE she had belatedly been awarded by the British, receiving it from Prince Charles on a visit he made to Mexico in 2000. She was bemused by these late accolades, but never impressed by them. Early on in her life she had decided there was only one thing she could ever rely on, and that was the steeliness in her heart: external events, the trappings of wealth and success, the opinions of others: all these were swept away, dismissed, ignored. She was as unconcerned by the approval of others as of their disapproval: she had learned to survive by burrowing herself ever deeper into a cocoon.

Most people who met Leonora now never got behind the brittleness, never were allowed beneath the hard shell that had so long been her armour against the world. She was an enigma, made more potent by the legends and fables that surrounded her. Those who did come close found her as I did: shield raised in defence, wary, circumspect.

But of course there was also vulnerability; she might have turned her back on our family seventy years before, but I could see that our shared heritage provided us with the sort of connection she hadn't had for decades. Perhaps this was a last chance: I was a link to a part of herself she had gone a long way to hide, and had worked hard to keep hidden; and yet it had always been a key to who she was.

'I'd like to come back,' I said, as we stood five days later in the dark hallway, with the taxi waiting outside in the sunshine to take me to the airport. 'I have no idea how, but I'll find a way.'

Because, I now realised, I'd been kidding myself. I

hadn't come to Mexico because I was a journalist, I'd come because I was her cousin. I was here because Prim – now Leonora – fascinated me. I also wanted to make amends for the schism that had separated her from our family; but more importantly, I simply wanted to spend time with her. I liked being with her. I thought she had enjoyed it too.

'Well,' she said. 'Come back when you can. I'll be here waiting for you.'

Had she been waiting, all these years, for someone from our family to come to find her? Was it possible that what Leonora had most wanted all her life was simply to impress us? One of the ironies of her story was that she had gone so far to get away from us, and then spent most of her time in Mexico exploring and explaining her childhood and adolescence in her art. Families are the hardest people to impress. You can create a myth with others, and it might work or it might not; but you can never create a myth with your relatives. And in our family, Leonora's reputation had nothing to do with her artistic prowess. She was a neglectful daughter, a selfish sister, an absent aunt. Nothing more.

But the Leonora I found became the best cousin I ever had. She welcomed me into her home and into her heart; she shared her story with me as fully and as honestly as she could. In the end I went to see her many times: between 2006 and 2011 (when she died), I visited twice each year. Sometimes I stayed a fortnight or three weeks, sometimes I stayed a month, and I spent every day with her. It never felt like a chore, and she never felt like an elderly relative; even in her nineties, she had the fire of youthful rebellion that had driven her away from us all those years before.

Leonora was indeed, as the art historian at the dinner party had said, one of the best-known artists in the country, and if we ate out in a restaurant there would always be approaches from fans and autograph-seekers. But she had been puzzling even herself and certainly others all her life. She told me about a day at her convent boarding school when she had come down to breakfast wearing mismatching shoes. 'There you are again, Leonora Carrington,' said one of the nuns. 'Always desperate to be different.' But the nun was wrong; Leonora had not worn the wrong shoes deliberately, and she was not desperate to be different. She simply *was* different, and she wasn't prepared to make the compromises most people do to fit in.

The key to Leonora was that she was a rebel, and a rebel to the very core of her being. By the time I met her, art history had already recorded her most spectacular and romantic act of rebellion, which was when she ran away with Max Ernst to join the Paris Surrealists; but that was only one square of the patchwork quilt that made up a lifetime of rebellions. To question what was expected of her was Leonora's raison d'être; everything was worthy of challenge and investigation. In childhood she rebelled against the strictures of being the only girl in a nursery full of brothers; in adolescence, she rebelled against the rules of the nuns, and was expelled – twice – from schools as a result. When her parents set in motion their ambitions for her as first a decorative debutante and then a dutiful wife, she rebelled again and bolted; and then in Paris, when she came up against the Surrealists' vision of her as a *femme-enfant*, a muse, she rebelled against them too. She told me the story of the day Joan Miró gave her some money and asked her to run along to the shops to buy him some cigarettes. 'I gave the money back to him and told him to do it himself. I wasn't daunted by them.'

Installed in Mexico a few years later, she rebelled against the Latino macho ideas about how women should behave, striking out on her own when her then husband neglected her. When her children arrived, she rebelled against any notion that motherhood meant she should slow down with her work: in fact, some of her best art was produced in the midst of a chaotic domestic life, painting, as she said, with a baby in one hand and her paintbrush in the other.

And then, gloriously and without a trace of regret, she rebelled against the very formula that would have helped her to become an established artist, falling out with important patrons and gallery owners, and refusing to grant interviews or be photographed for newspapers and magazines. In mid-life she rebelled against any notion of a settled or comfortable home, and instead set off alone on a peripatetic journey across America.

And finally, in the period when I knew her, she was embarked on her final rebellion of all: a rebellion against old age. She refused to be daunted or limited by it. She accepted its inevitability, but she was never going to bow to it, never going to be reduced by it, and never going to be faded by it. This, in fact, is why Leonora's life matters, and why it matters to tell her story: because she lived fearlessly, the kind of life so many yearn for and so few achieve. She felt fear, but she faced it down; time after time after time. As a result, her life was not limited in the ways people's lives are so often limited. But living fearlessly did not come without a price, as I was to discover; and if her story has a moral to it, that is it. We human beings can live more imaginatively and more freely than we suppose; but nothing is cost-free – neither the ignoring of that truth nor the playing out of it.

Leonora's reputation in our family could not have been more at odds with the reality of knowing her in Mexico. When I appeared on her doorstep she welcomed me generously into her life, and for the next five years she was my wise counsellor and a sounding-board. When I wasn't in Mexico we spoke on the phone; towards the end of her life her memory started to fade, and she always liked to reassure me she remembered who I was when I called. 'What's the weather like in London?' she would ask. 'It's still freezing in here, it's always freezing.' Whenever I called to tell her I was planning another trip, her advice was always the same: 'Make sure you bring plenty of jumpers, you know how cold it is in my house.'

One of the best things about being with Leonora was her sense of humour, which was always razor-sharp and often at the expense of someone else. Her wit was a complete mystery to many people, a problem made worse, perhaps, by the fact that it was bone dry and English, and her audience was usually Mexican and not tuned to the finer points of her humour. Many of her one-liners were delivered deadpan, without any clues as to whether she meant it to be funny or not; some of the time, she probably didn't know herself.

When I met Leonora I was in my early forties, a mother

of four and journalist living in London. Like most people, I occasionally thought how exciting, liberating and energising it would be if I could escape from time to time, and taste another kind of life. Because of Leonora I did just that; because really, what was stopping me from spending part of my life in Mexico? 'I couldn't do what you did,' people sometimes say. 'I've got children to look after/a job to do/no funds to travel/a home to run.' Well, me too. There is a way; but there is also a cost. And we all take risks with our lives, the people who stay at home as much as the ones who travel.

Meeting Leonora set my life on a different course, a course in search of her story. It took me to Mexico many times, as well as across Europe and to North America. It took me from a remote corner of Lancashire to an estuary in Cornwall; it took me from the smart streets of London's Kensington to the narrow, book-filled alleyways of the Parisian Left Bank. It took me from a spectacular, vine-covered hillside in southern France to a handsome port town in northern Spain, and from the art galleries of Madrid and the steep, tram-tracked streets of Lisbon to a palazzo by the Grand Canal in Venice. And in the end, as with all journeys, the real travelling happened inside myself, in my heart, just as it had for Leonora.

My travelling was through time as well as across lands: Leonora's story began in an England suffering the devastating losses of the First World War and moved to a France wracked by the chaos of the Second World War. She saw Spain in the early days of Franco, and Portugal in the days when it was overrun by refugees fleeing Hitler.

In war-time New York she was welcomed as one of the European artists in exile, and from there she travelled a thousand miles south to a Mexico whose art scene was still dominated by Diego Rivera and the muralists (no-one could possibly have foreseen, in those days, that it would be Rivera's wife Frida Kahlo who would go on to be the most famous Mexican artist of them all). And there she would stay, in a Mexico City that seemed sparse and empty when she arrived, but which would by the end of her life be the biggest city on earth; and she would make it her own, and become its unlikely darling.

Over the five years I knew her, Leonora said much to me that I will never forget, and that has changed my life. But the most important thing of all was this: 'Safety, under any circumstances, is an illusion.' She was one of those rare creatures who could see that illusion for what it is, and she lived her life accordingly.

I

The Debutante

It was the physical pain Leonora remembered most about the night of her presentation as a debutante at Buckingham Palace. 'I was wearing a tiara,' she told me. 'And it was biting into my skull.' She delivered that sentence in what I by then knew was quintessential Leonora: every word was elucidated, with her clear blue eyes fixed on mine. Two of the words were emphasised particularly: 'biting' and 'skull'.

The night she was remembering was a balmy spring evening in 1935. It was the first presentation at court that year, the year that would turn out to be the final one of the reign of King George V. A few months later George would be dead, and his eldest son would have embarked on the brief reign that would end in abdication. One of the few changes the new king, Edward VIII, would make would be to reduce the elaborate rigmarole of the annual 'coming out' of around a thousand debutantes, which had remained virtually unchanged since its instigation by Queen Charlotte in the eighteenth century. But for Leonora and her cohort of 1935, that rigmarole was still in full swing, and she was at turns appalled, horrified and humiliated by it.

In the photograph taken of her and her mother on the evening of her presentation, though, Leonora looks surprisingly acquiescent. She is wearing a dress that was described in *The Times* the following day as 'citron satin embroidered with the reversed side of the material'. It is cut on the bias, slim-fitting and elegant, with its short train draped fetchingly around her ankles. Her jet-black curly hair has been tamed and piled up on to her head, underneath that painful tiara. In her hand she is clutching a fan; her fingers are curled around it in a gracious pose. She is holding it as she has been instructed, and she is wearing the clothes she has been requested to wear. Beside her, her mother Maurie, in a long rose and silver gown, is holding ostrich feathers and looking wistfully, maybe even hopefully, off into the distance. Perhaps, she is thinking, this rebellious daughter of mine is finally about to be subdued. Perhaps at last we are going to be able to get her to behave the way we want her to behave, and in time she will find a suitably wealthy and landed young man who will marry her and carry her off into a life of privilege and advantage where she will settle down and stop causing us all so much difficulty. Because difficulty was what Leonora seemed to have been to the Carringtons for as long as anyone could remember: as the nuns at one of her boarding schools, St Mary's Ascot, had said a few years earlier when she was asked to leave: 'This girl will collaborate with neither work nor play'.

But Leonora's rebellion has hardly begun. Later, Maurie and her husband Harold will look back and realise that their daughter's early years – her expulsions from school, her inability to get on with anyone in authority, her complete disdain of so much that they held dear – were merely the warm-up to the full-blown explosion she would detonate a few years down the line. Today, on this spring evening in 1935, Leonora has allowed herself to be reined-in; but this will be the final occasion, the last time she ever does as she is told, or what they want her to do. Her face is serene, and she looks beautiful; her lips are painted a deep red, and she is staring straight into the camera. She has a Mona Lisa-esque look about her; whether she is smiling or stern isn't clear. But there is something in the set of her lips, and in the stillness of her stare, that says she is detached from all this. She is one month short of seventeen, but she knows her future, whatever it is, has nothing to do with being a member of the English upper class. She has tasted the London season, and she can see it for all it is, for all its snobbery, narrowness and conventionality.

The build-up to the night of her presentation began when an invitation, on thick card and with embossed lettering, arrived in the post at the Carringtons' London flat. 'The Lord Chamberlain is commanded by Their Majesties,' it read, 'to summon Mrs Harold Carrington and Miss Leonora Carrington to an evening presentation party at Buckingham Palace on 29 March 1935 from 5pm to 8pm.' Across the smart areas of London, in Mayfair, Knightsbridge, Kensington and Piccadilly, hundreds of other families were opening invitations to the same event.

Because 'coming out' was restricted to the daughters of the most privileged in the land: most were families whose pedigrees stretched back generations, who owned vast country estates, who had titles, wealth and armies of servants. Just a few invitees came from 'new money' families, like the Carringtons.

Preparing for the evening was time-consuming and demanding: Leonora and Maurie went for dress fittings to Mayfair, to top designer Victor Stiebel, who made their outfits and who was *the* designer for 1930s debs and their mothers. Leonora took lessons in how to curtsey from Betty Vacani, the doyenne of how to get a curtsey just right, with exactly the right side step and bob to precisely the correct depth. There would be two curtseys, one to the King and one to the Queen, in the throne room at Buckingham Palace. Everything, from the curtseys to the dress code to the timings, was subject to strict rules: trains were to hang precisely 2.5 yards from the shoulder, and three white ostrich feathers were to be attached to the tiara in *Ich Dien* motto fashion, slightly to one side. A long form from Buckingham Palace detailed how low the neckline and back of the women's dresses could be.

The Times noted that the overall mood that year was for Victorian-style frocks for debutantes and long, classical gowns for the older women. 'Frilled tulle and net and taffeta or ciré made most of the dresses for the young girls, the bodies sloping off the shoulders and finished with tiny puff sleeves or epaulettes,' said the report. 'In striking contrast were the older ladies' slim-fitting, severe gowns of lamé and tissue in rich colours, cut with short trains to the skirts.' Embroidery was an important feature of all the dresses; heavy incrustations of sequins, pearls or diamanté weighted the hems of many skirts and trains, and the design of most lace frocks was outlined with dainty beading. Queen Mary wore 'a gown of opalescent paillettes embroidered with crystal and diamanté', while the Duchess of York, who would by the end of the following year be Queen Elizabeth, wore a gown of gold and white silver ciré whose lace train was embroidered with gold and silver.

Leonora was still a teenager, but she already knew she did not want her clothes to ever be the most notable thing about her. While the London season may have made other girls feel secure and cossetted in their rarefied place in British society, the blatant inequality opened her eyes to the way women were regarded, and how they were treated. The most telling example of this came, for her, on a day at the races at Ascot, when she and her parents were guests in the Royal Enclosure. Horses were one of the great loves of Leonora's life, so a day at the races was more interesting than a day preparing for a ball or having tea at the Dorchester; but women were not allowed to place their own bets, nor to go to the paddock to see the horses before they raced. Furious, Leonora got out a book – Aldous Huxley's *Eyeless in Gaza* – sat in a corner and read it all the way through. Her parents were appalled by her very visible, if silent, protest; she was doing what she would do all her life, which was not being afraid to make her feelings known.

What the season most resembled, as Leonora saw it, was a cattle market. The expectations for young women of upper-class pre-war Britain were still extremely limited: they were to marry well, into another landed and wealthy family; for the so-called luckiest girls, there would be a title. There would be a town house to run in London and at least one estate in the country. There would be staff to direct, balls and parties to organise, and other ladies to visit for tea. In time there would be children to hand over to a nanny and then to boarding school. There would always be money, fine clothes, and good food at the best tables, and the most sought-after invitations would arrive in every post. And there would, eventually, be a kind of freedom: once children were born, love affairs would be tolerated, and little interests and pet projects would be encouraged. Ladies could ride and hunt; they could support charitable projects; they could travel.

But Leonora already had something most of the girls around her in Buckingham Palace that March night didn't have: she had personal ambition. She wouldn't have considered it an ambition, because it felt like the deepest and truest part of her; it was something she felt she already *was* rather than something she wanted to be. Leonora knew she wanted to make art. From as early as she could remember, she had drawn and painted what she saw around her, and how she felt. Her painting *Green Tea*, which dates from a few years later, 1942, offers plenty of insights. In the middle of a perfect, manicured English landscape, a young woman is mummified, bound in cow-patterned fabric, unable to move. The horses, which Leonora loved and would often identify with, as in this case, are tied to trees, unable to get away; in a surreal touch, the trees to which they are leashed are growing from the tails of one another's bodies.

The Carringtons lived in a splendour that was easily equal to that of most of the other 1935 debutantes; Leonora had been raised in a luxury completely unknown to ordinary workers like those who toiled in her father's extremely successful string of textile mills. The family home was a handsome, dove-grey Victorian mansion called Hazelwood Hall set on a hillside above Morecambe Bay in the lower reaches of the English Lake District. Everything about the place suggests plentiful wealth, almost opulence: the building has a wide, two-storey frontage, with huge bay windows at either end; in the centre is a balcony with wrought-iron railings held up by four stone columns. The main entrance was at the rear of the house in Leonora's time, and gave on to a panelled hallway leading through to several sunny drawing rooms at the front. And all around, created by Edwardian landscape gardener Thomas Mawson, was a magnificent garden with an intricate, almost geometrical assortment of terraces, box hedges, steps and pergolas.

I have a photograph of Leonora, which I found among my father's papers after his death, standing on the terrace at Hazelwood, and everything about the picture hints at the family's privilege. The photographer is standing on the lawn below the house, so that the huge bay windows of the drawing room and the master bedroom above rise up behind the figures of Leonora, who is standing alongside two of her brothers, my grandfather, George, and the uniformed family nanny. She was known to all as Nanny

Carrington, though her real name was Mary Cavanaugh; in the picture she is holding Arthur, the youngest of the Carrington clan. Standing beside Prim, lounging across the balustrade and looking slightly impish in a striped blazer, is her favourite brother and my father's favourite cousin, Gerard. Prim herself is to the left of the main group, slightly apart from the rest of them. She is about thirteen years old, and she is wearing a short skirt, a shirt and cardigan. Across her chest she has the strap of what looks like a small handbag, exactly the sort of handbag she always wore in Mexico City. The most striking thing about her is her thick head of dark curls, which fall round her face to her shoulders. She is half smiling, and looking into the camera; and there is something in her pose, and her slight aloofness from the rest of the group, that already seems to mark her out as a rebel.

Part of the key to Leonora's character lies in the fact that she had three brothers, whose freedom she was continually envious of, and no sister, with whom she might have conspired. Pat, Gerard and Arthur were given far more opportunities for rough and tumble fun, far more chances to play outdoors, than Prim. Her brothers were sent away to school, to the Jesuit-run Stonyhurst College in Lancashire, when they were seven or eight; but she didn't go to St Mary's Ascot until she was thirteen, and until then she had a French governess at home, and an education that was dominated by foreign languages and a knowledge of the arts. It would be a good grounding, as things turned out, for an artist who would go on to spend most of her life in a Spanish-speaking country with a French-speaking partner; but in the moment it felt as though she, alone of all her siblings, was being denied entry to the more exciting, wider world of boarding school, friends and opportunities to get away from the narrowness of home, and it was a discrimination she felt keenly.

And then there are the people who are not present in the photograph on the terrace at Hazelwood: Leonora's parents, Harold and Maurie Carrington. Harold was a hugely successful mill owner, running a company called Carrington and Dewhurst; he was rumoured to be the wealthiest man in Lancashire, and he was certainly one of the most influential. He had married his wife Maurie, née Moorhead, in January 1908, in her native Ireland; and now, almost two decades later, Maurie spent much of her time engineering the family's place at the top of the social ladder of the county, where she wanted them to belong. While Mary Cavanaugh shepherded the children outside to have their photograph taken, Maurie was quite probably having tea with one of the grander neighbours in the area. Connections mattered, and Maurie spent much of her life trying to make and keep good ones.

The pivotal fact about the Carringtons was they were not old money, not aristocrats, and not landed gentry stretching back generations. Harold was the grandson of a stationmaster, the son of a self-made millionaire; and Maurie was the daughter of an Irish doctor from County Westmeath. Theirs had been, in fact, a fairytale romance: they had met at a cricket match in Ireland in 1907, and were married the following year in Maurie's home town of Moate. It was an unusual wedding in those parts, because the man whom the pretty twenty-one-year-old, with her long, dark hair and bright, mischievous eyes, was marrying was a Protestant. That, in Catholic Ireland in 1908, meant the couple were only entitled to a brief wedding ceremony rather than a full-scale nuptial mass. Maurie's parents, Dr Henry Moorhead and his wife Mary, must have been saddened that their eldest child could only have what felt like a second-class service. The only consolation was that their new son-in-law Harold was taking Maurie back with him across the water to begin a life cushioned with the sorts of luxuries most girls from this backwater of a town could not have begun to imagine.

Harold's father Arthur was the son of a stationmaster called Thomas, and when on 26 March 1876 Arthur married Edith Hartley, Leonora's grandmother, at Holy Trinity Church in Habergham Eaves in Lancashire, he is described on his marriage certificate as a 'clerk', and she is described as a 'milliner' (which probably meant she made hats in a factory).

But Arthur Carrington did not remain a clerk for long. By the time his son Harold Wylde Carrington was baptised in September 1881, he had progressed sufficiently to describe himself as a 'manager', and was on the path to carving out a leading role in the most profitable business in Lancashire. When Harold turned thirteen, Arthur was earning enough money to send him to Rossall, the self-styled 'Eton of the North'; and when Harold left school on the cusp of the new century he followed his father into the now flourishing company, Carrington and Dewhurst.

As things turned out, it was the right business in the right place at the right time: in the run-up to the First

World War, the Lancashire textile industry was growing exponentially – at one stage its mills were said to be producing enough yarn and textiles to clothe half the people on the planet. The Carrington family became so wealthy so quickly in the early years of the twentieth century that Harold and Maurie struggled to keep up with the expectations their new-found fortune demanded. The first home of their married life was the relatively modest Westwood House in the village of Clayton-le-Woods near Chorley, where Leonora was born on 6 April 1917. But three years later there was enough money in the coffers to move to a much more splendid residence, Crookhey Hall at Cockerham, some fifteen miles north of Clayton.

Crookhey was a home on an altogether different scale from Westwood: it is a grand, large mansion, ivy-clad in parts and with tall, pointed roof points and turrets that give it a sharp and forbidding air. Designed by Alfred Waterhouse, who was also responsible for the Natural History Museum in London, and Manchester Town Hall, it has, like those buildings, a strong Gothic feel. At the gate stands a lodge, and then a sweeping carriage drive leads up through shrubberies to the main house. The main door is under a covered portico, and the lofty lounge hall has an oak floor and oak panelling. In Leonora's day there was a billiard room, a spacious conservatory (this, she later said, was by far the most beautiful part of the entire house), a boudoir, a huge drawing room, a library, dining room and study. Upstairs were six principal bedrooms and five dressing rooms, three of which had bathrooms, and there were a further ten bedrooms for the staff.

The grounds were as grand as the house itself. Surrounded by woodlands, and with views over Morecambe Bay, the gardens included tennis and croquet lawns, terraces and summer houses, an ornamental lake and rustic bridge, and a walled-in kitchen garden with a wide assortment of fruit trees as well as four vineries, a rose house and a tomato house. For Leonora, perhaps the most important part of Crookhey were the stables, where her beloved pony Winkie lived. Her father's great love was fishing, and there was brown and sea trout fishing in the River Cocker that flowed through the estate, as well as salmon and trout fishing in the nearby River Lune.

Of the Carringtons' wealth there can be little doubt; but the truth was that 1930s upper-class England was very difficult to penetrate socially, and Maurie Carrington did not find it easy to get access to the smartest drawing rooms of either northern England, or London. Strings were almost certainly pulled to get her invited to events during the debutante season, but that didn't equal general acceptance, and Leonora was only too well aware of Maurie's pain. She remembered how her mother had confided in her that she had once been ignored by a woman who considered herself grander than her when they met in the street, and how she had been grief-stricken as a result.

Leonora's life as an artist has usually been seen by art historians as a break from a family that couldn't contain her; and in many ways, that is true. But the fact that she was born into a family of outsiders, and that what she saw from a young age were relatives, her mother especially, who were desperate to break in to an inner magic circle, had various effects on Leonora. It made her feel humiliated; it made her feel depressed. But also, it inspired her. It made her realise that being an outsider had advantages, even attractions.

Everything came to a head for Leonora on that night at Buckingham Palace in 1935. What was really going on inside the pincer-gripped head, under the tiara, she told in her story 'The Debutante', written in the south of France three years later. 'When I was a debutante, I often went to the zoo,' the story goes. 'I went so often that I knew the animals better than I knew girls of my own age.' The animal she knew best at the zoo was a hyena, who was very intelligent ('I taught her French and she, in return, taught me her language'). When her mother announces that she is arranging a ball for the girl, she is horrified. 'I've always detested balls especially when they are given in my honour.'

Salvation from the ball comes in the shape of the hyena, who said she herself had never been to a ball, and would rather enjoy it. In her story Leonora freed the hyena from the zoo, transported her home in a taxi, and invited her to try on her ball gown and high-heeled shoes. The dress fitted, and the hyena was able to totter around on the heels; but in order to take Leonora's place at the ball, she had to be disguised as a human. How would that be possible?

It is the hyena, not the girl, who comes up with the answer. They must ring for her maid Mary, murder her, and make her face into a mask which the hyena can wear to the ball. It will be dark in the ballroom, and provided the face is human the swap won't be noticed. The killing goes

33

ahead, with the girl imploring that Mary is hurt as little as possible; the hyena eats her, all but her feet which she can't manage and leaves in a small bag for later in the day, and her face, which she stretches over her own.

When they can hear the music from downstairs, the girl sends the hyena down. 'Remember,' she warns her, 'don't stand next to my mother. She's bound to realise that it isn't me. Apart from her I don't know anybody.'

The girl spends the evening reading *Gulliver's Travels* by Jonathan Swift. Time passes, and she feels all must be going well for the hyena downstairs in the ballroom. But then – the first sign of trouble – a bat flies into the room, followed soon afterwards by the girl's now furious mother. As the party was sitting down for supper, she says, the hyena – which the girl has been worrying will give itself away by its strong smell – jumped up and shouted, 'So I smell a bit strong, what? Well, I don't eat cakes'. Then it tore off its face, and leapt out through a window.

Leonora told me that every piece of writing she ever did was autobiographical, and in this story – as, frequently, in her paintings – each of the main characters seems to me to represent a different facet of herself. And perhaps that is particularly true of the hyena: the beast ends up leaping dramatically through an open window, and disappears off 'with one great bound'.

2

Portrait of Max Ernst

On a spring morning in 1937, passers-by in Cork Street in central London 'were startled to see an elderly man laying a table for a meal in the window of an art gallery'. The man in the window – at forty-six, not exactly 'elderly' – was, the article in the *Daily Express* went on to reveal, 'the Surrealist painter Max Ernst, a German who lives in Paris (cooking his own food as well as any French man)'.

Max Ernst was in London for an exhibition of his work at the Mayor Gallery in Mayfair. The show would be well received; yet the most profound impact of his stay in the city that month would not be on the art scene, but on the life of a young student who, having failed to attract any marriage proposals during two seasons as a debutante, was now learning to paint under the tutelage of a French Cubist artist called Amédée Ozenfant.

Harold and Maurie had chosen to ignore all the signs

that their only daughter was ill-suited to life as an upper-class wife, and had ploughed on regardless with the parties, the balls, the trips to the races and the dress fittings. By the summer of 1936, though, they had to admit, if not defeat, then at least retreat. An alternative approach had to be found.

They knew that painting and drawing had been Leonora's greatest love since her earliest childhood; her notebooks from her years at Crookhey Hall, where she had lived between the ages of three and ten, are festooned with sketches and drawings of her favourite animals, horses, birds, and a host of other creatures that move and flit and dance across the pages. Now, at the age of nineteen, Leonora wanted some professional tuition. The Chelsea School of Art was mooted; it sounded respectable enough, and she could stay with friends in London, where an architect called Serge Chermayeff, whose acquaintance Harold had made, would keep a watchful eye on her (years later Leonora referred to Serge during an interview as a lover, probably her first).

Leonora had been at the Chelsea school for no more than a few weeks when Serge made another suggestion: Ozenfant, a French artist who had previously run an art school in Paris, had moved to London and was opening a new establishment in Warwick Road in Kensington. One of his former pupils from Paris, a young artist and mother called Ursula Goldfinger, née Blackwell, of the family who founded Crosse and Blackwell, was helping him to recruit students; her husband Erno Goldfinger was an architect and friend of Serge. Leonora signed up, and became

Ozenfant's first London student. The school was run out of a garage-like building; in the Goldfinger archives there is a photograph of Ozenfant and Ursula standing in front of what looks like a stable door, above which are written the words 'Ozenfant Academy of Fine Art'.

It was a grand title for a modest enterprise, but Ozenfant had far-reaching ambitions for his trainees. According to the prospectus, 'the role of the master is not to bring pressure upon his pupil to oblige him to think or paint like himself, but on the contrary to help him, first, to discover on his own behalf the general laws of art, for without them a work of art is only a fashionable article; then to reveal the student to himself by questioning him to know himself well, which is a way of making him discover at the same time the human constraints, and his own personality'.

Methodology and technique would be central to the school's raison d'être, the prospectus continued: indeed, decades later Leonora would recall that she spent an entire term at the school drawing just one object – an apple. Her time with Ozenfant would turn out to be the only formal art training she would ever have: but she made a little go a long way, and she always felt lucky to have had so exacting a teacher. 'Ozenfant worked me like a mule, he was a purist,' she said later. 'He did the following: you had to understand the chemistry of everything you used, including the paper and the pencils. He gave us an apple, a piece of paper and a 9H pencil. With this we had to do a linear sketch. He said he did not want to see the shell of an apple, it was an apple which had to be done with one single outline. I spent six months drawing the same apple which finally became a kind of mummy. He was a good professor with a clinical eye and he never left you disheartened.'

Stella Snead, who moved on from painting to photography and ended up living in New York, was the next student to join the academy, as she recalled much later in her life. 'There was one other student in the nicely spacious studio,' she wrote. 'She was Leonora Carrington at nineteen: beautiful, her eyes intense and mischievous. What people! I have never met anyone remotely like them. Other students soon joined us. Against the back wall was an immense mural-sized painting on which Ozenfant was still working; I was doubtful if I liked it . . . '

Ozenfant encouraged Leonora and Stella, and his other students, to make full use of being in London to visit museums, art galleries and exhibitions; these visits were crucial, he said in his prospectus, to ensure they remained 'in touch not only with the contemporary position of the arts but also with the existing state of philosophy, science and the most important results of modern industry'. One event he would most certainly have encouraged them to seek out was the show that opened at the New Burlington Galleries on 11 June 1936, and continued until 4 July that year. It was London's first International Surrealist Exhibition, organised by the artists Roland Penrose and David Gascoyne, and the influential art historian Herbert Read; and for the British public it was to be an explosive awakening to an art movement that, though it was well established in Europe and particularly in Paris, had not had much impact so far on the English side of the Channel.

Surrealism dates back coincidentally to the year of

Leonora's birth – 1917 – as that was when the word was first used, in a play called *Les Mamelles de Tirésias* by the poet Guillaume Apollinaire. As an intellectual and artistic movement surrealism grew from a deep dissatisfaction with bourgeois values, which were believed to have caused, amongst other outrages, the First World War; and it sought to promote the idea that humankind would be in a better place if much more emphasis was placed on unconscious rather than rational, conscious thought. Dreams, free association and techniques called automatic writing and automatic painting, which involved encouraging the spontaneous flow of words, thoughts and images on to a page or canvas, were highly prized by the Surrealists, whose lives centred on the cafés of Saint-Germain-des-Prés in Paris. Through the 1920s the movement had grown steadily, pulling in all the greatest names of the day. Their presence there made the French capital the centre of the global art world through the 1920s and 1930s; its founder and leader was the French writer André Breton, whom Leonora always referred to as 'the headmaster of Surrealism'. Her own definition of the movement is perhaps one of the best: 'Surrealism,' she told an interviewer late in her life, 'is a state of the spirit and no more; a state that can't be explained.'

Whatever it was, or is, surrealism spilled over from poems, words and discussions into art; and indeed, today it is best known as an art movement. As far as Britain was concerned, though, it didn't ever quite fire on all its cylinders; and in fact the 1936 exhibition was designed to launch it properly there. In the long term, this ambition was to fail; but in the short term, the show certainly made a significant impact, largely to do with the bizarre goings-on (some planned, others unexpected) that characterised its run.

The opening of the exhibition was a tour de force, with André Breton dressed for the occasion entirely in green. Sheila Legge, one of the few women in the Surrealist group, wore a long, white satin dress with her face obscured by roses and covered with ladybirds; she had been intending to carry a pork chop, but the weather was deemed too hot so she was clutching an artificial leg wearing a silk stocking instead. Composer William Walton pinned a kipper on to one of Miró's paintings, but the artist Paul Nash removed it because it smelled too strong. As the guests began to arrive, the poet Dylan Thomas went from one to the next offering teacups full of boiled string, asking, 'Do you like it weak or strong?' The pièce de résistance, though, was Salvador Dalí, who arrived wearing a deep-sea diving suit, to underline the fact that he was planning to make a dive into the subconscious, and proceeded to give a lecture entitled 'Authentic Paranoic Phantom' about a philosophy student who ate a wardrobe, including the mirror, over a six-month period; he delivered the lecture with two dogs on leads in one hand and a billiard cue in the other. But it was almost impossible to hear what he was saying, so the Surrealist patron Edward James translated from the front row. It was a while before anyone noticed that Dalí was slowly suffocating inside his helmet; a spanner proved useless, and eventually James had to prise off the helmet with the billiard cue. After he'd recovered, Dalí continued the presentation with a slide show; the slides, of course, were presented upside down.

More than thirty thousand people visited the show during its short, three-week run; on the opening day, the traffic was brought to a standstill on Piccadilly due to the crowds. But for all the attention it attracted, and for all its eccentricities, its architects were deadly serious about Surrealism and its ambitions. 'Do not judge this movement kindly,' wrote Herbert Read in his contribution to the catalogue. 'It is not just another amusing stunt. It is defiant – the desperate act of men too profoundly convinced of the rottenness of our civilisation to want to save a shred of its respectability.' So far artists had only interpreted the world, he said; 'the point, however, is to transform it'.

The show brought together almost four hundred paintings, collages and sculptures, and those represented read like a roll-call of twentieth-century art: Salvador Dalí, Pablo Picasso, Marcel Duchamp, Paul Klee, Man Ray, René Magritte, Henry Moore, Méret Oppenheim, Paul Nash, Roland Penrose, Francis Picabia, Dora Maar, Joan Miró, André Masson, Edward Burra, Giorgio de Chirico, Wolfgang Paalen, Graham Sutherland, Yves Tanguy and Toyen: all of them were there. And, of course, Max Ernst; he had sixteen works on display including a painting in oil dating from 1926, which according to the catalogue was lent by the poet Paul Éluard, one of his closest friends. The piece is entitled *The Bride of the Wind*, and what it shows is a jumble of two horses engaged in an act that seems simultaneously to be love-making, combat and co-operation. It's impossible to see where one horse ends and the other starts; their legs, tails and heads are all scrambled together, and they seem to be flying, as though fate has brought them together in a chance mid-air encounter, by the rimmed light of an eclipsed moon. They are dancing and coupling, ravelling and unravelling, crashing together and pulling apart. Whatever has happened, it's clear that this painting represents a moment of extreme urgency, unbridled passion and powerful energy. By the light of a surreal moon, two horses rushing headlong through time have clashed and realised instantly the need to make the most of every nanosecond they can be together.

Leonora often spoke of how she fell in love with Max Ernst the artist long before she fell in love with Max Ernst the man; but it wasn't *The Bride of the Wind* that brought him to her notice, it was a piece entitled *Two Children are Threatened by a Nightingale*. Today that work is at the Museum of Modern Art in New York, a small collage whose dark wooden frame seems initially too heavy for what might, with its azure sky and garden gate, be an idyllic scene. But nightmares happen, even on a cloudless day; maybe especially on a cloudless day, when our defences are down and our expectations are high. And this image tells the story of one such nightmare, on one such day. There are three female figures in the scene: one is lying unconscious on the ground, another is being carried away across a rooftop by a faceless man; and a third is brandishing a knife in the direction of the speck in the sky that seems to be the menacing instigator of all this danger: a solitary nightingale, or *rossignol* as Ernst has written in French underneath. To many who see it, the painting is an enigma, a riddle that raises more questions than it answers. But for Leonora, it made perfect sense the moment she set eyes on it. 'I thought, ah, this is familiar; I know what this is about,' she said. 'A kind of world which would move between worlds . . . the world of our dreaming and imagination.'

Oddly (or perhaps in the spirit of surrealism, not very oddly at all) it was Leonora's mother who inadvertently brought the nightingale painting to her daughter's attention. Maurie bought her a book edited by Herbert Read, published to coincide with the exhibition at the New Burlington Galleries; among the works Read discussed in it was the Ernst collage that so imprinted itself on Leonora's mind.

Its creator was a German, born in 1891 in Brühl near Cologne, one of nine children in a devoutly Catholic family. Max Ernst's childhood was full of incidents and events that would later be used in his art: one significant moment was the coincidental death of a pet cockatoo the same day as the birth of a new sister: this led him, Ernst said later, into 'a dangerous confusion between birds and humans' and influenced his choice of a mythical bird, Loplop ('the most superior of the birds') as his alter ego. His father, Philipp, was an amateur painter, which was connected to his son's decision to take up art as a career; but more significant to his development as a Surrealist was the fact that Philipp was an unbending and often unreasonable disciplinarian, which nurtured in Max a deep need to defy authority; this was to characterise his art and views throughout his lifetime.

The young Max studied at Bonn University, before

turning to painting; and in 1912 he visited an exhibition in Cologne where he saw for the first time the work of Picasso, as well as the Post-Impressionists with whom he was already very familiar, including Van Gogh and Gauguin. The show made a deep impression on him and served as a turning-point in his commitment to his art. So too did the First World War, when he was drafted into the German army and served on both the Western and Eastern fronts.

After the war Max returned to Cologne where, in 1919, together with colleagues including the social activist Johannes Theodor Baargeld and artist Hans Arp, he formed the Cologne Dada group. Dadaism was the womb that gave birth to Surrealism, and entwined in its umbilical cord were the same core questions, questions that focused on the madness of war, the emptiness of bourgeois values, and the proper place for intuition and irrationality in human society. Its most controversial event in Cologne was an exhibition featuring a row of urinals which visitors were required to walk past while listening to lewd poetry recited by a woman in a long, white communion dress; the show was closed by the authorities on the grounds that it was obscene, though when no charges were brought it reopened.

A few months before that show Max had married an art history student, Luise Straus, and their son Ulrich, known as Jimmy, was born in 1920. The marriage was short-lived: two years later Max left Luise and Jimmy, and moved to Paris to join André Breton and other members of the burgeoning Surrealist movement, who were about to launch themselves on the art world with the publication in 1924 of the first *Surrealist Manifesto*. Among the friends he had in Paris was the French poet Paul Éluard, whose wife Gala was the central and in many ways the essential Surrealist muse, an exponent of free love with a voracious appetite for sex. Across her lifetime she would boast many lovers; and they would include some of the leading figures of the Surrealist movement: Giorgio de Chirico and Man Ray, as well as Éluard and, her most famous partner and husband, Salvador Dalí. Now, though Éluard's wife, she became also Ernst's lover, and they embarked on a ménage à trois; Éluard even used to tell his friends 'I love Max Ernst much more than I do Gala'. The bohemian arrangement came to an end in 1924, and in 1927 Ernst, having divorced Luise the previous year, married a twenty-one-year-old called Marie-Berthe Aurenche.

Artistically, Ernst was a whirlwind – inventive, exploring, always pushing at boundaries and constantly eager to try out new techniques. As a Surrealist he wanted to record the subconscious; but more than just recording it, he wanted to promote a dialogue between the conscious and the unconscious. One of his early experiments was in the creation of collages, an idea he got from studying mail-order catalogues and teaching manuals: the dreamlike appearance of collages suggested the possibility of attacking contemporary values, and especially the reliance on reason.

Ernst had made an impact in Britain with his prominence at the 1936 Surrealism exhibition, so it was unsurprising that, a year later, he travelled to London for an exhibition of his work at the Mayor Gallery in Mayfair, his first solo show in England. It featured pieces of work produced since 1923, including a painting of the bird Loplop, his alter ego, which was priced at £200. The table in the gallery window which the *Daily Express* of 9 June 1937 described him laying for a meal was not an ordinary one: Ernst had removed the legs from one end and nailed them down on the top so they stood on their head. The table was set with dishes and cutlery, the chair he covered with broken glass. 'A Surreal banquet,' declared the *Scotsman*. But if Ernst meant to challenge the British public (and surely he did, for what else was his art for?), he seems to have failed as far as the *Sunday Times* reviewer was concerned. 'Little though it may please a Surrealist to be called charming, charm is Ernst's ultimate quality,' he opined in its edition of 13 June. 'His attempts at the horrific are no more frightening than the Jabberwock with his attendant Borogroves.' Anthony Blunt, writing in the *Spectator*, also had reservations. 'With Ernst as with Dalí,' he wrote, 'one is compelled to admire a certain technical dexterity (no-one, with the possible exception of Klee, can give to paint a more attractive quality) but when one has done wondering at this, what is left? A gift for dream creation perhaps: but the term seems to have lost its vitality; and anyhow are we to be content with dreams?'

During his time in London Max was a guest of his friend Roland Penrose; but another friend he saw during his stay was Erno Goldfinger, whose wife Ursula had become a friend of Leonora through Ozenfant and the art school. Goldfinger was a Hungarian-born naturalised British citizen and the architect who went on to design the controversial tower blocks that rose up as part of the London landscape after the Second World War, including Alexander Fleming House at the Elephant and Castle, Trellick Tower in Ladbroke Grove and Balfron Tower in Tower Hamlets.

Goldfinger's most enduring fame would be as the inspiration for James Bond's most notorious adversary; and the real-life Goldfinger seems not to have been popular with his acquaintances, given to frequent rages, and was remembered by Leonora as arrogant and controlling. In June 1937 Erno and Ursula, with their two young children, were the inhabitants of a strikingly beautiful flat in the first Modernist building in England – a tall, whitewashed, elegant block that stands like a swan at the top of Highgate Hill in north London. Highpoint was the flagship work of the Georgian emigré architect Berthold Lubetkin, who was the pioneer in Britain of what became known as the International Style: all rectangular on the outside, inside it was full of surprising curves, cork floors, columns, dove-white walls and glass bricks that combined to give an irrepressible feeling of light, space and weightlessness. The Goldfingers inhabited Flat Number 3 on the first floor. It's a three-bedroomed dwelling whose front door opens into a generous-sized public area, with concertina windows along the main wall opening on to a narrow balcony; below are the shrubs and trees of the garden, and beyond that the whole of London is laid out to the horizon.

It is to this flat, Number 3, Highpoint, that the celebrated Surrealist Max Ernst hurries one evening in early June 1937. He is probably distracted, because on his mind is his show at the Mayor Gallery and the reviews it is getting, and he is thinking about how it is being received by his fellow artists across London as well as those further afield in Paris. He's said yes to supper because the invitation came from his friend Erno Goldfinger, who spoke of a young art student, a friend of his wife, who will also be there. Max's interest has perhaps been piqued, because here is a man who falls often to the charms of beautiful women, and is rarely without an amour: his current marriage to Marie-Berthe has been on the rocks due partly to his affairs with, amongst others, Méret Oppenheim in 1933, Lotte Lenya in 1934 and Leonor Fini in 1935. All the same, it is extremely unlikely that Max knows anything like as much about Leonora as she knows about him; which begs the question, whose idea was the dinner party in the first place?

Art historians have long speculated that the Goldfingers set the couple up; but my guess is that Leonora has engineered this opportunity to meet for herself an artist whose work she had come to admire deeply. If so, it was a bold and confident move from a young woman still aged only twenty. She could not possibly have known what she was unleashing, in herself or with Max; but if my surmise is true, what it showed was her irrepressible enthusiasm to take an opportunity where she saw one, her ability to put her faith into the unknown, and her potential to embrace the possibility of adventure and to walk into that adventure with her head high. On that day in June 1937 she was looking not just forward, but way into the future.

Max will almost certainly have travelled to Highpoint from Mayfair, probably getting the tube to Highgate and walking from there. Leonora arrives by car, driven by her friend Joan Powell who is intrigued about the fascinating-sounding dinner party, and is hoping she will be invited in for a drink at the start of it. She is not: Leonora thanks her, gets out of the car and walks purposefully into the building. Perhaps she knows she is stepping into the ante-room to a whole new world.

It's a warm June that year, and the Goldfingers have prepared their airy and spacious Highpoint flat by opening their concertina windows, so one entire wall is open to the evening, the view, and the sights and sounds of London; the great city below can be a witness to the momentous introduction that is about to take place. The stage is set; and no-one in the audience will be disappointed. From the second they set eyes on one another, the electricity is palpable between the beautiful, sparky young woman with her dark eyes, crimson lips and cascade of raven curls, and the white-haired, slim, middle-aged man with his lined forehead and kind-looking eyes. He is old enough to be her father, but how different from her actual father he is; and how irresistible that makes him. He is courteous, attentive, interested and enchanted; she is excited, hopeful, optimistic and charmed. Erno asks what they would like to drink; they decide on champagne. They stand facing one another; Leonora would never forget this moment, and described it to me. She has in her hand her glass, and Max has his in his. But Erno has poured the champagne too quickly; it is bubbling up in the glasses, its effervescence about to spill over, its spirit too strong to be contained. Max looks at his drink and then at Leonora; he takes his finger, and he puts it into the swelling liquid in his glass. Leonora's eyes are on his; she watches what he does, and then she takes her own finger and does exactly the same. The couple, Leonora said later, became lovers 'almost instantly'. Three decades later, Max seems to have had the same memory; in a book drawn from conversations between the author and himself, the meeting with Leonora is described as an 'encounter that had upon both parties an instantaneous and irresistible effect'.

Max Ernst has met his bride of the wind, and Leonora Carrington has met her saviour. These two creatures running headlong through space have become entwined. Soon it will be impossible to see where one starts and the other stops, as their dancing and coupling, their ravelling and unravelling, their crashing together and pulling apart begins. They have found one another, and now they are hurtling onwards on their journey through time and ideas, space and surroundings, friendships and art.

3

The Lovers

The couple's friends – Erno and Ursula Goldfinger, Joan Powell, Roland Penrose, Paul Éluard, Amédée Ozenfant – were thrilled with the new romance, enjoying the delightful anti-symmetry of the mature, white-plumed bird and his youthful, black-maned, untamed horse.

It was, in every sense, a surreal match; a romance that could have come straight from the surrealists' favourite parlour game, Exquisite Corpse. In the game players pass around a piece of paper on which each participant adds a word, series of words or a drawing, before folding the page and passing it on to the next player. The words, sentences or drawings are unconnected, disparate, random; and at the end of the game, a sentence, paragraph or series of images is revealed. A sentence that emerged from one of the early games was *Le cadavre exquis boira le vin nouveau* (The exquisite corpse will drink the young wine), which was how the game got its name. According to André Breton, the objective was 'to provide the most paradoxical confrontation possible', and to disrupt and confound logic and expectations. Leonora and Max were a real-life *cadavre exquis*, and the playing-out of their story seemed in every way emblematic of Surrealism and all that it stood for.

The pair were not the only ones on the threshold of an absorbing new relationship in that early summer of 1937. A few weeks before the fateful meeting at the Goldfingers' flat, Max had been in France with the friend with whom he was now staying in London, Roland Penrose, and the two had been invited by the art dealer Julien Levy to a fancy-dress ball at a hotel in Paris. Max and Roland dressed as bandits for the party, dyeing their hair (Max's was blue, Roland's was green) for the occasion. And there, across the room, Roland noticed a striking woman with blonde hair who had just arrived from Egypt via Marseilles: Lee Miller, the model-turned-photographer who would go on to produce some of the most memorable, and important, images of the Second World War.

A few years earlier Lee, who had recently turned thirty, had been the lover of Man Ray; for the last three years she had been the wife of a wealthy Egyptian called Aziz Eloui Bey, and had been living with him in Cairo. Now, however, she had left him, and was in search of a new life in Europe. She found it that night at Levy's party; she and Roland would spend the rest of their lives together. Like Leonora and Max, Roland and Lee became lovers immediately, and were inseparable; so to hear his friend had been struck by a similar thunderbolt just a few weeks later probably seemed rather wondrous to the happy Roland.

The Carringtons, meanwhile, were appalled. Harold and Maurie had hoped that by pandering to Leonora's fascination for art they could win her round. As far as they were concerned, art was a phase, an emblem of her dissatisfaction with their world, her attempt to strike a note of independence. They had no idea that art was the very fire in her soul. And they could never have understood what she told me one day in 2006 in her kitchen in Mexico City, though I suspect she could have said it to them it even when she was a young child: 'You don't decide to paint. It's like getting hungry and going to the kitchen to eat. It's a need, not a choice'.

Art historians have tended to paint the story of Leonora's younger life by bracketing her parents together, and examining her relationship with the two of them as a single turbulent entity: but in fact, her interaction with each was quite distinct, and her father and mother were important in her life and in her artistic development in separate and different ways. Harold, whose mills employed hundreds of people across Lancashire, came from a professional world where hierarchy was respected and where the company chairman's word was never questioned; and in his personal background he came from a working-class world where women did as they were told. At home he expected to be obeyed, especially by his daughter; he was perplexed by this young girl who had become his most vociferous critic, always ready to rail against his plans and to confound his expectations. At the end of her life Leonora acknowledged that father and daughter were extraordinarily similar: strong-willed, determined, unflinching, hard-nosed. Neither was willing to back down; Harold thought his wealth and position, both in the wider world and as head of the family, meant he held all the cards. In the end he was to realise, as all parents do who push their children to their limits, that his cards were worthless; but by then, it would be too late.

The depth of Leonora's feelings for her father are told most comprehensively in her short story 'The Oval Lady', written in 1939, which tells the tale of a young girl aged about sixteen named Lucretia who is locked in an epic battle of wills with her father. When the narrator chances upon Lucretia she is all alone in a very grand room, surrounded by elegant furniture and trinkets, but clearly very sad. The narrator suggests a cup of tea, which might make her feel better. 'I don't drink, I don't eat,' Lucretia says in reply. 'It's a protest against my father, the bastard.'

She soon capitulates and has some tea, and somehow one cake turns to twenty; but her father must never know, she says. 'Even if I die of hunger, he'll never win . . . I'd like to starve myself to death just to annoy him. What a pig.'

Lucretia's favourite playmate is Tartar, the old rocking horse in her nursery; Tartar is able to move, and to travel, and then return to the nursery with stories. Lucretia herself can turn into a horse; when her French governess comes into the nursery and finds her playing there, that's exactly what happens. The governess is angry, and says Lucretia's father has forbidden her to play on the horse; 'You aren't a child any more'. Lucretia, 'neighing with rage', is taken to explain herself before her father, who issues a shocking punishment. 'What I'm going to do is purely for your own good, my dear,' he tells her, in a voice all the more chilling for its gentleness. 'You're too old to play with Tartar. Tartar is for children. I am going to burn him myself, until there's nothing left of him.'

Lucretia gives a terrible cry and falls to her knees. 'Not that, Papa, gives that.' She weeps and begs; but her father goes out of the room, and up to the nursery; and Lucretia has to put her fingers into her ears 'for the most frightful neighing sounded from above, as if an animal were suffering extreme torture'.

Harold did not burn Leonora's rocking horse, because it was still there in the nursery at Hazelwood Hall when my father was a child. But clearly, he was able to deliver punishments that sliced into his daughter's heart. Worse, his employment of these sanctions forced her to cry and to beg. Whatever Harold did to admonish her, he wounded her to the core; and, worse, he did it by attacking something she held sacred. That, for her, was unforgivable. Having forced her into such a humiliating situation – and there was surely a real-life incident on which Leonora drew in 'The Oval Lady' – it could only be a question of when, rather than if, there would be a final, seismic show-down between father and daughter.

Leonora's relationship with Maurie, though tumultuous at times, fitted into a more usual spectrum of mother/

daughter relationships; it was complex, and each had criticisms of the other, but Leonora respected Maurie in a way she did not respect Harold. Maurie was always aware of, and proud about, her heritage through her female line. As a child Leonora spent her summers in Moate in County Westmeath, staying with her maternal grandparents; and in the kitchen in the whitewashed doctor's house at the church gate she would hear stories from her grandmother, Mary Monica Moorhead, about her female antecedents. Most notable of these, certainly as far as Mary Monica was concerned, was Maria Edgeworth (1767–1849), a novelist sometimes referred to as the Jane Austen of Ireland. In her 'Essay on the Noble Science of Self-Justification' (1795) she writes that women should use their wit and intelligence to continually challenge the force and power of men.

The Edgeworth connection was through Mary Monica's mother Jane Somers, born Jane Usher, and it was much cherished by Mary, suggesting a deep strand of feminism at the core of our family long before it was fashionable or even remotely respectable. So much so that, when Mary Monica's first child Maurie was followed two years later by a second daughter, she was given the name 'Leonora' after the eponymous heroine of one of Edgeworth's novels. Two decades later, when Maurie came to have her own daughter, she passed on the name; by this time, the first Leonora (always known in our family as Leo) was a nun, a Sister of Charity in a convent in Dublin. But like her namesake, Sister Mary Monica (she took her mother's names as her name in religion) was a rebel whose finest hour came when she went head to head with the much maligned, authoritarian Dublin archbishop John McQuaid. Their row, which Aunt Leo apparently won, was followed by a punishment in which she had to clean the convent floors. In 1951, Leonora remembered her aunt's disgrace in a painting called *Clean Up at Once Said the Archbishop*. The painting shows two figures, presumably Archbishop McQuaid and Aunt Leo, in the middle of their argument, their faces pressed up against one another. Leo's blue robes flow down from her shoulders like angelic wings; the prelate is wearing dark robes, and his neck, face and hair are flame-red, rising to a phallic point above his head. He is pointing a long, spindly finger towards the penance to which Leo must go; she, meanwhile, is upright, dignified, unyielding.

Aunt Leo was a legend in our family: like so many nuns of past generations, she probably saw the convent as a liberation from the only alternative life to which she could aspire, that of being a wife and mother. Embracing a future in a convent brought a kind of autonomy and independence that was lacking in her sister Maurie's life as a wife, even the wife of a wealthy man. Leonora Carrington never forgot her aunt, whom she visited on those summer trips to stay with her grandparents in Ireland. Leo was, in a strange way, an early role model; another example, along with Maria Edgeworth, of female rebellion close to home.

If Maurie's family brought interesting female relatives into the frame of Leonora's early life, they also brought a magical prism through which to view the world, which would prove invaluable to her development as an artist.

Maurie was a fabulist who loved to tell stories about connections with ancient Irish figures, real and mythical; and Leonora sometimes countered her mother's fantasies with one of her own, suggesting the Moorheads were 'probably gypsies, handymen'. This is unlikely: the Moorheads moved to Ireland from northern England during Tudor times, and by the nineteenth century were comfortably off; both of Leonora's Irish great-grandfathers were doctors. What's interesting, though, is that Leonora chose to link her Irish family to the gypsy or traveller community; that suggests she found it exciting to be related to them. In this respect she was emulating exactly her mother's instinct to link herself to an exotic family history. Leonora used to tell me that when the nouveau riche Carringtons moved to the grand and gothic Crookhey Hall in the early 1920s, Maurie attempted to create a back story of distinguished-looking forebears by buying up portraits from art dealers. Sometimes, Leonora said, she was even taken along too so they could look out for portraits with a family resemblance; 'We'll have that one! She looks like you, Prim.'

The fables and half-truths extended beyond the portraits on the oak-panelled walls at Crookhey, to more family history in Ireland. Both Maurie and the Carrington family nanny, Mary Cavanaugh, were rich and irrepressible storytellers, and Leonora's childhood was steeped in tales from both Irish and family history, supplemented on her summer breaks to County Westmeath by total immersion in her grandmother's world of Irish legends and myths, a world in which it was virtually impossible to separate fact from fiction. The so-called 'little people', known in Celtic mythology as the 'Sidhe', played a role in the lives of the Moorheads of Moate that can still be recalled by older members of our family to this day. There are stories that continue to be told about a funeral cortège that had to be halted in order to allow a procession of little people across the road in front of it. It's easy to imagine how powerful a story this would have been for the young Leonora, sitting by the outsized range in Moate while her grandmother stirred her pots and wove her narratives; many years later, she would return to this scene as the setting for one of her best-known paintings.

What her mother and grandmother gave Leonora was the raw material for her life: a way of looking at the world that allowed an unusually wide berth for the inexplicable, the spiritual, the mystical, the bizarre. In essence, it was a world that was naturally surreal, long before Leonora ever heard the word 'surrealism'; indeed Ireland, like Mexico, was surreal centuries ahead of the coining of the word by Guillaume Apollinaire, or the writing of the Surrealist manifestos by André Breton et al. So perhaps it's not remotely surprising that it was Maurie who gave Leonora the Herbert Read book that was her introduction to Surrealism and to Max Ernst. And perhaps the truth about her relationship with Maurie was that it was nuanced and complicated but that it contained mutual respect and understanding. And maybe too Maurie – for all her social climbing, and for all her ambitions for a 'good marriage' for Leonora – had, somewhere inside, a secret pride in her daughter's spirit; because it was, after all, her family's spirit, the Moorhead spirit; the spirit of the *Tuatha Dé Danann*, the spirit of the Sidhe, the spirit of Maria Edgeworth and Aunt Leo. Maurie had allowed herself to be tamed by marriage to Harold; but inside perhaps there somewhere lurked a rebel who had never had an outlet, but who had produced one par excellence as her only daughter; and perhaps, mingled with her horror, astonishment and incredulity at Leonora's actions, there was sometimes the hint of another emotion: admiration.

In June 1937, though, terrible news reached Hazelwood Hall: Leonora had taken up with a penniless German old enough to be her father. Serge Chermayeff (who may have had his own reasons for feeling bitter about her new affair) told Leonora to her face that she was a cheap slut; 'I told him, cheap slut or not, that's the way things are, what do you want me to do, Serge?' she remembered. Presumably he was as damning as he dared to be in his report to Harold Carrington; in any event, the message was clear. Leonora and Max were now together; they were engaged in a sexual relationship and they were doing nothing to hide the reality of that relationship from those around them in London. Maurie was distraught, and Harold was apoplectic. Just as in 'The Oval Lady', he decided to wound Leonora in the heart; he decided to attack what she held most dear, and it was very clear who that meant.

Two hundred miles south of Hazelwood in London, Leonora and Max were spending every minute they possibly could together – in bed, out of bed, in cafés and restaurants, at art galleries and theatres, on walks in the parks. Very early on in their relationship, Leonora remembered, they had a day out in the country, and

Max taught her frottage, the artistic technique he had invented a few years earlier: it involves placing paper randomly over wood or another surface – in this case, leaves – and rubbing with a pencil on the back. Max's frottage drawings are some of his finest work, though not his best known: he used it to produce pieces of art that are intricate, striking and thoughtful: caged birds, detailed close-ups of the human eye, a female form within whose breasts birds flutter.

And teaching Leonora how to do frottage was an important indication as to what this relationship would be about: not simply love, not simply sex, not simply physical attraction, not simply fun: work was right there too at the centre of the mix. Leonora and Max slotted together, in that what she needed, he had to give; and what she had to give, he needed. And one part of that was knowledge about the world Leonora had begun to glimpse during her time in London, but was now with Max's help able to begin to see properly for the first time: the world of art, ideas, politics and literature. It was the world of intellectual thought, a world that had not much impinged on her life so far. 'Intellectualism' was not an ambition in her convent boarding schools, nor in the schoolroom at Crookhey, and it certainly wasn't on the agenda at Hazelwood, where life revolved around tennis on the lawn below the drawing room and dinners to which local notables and Jesuit priests from Stonyhurst College, where her younger brother Arthur was at school, were invited. There was no value, in the Carringtons' world, for intellectual thought; it was neither sought nor welcomed. But this was the stimulation Leonora now realised she craved; and in Max, she had the perfect teacher.

When love moves in it often moves quickly; and it moved quickly now. Leonora was not particularly committed to one group of friends or another; she had often felt rudderless in London, the Ozenfant school her only haven. So now, with Max, she was able to move almost instantly into a new existence in which her life was entirely wrapped up with his.

His show at the Mayor Gallery was on through the whole of June; the Goldfingers' dinner party had been at the start of the month, so the first weeks of the couple's relationship centred on London, and involved many trips to the gallery. It was all a long way from Hazelwood, but from his study there Harold Carrington had begun to take a close interest in the Ernst show. He read the reviews; he asked Serge Chermayeff to visit and report back. He spoke to other contacts in London about the content and the style of the exhibits. And before long, he came up with a verdict on the German artist and his work: it was filthy! Not merely filthy; pornographic. And if it was pornographic, it was illegal; and so Harold decided to involve the police. What were they doing, he asked, allowing this pornographic exhibition to be open to the public in central London? And what was the status, precisely, of the German artist who had created it? What right did he have to be in Britain, showing the distasteful images he regarded as art? Shouldn't the police be investigating? Should they not, in fact, be questioning the German about his motives, and challenging him as to his right to be here, and to the use of his art in this way?

Harold Carrington was a powerful man, and not only in Lancashire. He was a prominent member of society, and a regular visitor to London (where he always stayed in a suite at Claridge's). He was someone who could wield power and who people like police officers respected and listened to; and when he shared his concerns about the porno-graphic work of a German artist they listened gravely, and decided to act. Max Ernst, like Tartar, had to be sacrificed. Harold would explain it all one day to Leonora, in a voice that was as gentle as it was chilling. He had no option, he would tell her, other than to have Ernst arrested; and yes, it was unfortunate that he had ended up deported back to Germany, a Germany run by Hitler, but couldn't she see why he'd had to do it? It was purely for your own good, my dear; purely for your own good . . .

Quite how Max learned of the arrest warrant isn't clear; but he did learn it, and soon. There was, as Roland made clear, no time to lose; London was no longer safe for him, and he had to get away – as far as possible from the capital. As luck would have it, Roland had the perfect hideaway: Lambe Creek near Falmouth in Cornwall, where his brother Beacus had a house. Fortunately, Roland had already arranged to borrow the house for three weeks, and was about to set off there with Lee. The simplest and most secure solution was for Max and Leonora to join them.

If Lambe Creek House had been designed as a bolt-hole for an artist on the run from the police, it could not have been more perfectly situated. It's a handsome, whitewashed

Victorian building with large bay windows looking out over a tiny inlet on the River Truro. To reach it takes about six hours from London even today; in 1937, it would have taken far longer. After Truro town you drive down windy lanes with high hedges on either side; in June the hedges and trees would have been in leaf, making the whole area seem even more hidden, even more screened off from the outside world. The house is outside the village of Kea, which features in some versions of the story of Tristan, the Cornish knight who falls in love with an Irish princess called Iseult (the story inspired the Arthurian tale of Lancelot and Guinevere).

If the remote and tranquil surroundings were not quite enough to distract Max and Leonora from their troubles, the other guests who joined them surely did precisely that. Because the next three weeks turned into what the artist Eileen Agar later described as 'a delightful house party ... with Roland taking the lead, ready to turn the slightest encounter into an orgy. I remember going off to watch Lee taking a bubble bath, but there was not quite enough room in the tub for all of us ... The Surrealists were always supposed to be such immoral monsters, but I for one did not go to bed with everybody who asked me. When would I have found time to paint?'

Agar was just one of those who motored down to Truro that summer to take part in what some art historians have described as the biggest ever gathering of British surrealists on English soil. As well as Max and Leonora, Roland and Lee, and Agar, there were visits from Paul Éluard and his wife Nusch (his former wife Gala, part of the ménage à trois with Max from a few years earlier, was now with Dalí), the poet Joseph Bard, the photographer Man Ray (Lee's ex-lover) and his new partner, a Filipino model called Ady Fidelin. The sculptor Henry Moore and his wife Irena, who were on holiday in Cornwall, called in for lunch one day; the Belgian poet and art dealer Edouard Mesens stayed for longer. The weather in the south west was dull and cool that month, but it didn't seem to dampen anyone's spirits: there were walks around the peninsula, a car trip to Land's End, and visits to the local pub, the Heron, in a rowing boat, across a piece of water from which the next village, Malpas, took its name (bad crossing). There were group postcards, signed by everyone, mailed to friends who couldn't be with them: Monsieur Pablo Picasso on the Rue de Grands Augustines in Paris VI, and Gala, who with Dalí was also in Paris. 'If you were here we'd behave better,' they wrote to Picasso; and 'it's very healthy in this wonderful country, but not too hot,' they reported to Gala.

But the most telling and revealing legacy of events in Lambe Creek that summer was not written down but photographed, mostly by the talented and perceptive Lee. Her archive is packed with photographs from those weeks in Cornwall, and they bear witness to what an extraordinary amount of fun everyone was having. It was as though they had found themselves their own kingdom, and it was one where other people's rules were forgotten, and everyone's defences were down. Lambe Creek was their playground, and the games were by turns clever and sophisticated, abandoned and sexy. There is Max, covered in seaweed, up to his waist in the water of the creek; there he is again, covered in something white and woolly, aping an old man's beard, creeping up on the camera and then, in a shot taken by Roland, embracing Lee and pushing his tongue playfully into her ear. There is the ever cheerful Ady smiling down from an open sash window, next to Man who is holding his camera (taking photographs of Lee, while she takes photographs of him). In another shot taken by Roland, there is a naked Lee leaning out of an upstairs window, the sun lighting her hair like a halo. There is Man in his beret, rowing the boat; there is Mesens, bare-chested, one arm around Max, his eyes obscured by swimming goggles.

And then there is Leonora: Leonora and the other women – Lee, Ady and Nusch – on deckchairs, cups in hand, eyes shut, as though they are sleeping beauties who were in the middle of a tea party when the fairy cast her spell. Leonora with Max, lying on a grass bank, her reclining into him, him crouched down at her head, her shoulder against his knee, his hand pulling her face towards his, his lips on hers. In the foreground is Lee, her everyday smile belied by the glass gun she is pointing at her own head; this is surrealism, up close on a sunny day in an English field. In another shot, one of Lee's carefully constructed groups, Leonora is at the centre of a trio of adoring men. Mesens is behind her; Éluard beside her; Max, his doe eyes turned towards her, resting his head on her shoulder. Leonora is in control, cool and confident: she is looking straight at the camera. She is in charge; she is soaring; she looks splendid. The view from Cornwall that summer contained more than fields and flowers and birds and boats; it was a view into the future, a view of what life not only could but was now undoubtedly going to be. It was a vision of a way people could live, if they tried, as the Surrealists tried, to leave their preconceptions and the expectations of others behind them. For Leonora, this was a golden time; a validation of all she had ever hoped for, all she had dared might be possible. There was another world out there, beyond her parents' world, beyond most people's world; a world she had now entered, and was determined never to leave.

The most beautiful photograph from Lambe Creek that summer is a perfectly composed portrait by Lee of Leonora and Max which entirely captures the spirit of their love, and of their Cornish honeymoon. It's a sunny day, and they are sitting on the unofficial balcony that features in many of the shots, a flat roof accessed from a first floor window. Leonora is wearing knickers and an open robe; in her left hand she holds a lighted cigarette. She is leaning back against the window-sill, and sitting on it behind her, wearing shorts and a shirt, is Max. He has his arms across her chest, his fingers fanned out across each of her breasts, his strong, veined hands old and lined against the alabaster sleek of Leonora's smooth, young chest. Her eyes are closed, her eyelashes creating feathery shadows on her face; one lock of her tightly-sprung, jet-black hair, which Max is nuzzling up against with his right cheek, curls down like a droplet on her forehead. She is in a perfectly-contained, contented reverie. Max's eyes, though, are open, searching. He is her guard, her protector, her lookout. She can dream her dreams; he will keep danger at bay.

That photograph points up a truism about the group at Lambe Creek, and the differences between the men and the women. The women had beauty and youth in common; the men, more disparate in looks, were older, more ragged, less aesthetically polished. In most of the photographs the women could have been professional models (as indeed Lee and Ady had both been); in one picture Ady and Nusch are wearing similar bikini and sarong sets, standing either side of a rather bemused and crumpled-looking Roland, who is glancing from one to another in a gesture that seems to say, how did I get this lucky? How *did* these men get this lucky? In another frame is the incongruous-looking Man Ray ('he was no oil painting,' as Leonora told me) standing looking awkward and formal in a tweed jacket on a boat; beside him, the gorgeous Ady is relaxed and perfectly attired, in a sailor-style jumpsuit.

How these men got so lucky in the summer of 1937 in a corner of Cornwall is the story of men and women through-out and across humanity. It's the story of men's power and women's power, and the difference between the two; it's the story of male wealth and experience versus the power of female sexuality and youth. It's the story of the Surrealist idea of the *femme-enfant*, the woman-child who could inspire great art but who was never going to be expected to create anything herself. It's the story too of intimate ownership, because there was a certain amount of partner-swapping during those weeks in Cornwall; Eileen Agar had an intense affair with Paul Éluard, while Joseph Bard had a relation-ship with Nusch. Max and Paul, of course, already had form – their ménage à trois with Gala – but in this moment,

Leonora and Max were interested only in one another. There was a part of Leonora that was strangely traditional when it came to sex; oddly enough, she told me once that she felt she had inherited a streak of Puritanism from, of all people, her father. But she was also loyal to Max; and perhaps she also felt she needed to keep things in her love life simple so she could concentrate on other things, like art.

Towards the end of the three weeks talk turned, inevitably, to what would happen next. Four of the couples – Lee and Roland, Ady and Man, Paul and Nusch, and Eileen and Joseph – decided to reconvene in France, in the village of Mougins in Provence where Picasso was spending the summer with Dora Maar. Max needed to return to Paris to see his wife Marie-Berthe, who he knew was increasingly distressed at his absence; and London remained an unsafe place for him.

Long before the plans were settled, Leonora had decided on her next step. She would return to Lancashire, to Hazelwood, where she would confront her father. Once Max was in Paris he would be out of Harold's jurisdiction; he was safe, taking Leonora off limits from any sanctions her father might try to employ. She had tasted another way of being, a different way to live. She had made her choice.

I feel almost sorry for my great-uncle, and I certainly feel sorry for my great-aunt, as the train carrying Leonora trundles north towards the Lake District. Maurie thinks she will stay out of it, thinks this is between Harold and Prim and that Harold will deal with it. Almost certainly she believes, as he does, that Leonora has gone way beyond what is acceptable this time.

Leonora described to me the moment she and Harold confronted one another at Hazelwood Hall, both of them angry and passionate.

I am going to Paris, says Prim (she is still Prim; this is the last day she will ever be Prim). I am going to live with Max. I am going to be an artist.

You can't go, says Harold. It's a preposterous, ridiculous idea. You have had your wild interlude but this has to be the end of it. You must come back home, re-immerse yourself in our family, and remember what your life is going to be all about.

But Prim knows now what her life is going to be about: it will be about art, Max and Surrealism.

Harold is making no headway; he is furious. Artists, he tells her, standing there in the heart of his mansion, are penniless. If she does this, Leonora will live and die without money. She will die penniless in some attic. She will have nothing.

Leonora laughs: money is his obsession, it has never been hers. Harold delivers his coup de grâce. There will be no further funding, he tells Prim, if she goes to Paris. If she takes up with this German in Paris, she need not bother coming back. Their relationship will be broken; it will be over.

Harold only means to frighten Prim: that's what he's always done, frightened her so she will see sense.

Prim does not care. She is leaving. In truth there will be no winner, but it will be many years before she will realise that. For now she is doing what Lucretia could not do: she is teaching her father, the bastard, a lesson.

It is August 1937. Leonora Carrington is leaving

Hazelwood, leaving England, and is headed for Paris. She is not eloping, although that is how art historians have described her departure, because she is not leaving with her lover. Rather, she is going alone. 'I always did my running away alone,' she tells me, decades later, in her kitchen in Mexico City. She is leaving not so much for Max, as for a whole new beginning, a whole new life. This is much more about Leonora the individual than it is about Leonora and Max the couple. As Paul Éluard is to write, in a poem inspired by the holiday in Cornwall, 'I accept the danger of being in love. I live.' Leonora accepts the danger of being in love, and she accepts the danger of being in life.

Leonora is twenty years and four months old as she boards the boat train from London to Paris. She is leaving behind her home and her friends; she is leaving behind her mother and her brothers. She is leaving behind her father Harold; and though he will live for another thirteen years, the two will never meet again.

4

The Inn of the Dawn Horse

By the autumn of 1937 Paris was more than the principal city of France: in artistic terms, she was the capital of the entire world. Since the beginning of the century artists and thinkers of all kinds had been gathering there. Painters and writers, poets and activists, film directors and political radicals; they clustered in the cafés of Montmartre and Saint-Germain-des-Prés to debate and deconstruct, critique and condemn the rapid developments in technological, social and economic life that were transforming not only Paris, but the whole of Western Europe. Only rarely in history has a time and a place fused to provide a cradle for so many art movements and such a wealth of artistic directions. There was Cubism and Fauvism, Dadaism and Orphism; there were the artists who became known collectively as the École de Paris, a label that covered all these movements and more; and there was Surrealism.

The artists who had flocked to the City of Light in those early years of the twentieth century were the mould breakers of art history; this was, in all truth, a renaissance. Pablo Picasso and Georges Braque were there to overturn all the conventions of painting; Robert Delaunay to reinvent the use of colour. Wassily Kandinsky came to Paris to forge the spiritual link between the artist and the viewer and the canvas; from Constantin Brâncuşi's studio appeared the clean, elegant geometric works that would redefine what sculpture could be. A few years earlier in the century Amedeo Modigliani had been in Paris to elongate the female form; Marc Chagall had been there to create his colourful dreamworks; Piet Mondrian had moved in to distil his block basics and Henri Matisse had arrived to put together his contrasts of pure, unmodulated colour. Among the surrealists, Yves Tanguy was now preoccupied with the place that was the unconscious; Jean Arp was toying with the revolutionary notion that random chance played its part in the creation of a piece of art, and Joan Miró was finding out what happened when meticulous planning was fused with the automatism so beloved of the movement.

And then there was Max, as talented as the best of them, and even in this company a stand-out figure in terms of his radical inventiveness; he was truly the cream of the avant-garde. Always trying out some new artistic technique, someone who would rather die than play safe; the inventor of frottage and grattage, who now had a new idea, decalcomania, which involved pressing the paint between the canvas and a smooth, glassy surface. Max, with milky-white hair, sky-blue eyes and his beak-like nose: if he had not likened himself to a bird in a spiritual sense, others surely would have made the connection. He was slim, athletic-looking, handsome, and he was charming; according to the art collector Peggy Guggenheim he had 'a terrific reputation for ... his success with women, besides being so well known for his Surrealist paintings and collages'. According to Breton, Max had a gift for projecting an inner light on to those around him; Leonora agreed with this description, saying he 'irradiated light' and that he 'was always smiling'.

Max was intellectual, popular and urbane; along with André Breton and Paul Éluard he was a central figure of Surrealism, usually to be found in the middle of the group at the Café Les Deux Magots or the Café de Flore in Saint-Germain, or at the Café de la Place Blanche in Pigalle. So it was that the feisty twenty-year-old former debutante, with her wild black hair, her pale, alabaster skin and her red lipstick, found herself at the centre of the most exciting group, artistically speaking, on the planet. Within days of her arrival, suitcase in hand, at the Gare du Nord on the boat train from London, she was having supper with Pablo Picasso, Salvador Dalí, André Breton, Paul Éluard (whom she already knew, of course, from Cornwall), Marcel Duchamp and Yves Tanguy. It was thrilling, fascinating, compelling; the whole ethos of the group, she said later, was 'incredibly productive', focused, industrious. These were artists intent on changing the world, and she was now at the centre of their deliberations about how they were going to do it.

Max was delighted to have his new love by his side; he

was proud of her, delighted by her, in awe of her youth and her beauty. For Leonora the twenty-six-year age difference between them was irrelevant. 'He didn't seem that old to me,' she told me. 'We were lovers,' she continued, as though that explained everything; and it *did* explain most of it. Because she and Max were hopelessly, totally and entirely in love, although to separate their love from all that went with it – the discussions in cafés, the chat about art, the sense of being at the heart of something important and meaningful – might, for Leonora, have been difficult. Along with being in love with Max was Surrealism. Not that Leonora needed or desired a label. Indeed, on the contrary, she said later she was only in the Surrealist group because she was in love with Max; she didn't feel she had to fit in and it made her feel free, not constrained or worried about how she appeared. But what was vital to her was his ability to show her a new landscape. As she put it years later, in a typically understated summation of all that Paris was about for her: 'He was a great artist, and I knew that from the start. He was intelligent.' We were looking together at pictures of the two of them; Max looked a bit impish, I said. She laughed: 'He was a lot older than me so I probably out-imped him. I think he taught me a lot. Especially about writers and artists – he told me about people I wouldn't have known about otherwise, he introduced me to them. They weren't the kind of people my family were around. He educated me a lot. Really educated me – a proper education, not a convent education.'

As well as being with someone who was, in Leonora's words, 'an extremely interesting person', there was the wider group of the Surrealists. 'I was working in a new place and alongside new people, wonderful new people,' she told me. 'I felt an affinity with them. I felt at home.' All the same, from the point of view of her work she was still on her own. When I asked her whether she felt nurtured in Paris, she said she didn't, not really. 'They were all doing their own thing. With Max, yes, I was nurtured a bit. But he was doing his own thing as well. They weren't that interested in me.' For the wild child from Lancashire, now on the threshold of a lifetime as an artist, Paris was an opportunity to observe, from the sidelines, the mature period of one of the world's great art movements: to watch carefully how its artists behaved and worked, how they interacted and where they found their inspiration. And for the first time in her life (and what a relief this must have been) there was no-one watching *her*; no-one obsessing over whether she was behaving in the right way, or doing the right thing, or mixing with the right people. This was freedom, and Leonora cherished it.

The couple found an apartment to rent on the Rue Jacob in Saint-Germain, in a building with an interior courtyard reached from the street via a large wooden door. The two cafés, the Deux Magots and the Flore, where they spent much of their time, were a five-minute walk away; the Seine, and the view across it to the Jardin des Tuileries and the Louvre, was a short walk in the opposite direction. Picasso was living at the time just a few metres away; he was a frequent visitor to their flat, and Leonora remembered him dancing round it one evening after supper with a bottle of wine in his hand. She liked him, found him impressive. Unlike Max, he did seem older (Picasso was fifty-six at the time). 'He was very Spanish, very macho,' she recalled. 'He thought all women were in love with him, and he seemed to think women were useless on other fronts. But then again,' she added, 'a lot of men are like that.'

Duchamp she liked very much: he was 'the one I found to be fun; he never took himself seriously'. Salvador Dalí she said 'looked like an ordinary Spaniard; he wasn't extraordinary-looking at that time, he only became that when he moved to live in the US. He was living with Gala then, and I remember that she didn't like me. But he liked me all right, I remember that ...' Dalí wrote later that Leonora was 'a most important woman artist'. Leonora would not have forgiven him the word 'woman' in that phrase.

She had not long arrived in Paris when she had a visitor one day when Max was out. The young man who arrived at the door had hoped to see Max, and was initially disappointed to find he was not at home. But his sadness soon dissipated as he got chatting to the person he described as 'one of the most beautiful women I had ever seen' who spoke 'in English-accented French'. She made tea, 'and in the course of the conversation told me that she loved Max and that they were living together'. Before long, the young visitor found himself unable to speak coherently, so affecting did he find Leonora's 'dark, glowing beauty'. When she told him she hoped they would become very good friends, and kissed him warmly on both cheeks, he knew his 'hammering heart' would take a while to recover.

The young man who arrived at the Rue Jacob that day in search of Max was his son, Jimmy Ernst, and from the way he described their meeting it sounds very much as though Leonora had exactly the same effect on him as she had had on his father a few months earlier at the Goldfingers' flat. Jimmy had just arrived in Paris from Germany with his mother, Luise Straus. The marriage between Max and Luise had been over for many years, and they had converted their romantic feelings into a warm friendship, and a shared concern for the now seventeen-year-old Jimmy. Far more tempestuous, though, was Max's relationship with his current wife, Marie-Berthe, and Leonora's arrival in Paris was about to ratchet up the stakes considerably where that was concerned.

Max and Marie-Berthe had been married for ten years, and what is most striking about the story of their relationship is how similar her tale is to that of Leonora. When the two met Marie-Berthe was twenty years old. She came from a wealthy Catholic family who, like the Carringtons with Leonora, opposed the relationship; when it was obvious that it was serious, they tried to get Max arrested – he had to go on the run with the help of friends after a warrant was issued for his arrest. They later lived on the Rue Tourlacque in Montmartre; Marie-Berthe, like Leonora, was a painter, but more of a dilettante than a serious player. She, much more than Leonora, fitted the Surrealist ideal of the *femme-enfant*; but she had stayed too long, and was now no longer *enfant* enough for Max. Jimmy Ernst described her as a 'fragile, bird-like figure' who, he said, had shown him much affection. When Jimmy did eventually get to see his father that day in the Rue Jacob, Max explained to him that Marie-Berthe had become completely immersed in the Catholicism of her youth, and was even considering entering a convent. In the meantime, though, she was horrified by Max's open relationship with Leonora, and had taken to following them to public places and sometimes creating embarrassing scenes. The situation had also reignited the Aurenche family's anger over Max, and they had made what Jimmy said were successful attempts to blacken his father's name in Paris, seriously denting sales of his work.

All this meant it was doubly important that the event the Surrealists were now planning should be a success, and especially a success for Max. It was a new exhibition of Surrealism, this time in the Galerie Beaux Arts in central Paris. Along with Salvador Dalí, Max was listed as a 'technical adviser'. Man Ray was in charge of lighting; Wolfgang Paalen was the 'expert for water and foliage'. Marcel Duchamp was the curator, and André Breton and Paul Éluard were the organisers.

It was a show that would rewrite the manifesto of what an exhibition could be: and it began where a successful art exhibition should always begin, by creating a buzz. Visitors were invited to attend the opening at 10pm on the night of 17 January 1938; but when they arrived on the Rue du Faubourg Saint-Honoré they found the gallery still locked, and a well-dressed but confused-looking crowd milling about, wondering what was going on. Salvador Dalí was running up and down telling people that they should come back in an hour; in fact, it would be midnight before the doors were opened.

As they filed into the exhibition the crowd passed through a forecourt that contained a work by Dalí called *Rain Taxi*. It was a real-life Fiat taxi and it contained two mannequins: one in the front seat wearing a peaked hat and dark glasses and holding the wheel, the other a scantily-clad female reclining on the back seat. She was covered in ivy and crawling all over her were live snails; they were leaving slimy traces as they criss-crossed her body. But the most significant element was the rain, which was drenching both occupants of the taxi because it was an internal storm, pouring in from the taxi roof.

From there the visitors passed into the gallery proper, where they were informed that the lights had failed and that they would have to look at the exhibits using torches. With these in hand they continued their tour along a corridor made to resemble a Parisian street, along which – lined up to resemble prostitutes soliciting for clients – were a row of mannequins, each designed by a different artist. The head of André Masson's mannequin was enclosed within a bird cage, referencing a Magritte painting called *The Therapist* dating from the previous year; Dalí's wore a bright pink hat designed by the surrealist designer Elsa Schiaparelli, with a broken egg splayed across its chest and tiny coffee spoons dotted down its torso and legs. Duchamp's model, meanwhile, was androgynous, wearing a man's waistcoat, jacket and tie on top, but with its lower half exposed. Max Ernst's work was fascinating: his mannequin was a female figure wearing a black dress, her face partly obscured by a dark veil, who was standing looking triumphant and imperious above the figure of a white-haired male who was lying prostrate at her feet.

The exhibition continued into a room designed by Duchamp. He had hung 1200 coal bags from the ceiling, and the result was a womb-like environment with a bed in each of the four corners of the room. True to the essential spirit of Surrealism, the underlying story of the show was all about sex, and the subconscious; it was about life and death and desire, and it perfectly displayed the central ambition of the movement, which was to be both playful and disturbing at the same time. But most important of all, for the future of art history, was that this show was the first proper example of what might be called installation art. No longer did an exhibition have to be about looking at paintings on pristine white walls: this was the show that deconstructed that idea completely, making the event an experience and forcing its visitors to be participants, players, not mere spectators. Surrealism was all about separating people from their expectations, forcing them to confront their deepest feelings and desires, the feelings and desires they worked so hard to keep hidden, or had never had the imagination to unlock. Life can be different from the way it has been up to now, the Surrealists promised; an art exhibition can be different from the way it has always been. Come with us, they beckoned, and we will show you how.

For Leonora, the exhibition was a ground-breaking moment: aged not quite twenty-one, she had joined the greatest names of twentieth-century art to take part in a seismic exhibition. As achievements go, it was no mean feat.

Painting, of course, was essential to Leonora in her

exciting new surroundings in Paris; but so too was writing, and in the spring of 1938 she became for the first time a published author, with a short story published in pamphlet form called 'The House of Fear'. As with all Leonora's writing, the story weaves a dry, everyday sense of humour through a fantastical tale, in this case a visit to a woman who had one huge eye that was six times the size of a normal eye, and whose fluttering dressing gown was made of live bats sewn together by their wings. There is a hint in the story of the loneliness she perhaps sometimes feels ('I have few friends and am glad to have a horse for a friend') and a self-reproach for being a recluse; but even in England Leonora had always been on the edge of any group she was connected to, and being on the sidelines of the group in Paris would not have felt strange or unfamiliar to her. What she never did was kowtow to the grandeur of the older men who dominated Surrealism.

The publication of 'The House of Fear' (which had a tiny print run of 120 copies) was a kind of public acknowledgement of her relationship with Max, who contributed both its illustrations, and an introduction. The opening image shows a woman's body with a horse's head, its head turned slightly to one side; and in his introduction, Max quite clearly makes the connection between the painting he displayed in the London exhibition the previous year, and his new, young love. He describes two people walking slowly down a street: is one of them, he asks the man people call Loplop, 'the Bird Superior', so-called because his temperament is at once both kind and savage? On his hat sits a bird with deep red feathers, a hooked beak and a stern look. The man is fearless, but he has come, says Max, from 'the house of fear. And the woman . . . must be none other than the Bride of the Wind'.

But who, he continues, is this Bride of the Wind? His description seems to hint at their intimate life, a life in which he teases her about her inadequate French (which is the language they speak together), her lack of education and perhaps even her domestic shortcomings. Can she read, he asks. Is she able to write French? Does she know how to put wood on to the fire so they can keep warm?

And then Max goes on to answer his own questions. His Bride of the Wind herself provides warmth with 'her intense life, her mystery, her poetry'. Even though she is not well-read, she has absorbed everything. The nightingale, he says, has seen her reading; horses and other animals were gathered round, listening to her with approval.

Another visitor to the Rue Jacob around this time was the wealthy collector Peggy Guggenheim, who arrived accompanied by Howard Putzel, the American dealer she had recruited to help her in her quest to amass what would become one of the finest collections of modern art, the collection that today is the backbone of her epony-mous museum in Venice. Peggy's ambition at the time, she writes in her autobiography, was to buy a picture a day: so when she arrived at Max's studio, his hopes must have been high. Leonora was there beside him: 'At the feet of Ernst sat his beautiful lady love and pupil, Leonora Carrington,' Peggy records. 'They looked like Nell and her grandfather in *The Old Curiosity Shop*.'

Max spoke very little during the visit, so Peggy was 'forced to carry on a continuous chatter'. She settled on a painting she would like to buy, but it turned out to belong to Leonora and was not for sale. Another piece she liked was declared by Putzel, slightly bizarrely, to be 'too cheap'. In the end, Peggy did buy – but it was one of Leonora's works, not one of Max's. 'She was unknown at that time, but full of imagination in the best Surrealist manner and always painted animals and birds,' Peggy wrote later.

The sale to Peggy was her first ever. Perhaps it was partly because of this that Leonora always held Peggy in great regard; and indeed, though there would go on to be plenty of reasons why the two women could fall out, surprisingly they never did.

The painting Peggy took away from the Rue Jacob was entitled *The Horses of Lord Candlestick*, and it showed four horses – one white, one grey, one chestnut and the other olive green – against a turbulent, stormy landscape, frolicking while other horses watch from a distance. 'Lord Candlestick' was Leonora's name for her father Harold Carrington; in another painting dating from the same period, *The Meal of Lord Candlestick*, a group of figures are seen feasting on birds, fruit, flowers ... and a human baby, into whose body one of the diners is prodding her fork. 'What desire for extravagance!' Breton remarked, on seeing it. It was an extravagance from which Leonora had now escaped, as perhaps the frolicking horses of the Guggenheim painting convey.

Though her relationship with her father Harold had been damaged beyond repair by her relationship with Max, that with her mother Maurie was more robust. At some point in that spring of 1938 Maurie crossed the Channel to spend a few days in Paris so she could see Leonora. It was an act of defiance, for a wife like Maurie, who one imagines did not have her husband's blessing. Throughout the rest of Maurie's long life, mother and daughter never lost touch; and throughout the turbulence of the next few years in Europe, Maurie (with the help, at times, of Harold) did all she could to support Leonora, even from afar and even in the midst of war. On her trip to Paris in 1938 Maurie was already worried about what the uncertain political situation in Europe might mean for her daughter and her partner; as things would turn out, she was entirely right to be so concerned.

The most significant barometer of Leonora's feelings during her time in Paris is contained in a painting that is one of the most important of her lifetime: her *Self-Portrait*, or *The Inn of the Dawn Horse* (1937–8) which today hangs in New York's Metropolitan Museum. The location is a large, empty room with a tiled floor and an aperture with grandly draped ochre curtains which transform it from a mere window into a stage, the stage on which Leonora's future life is being played out.

She herself is sitting on a delightfully surreal upholstered blue and crimson chair, its fulsome skirt protecting the modesty of its dainty little high-heeled feet. But the chair is more ostentatiously female than its sitter: she, and she is clearly Leonora, is almost androgynous, with a brown, high-necked shirt under a moss-green riding jacket; there is no hint of breasts, let alone cleavage. Her shapely, jodhpur-clad white legs are splayed and her pointy boots are wide apart. Her hair, always a symbol of her rebellion, is wild, mane-like and luxuriant around her determined-looking face. She is pointing an elegant, long finger towards one of the three other creatures in the picture: it is a hyena, like the hyena from 'The Debutante', only this time it is a lactating hyena with three milk-filled breasts.

The other two creatures are both horses, and at first glance they appear similar: both white, both captured mid-gallop. But the horse behind her, suspended in mid-air, is a wooden horse, a rocking horse like Tartar, and like the horse she bought for the apartment on Rue Jacob, on which Max was photographed in 1938. The rocking horse is elegant and handsome but, ultimately, it is constrained, suspended in that moment, unable to move or to roam free.

The second horse is outside the window. She is in a garden with green grass and tall trees, and she is running freely; in another second she will be out of the picture, gone from the frame. This horse is the new Leonora; and the androgynous woman in the chair is the new Leonora as well. Everything about this image points to how thrilled Leonora is to have escaped from the confines of her birth; everything about it hints at her hopes for her now autonomous future. This is not the painting of a muse, and nor is it the work of a handmaiden. This is the work of a rebel who has already completed one rebellion and who hints there are more rebellions in store.

Leonora and Max's first fall-out was with Breton, who as soon as the exhibition at the Galerie Beaux Arts was finished, left to visit Mexico where he met the muralist Diego Rivera, his wife and fellow artist Frida Kahlo, and her lover Leon Trotsky, who had by this time moved out of the Blue House occupied by Rivera and Kahlo (after Rivera objected to their affair) to the fortified villa where he would be murdered, on Stalin's orders, two years later. But Éluard had become an apologist for Stalin, and he attempted to interfere with Breton's siding with Trotsky, leading to a disagreement on Breton's return to Paris that saw Éluard removed from the Surrealist group. Max was no Stalinist, but Éluard was his closest friend, and he now found himself in disagreement with Breton.

The second, more immediate conflict, however, was with Max's second wife Marie-Berthe. On at least one occasion in the Café de Flore, Leonora and Max's favourite café, she caused a scene that ended in the throwing of cups and saucers. Leonora, as she later recalled, gave as good as she got, and sent her own crockery flying straight back in Marie-Berthe's direction. But the combination of difficulties in his private life and disagreements with his fellow artists meant Paris had, within nine or ten months of Leonora's arrival, become an uncomfortable place for the couple to be. 'All I want now,' Max told Jimmy, 'is to leave Paris for a long time and live with Leonora in the Ardèche . . . and to love her . . . if the world will only allow it.'

It was an ambitious hope, and both of them knew it: but they had come this far, and now certainly wasn't the moment to turn back.

Leonora's father, Harold Carrington

Leonora with her mother, Maurie,
at the presentation at the court of
King George V

Leonora with her brothers Gerard and Arthur, Nanny Carrington, and the author's
grandfather, George Moorhead, on the terrace at Hazelwood Hall

Leonora and Max Ernst during their stay in Cornwall in the summer of 1937

A surreal pose: Leonora (front) with (from left) Lee Miller, Ady Fidelin and Nusch Éluard, in Cornwall

Leonora with (from left) E. L. T. Mesens, Max and Paul Éluard, in Cornwall

Lee Miller with glass gun in the foreground; Max kissing Leonora in the background. Cornwall, 1937

Leonora and Max in the midst of their idyllic summer:
Saint-Martin-d'Ardèche, France, 1939

The artists in exile in New York, 1942, in a photograph taken at Peggy
Guggenheim's home. (From left to right) front row: Stanley William
Hayter, Leonora Carrington, Frederick Kiesler, Kurt Seligmann. Second
Row: Max Ernst, Amédée Ozenfant, André Breton, Fernand Léger,
Berenice Abbott. Third Row: Jimmy Ernst, Peggy Guggenheim, John
Ferren, Marcel Duchamp, Piet Mondrian.

Leonora and Chiki's wedding day, Mexico City, 1946. Seated from left to right: Kati Horna, Chiki Weisz, Leonora Carrington and Gunther Gerzso; standing by the window: Benjamin Péret and Marianne Frenkel

Leonora turns artist's model for Kati Horna in this photograph from a series entitled *Ode to Necrophilia*, 1962

Leonora with her sons Gabriel and Pablo, by her husband, Chiki Weisz

Leonora in her home in Mexico City with the author, next to a maquette of *How Doth the Little Crocodile* and Yeti's tail

Leonora in her studio in Mexico City in 2010, the year before her death

5

Little Francis

They were looking for somewhere beautiful, cheap, remote and a long way from Paris; and Max knew exactly the place. Marie-Berthe had relatives in the Ardèche, an area he had visited with her. He remembered the endless verdant countryside, the vineyards, the tiny medieval villages perched on hillsides. He remembered the starry night sky – this was Van Gogh country, after all – and the inns where the wine was served like water; and most of all, he remembered how far it all seemed from Paris.

They caught the Rapide from the Gare de Lyon to Orange, left their suitcases there to be sent on later, and bought bicycles on which they rode south, taking it gently. The weather was warmer than in Paris, the air was filled with a chorus of crickets, and after a journey of about thirty kilometres they arrived at a village where the river was wide, with a stony, white shore. Leonora had never seen water like it, so brilliant and deep and green.

This was Saint-Martin-d'Ardèche, population around one hundred and fifty, a village whose inhabitants worked on the land and had never heard of Surrealism, or Pablo Picasso, Salvador Dalí or Max Ernst. They did, though, think he seemed like a very strange man indeed, this white-haired new arrival with the young girl who at first they thought was his daughter, but who it quickly became clear, from the way he looked at her over their glasses of wine at the Hôtel les Touristes, was his lover. The couple spent their first few nights there, in a room that was dirty but pleasant; but then Max did a deal with some campers who were returning home to Marseilles, and bought their tent. He and Leonora took the tent to the opposite side of the river from the village and pitched it there; it seemed to her as though it was a different world, this other side of the river, a private, secret and almost perfect world, in which she and Max were finally alone, safe and completely happy. There was time to talk and to make love; time to laugh and to tease one another; time to swim and to fish; time to sit gazing at the beauty of the surroundings. When the sun was too hot in the middle of the day Max stayed in the water to keep cool, emerging eventually with his eyes looking 'like two beautiful blue fish'. His hair would then dry 'into fluffy white plumes in the sun', as he stretched himself out on the warm stones. He had made a bed for Leonora out of sand; after a late lunch of bread, cheese and wine they would sleep until the buildings of the village were turning purple, which was their signal to wander back to their favourite bar, Chez Le Foufou, for more wine, and chat into the night with the eccentric owner, a woman with whom they were striking up something of a friendship.

But the idyll was almost over as soon as it had begun. The descriptions above are taken from a novella called *Little Francis*, which Leonora wrote as a roman à clef to describe the love triangle between herself, Max and Marie-Berthe. Because as it turned out, four hundred miles was not enough space between them and Max's wife. *Little Francis* disguises its true tale by presenting Max as the kindly Uncle Ubriaco whose fourteen-year-old daughter, Amelia (Marie-Berthe), is insanely jealous about his relationship with a young nephew, Francis (Leonora). When Amelia realises the boy has arrived in Paris she tries, unsuccessfully, to get him sent home to England; when that fails she lies on the floor screaming, and Ubriaco bundles Francis out of the house, whispering in his ear 'Café de Flore, Boulevard Saint-Germain, in an hour's time'. After they rendezvous there, uncle and nephew slip away from the city to the south, to a village called Saint-Roc (Saint-Martin), where they camp by the river and lead a simple, happy life. It is a magical interlude for Francis, who knows these are times he will remember for ever. One day, as he watches his uncle standing by the river, naked apart from his green fishing hat, Francis feels 'slightly sad ... he felt he would never love anybody so much as Uncle Ubriaco'.

Leonora's novella does not flinch from the truth about her situation. In making Amelia Ubriaco's daughter she acknowledges that Marie-Berthe has the stronger claim on Max; but in describing how comfortable and contented Ubriaco is with Francis, and how easily the two co-exist in their secret world, she is paying tribute to the depth and simplicity of the love between her and Max. What is also fascinating, and again resolutely honest, is her portrayal of Max as a father/uncle figure, to both Marie-Berthe and, more importantly, to her. There was no disguising in Leonora's mind about the role Max occupied; of course Max was a father figure; and unlike her actual father, who had wanted to, as she always put it, 'diseducate' her into the ways of the English upper classes, Max was intent on educating her in every way he could. All her life, Leonora would remember how much she learned from Max: 'It was more or less everything,' she told me.

But one evening, in the story of *Little Francis*, the son of the local aristocrat appears in the mêlée of the village inn to say Ubriaco is wanted on the telephone; his daughter is calling him. Uncle and nephew escape again, taking refuge with a friend in a neighbouring region; eventually they return to Saint-Roc, only to be woken on their first morning back at the inn by the landlady. Amelia has arrived; Ubriaco cannot ignore her any longer. She only wants him to stay with her for three days, he tells Francis, after which he can deposit her with an aunt in Valence. But three days turns into a much longer period when Ubriaco ends up taking his daughter back to Paris; and Amelia then tricks Francis into returning to Paris at precisely the moment Ubriaco decides to go back to Saint-Roc to be with him. The coup de grâce is the killing of Francis by Amelia when he goes to his uncle's flat and finds her there instead of Ubriaco.

Like all of Leonora's fiction, much of the narrative is true. Marie-Berthe did follow her and Max to the south; Max did end up having to take his wife back to Paris; and Leonora, like Francis, was left bereft, angry and afraid in the village inn. It is those feelings, ascribed to Francis in the novella, that reveal the depths of Leonora's turmoil. To have got this far on their tumultuous journey, only to have her lover appear to have returned to his wife, seemed an impossible burden to bear. She had, in effect, pinned all her hopes on this relationship; she must have realised how precarious her situation was, and how dependent she had made herself upon this man. When Ubriaco tells Francis he is going to spend three days with Amelia, the boy is furious, and reacts no doubt exactly as Leonora did when Max told her he was returning to Paris with Marie-Berthe: 'Don't talk to me as if I'm a door-knob. I'm going if you do – in the other direction.' If Ubriaco manages to arrange his 'genital responsibilities' (Leonora at this point seems to be reverting to truth rather than fiction) then Francis might come back to see him. But her unhappiness is only too apparent through the wretched response of poor Francis, who oscillates from hope to despair as Ubriaco worms this way and that, seeming at one turn to be about to stay with Amelia, and at another to be returning to his nephew.

In the fictional version of the story Francis/Leonora is destroyed; but in the true version, she survived and, indeed, won the battle for Max. In January 1939, having spent most of the previous month in Paris with Marie-Berthe, he returned to Saint-Martin, and would not return to his wife again. Leonora, for all he had put her through – or maybe *because* of all he had put her through – was more in love with him than ever. On 16 January, she wrote in the journal she was keeping at the time: 'I'm in my house with Max. For two years, I have been desperately and madly in love ... I'm still painting but only to keep me from going crazy. Every second I want him to live only for and with me. I wish that he had no past. I want him for ever. I want to be in the same body as him ...'

The house in which she wrote this was an old and decrepit stone building just outside the village, in an area known as Les Alliberts. It is situated up a narrow lane, halfway up a hillside; a rather ramshackle farmhouse with the date '1640' chiselled roughly above the doorway. The house is entered via a staircase, above which is a terrace with breathtaking views across the treetops and the valley; from there, through a windowless aperture, the Ardèche in all its lushness and with its vineyards and huddles of habitations is laid out. Turn into the house and there is a dark kitchen, with bedrooms and a sitting area upstairs. The house is a perfect size in an ideal location for a couple who want to spend most of their days à deux, but who will from time to time be hosting guests from Paris.

Leonora and Max fell in love with the house the first time they saw it. Buying it wasn't difficult; Max had no money, but Maurie was still prepared to fund her daughter, possibly without Harold's knowledge. The money was wired from Lancashire; the deal was quickly done. The couple sent for the rest of their belongings from the Rue Jacob, and moved in. The happiest interlude of both their lives was about to begin; 'a kind of paradise time of my life,' Leonora called it many years later; and it would be dominated not only by joy, although there was to be plenty of that, but also by an extraordinary amount of inventive and intriguing art; for both Leonora and for Max, 1939 in Saint-Martin would be one of the most intensively productive periods of their lives.

The house was more than just a home. It was a haven, a safe house not only from all the difficulties they had encountered, but also from the cloud that had been gathering with an increasing sense of danger during their time in Paris. That cloud, which had begun to dominate more and more the late-night discussions in the Café Les Deux Magots, concerned the threat of the encroaching force of Nazi Germany and Adolf Hitler. But as the spring gave way to summer, all these dangers seemed a very long way indeed from the remote farmhouse perched on the hillside above Saint-Martin, where the sounds were the bells of the goats in the fields, the buzzing of the bees and flies, and the crickets at night chirruping into the darkness lit by a thousand stars above the vineyards.

The couple hired some help from the village and set about making improvements: on Tuesday 13 June 1939, Max and Leonora wrote to their friends Paul and Nusch Éluard inviting them to stay; they would, they said, be 'thrilled' to see them. 'For now it [the house] is completely lacking in comfort, but in a month or five weeks it will be better ... ' The first thing they wanted to create was a terrace where they could sit late into the cool of the night, looking down on the valley. They bought a pair of peacocks to grace the grass below, and a dovecote and some birds. And once the building work was completed and the terrace was finished, their attention turned to the house itself. It was to be their canvas: over the coming months they would fill every nook and cranny of it with their art, making it a testament to their journey together and their love for one another. Terrace, kitchen, cupboards, walls; everywhere had the potential, at Les Alliberts, to become a Surrealist work. Behind the wooden frame of a kitchen cupboard door, as though it was passing by this very second, on the other side of the wall, is a blood-red unicorn, with a fierce orange mane and a wispy beard. This is by Leonora; so too is the image on the outside of another cupboard door, where a she-figure stands sheathed in a purple dress, her head that of an elegant black horse, her mane cascading freely (of course!) down her back. And the creature has wings, too: she has joined forces with a bird, and has taken flight. Open the cupboard doors and strange lizard-like creatures are waiting to greet you; move through the house, and there are more figures at every turn. One, in green, is a resting horse-like female, a she-mare, this time with the image transposed so the body is that of a horse, and the face is that of a woman. But the horse has human breasts and a fish's tail; and the expression on her face is steely and fierce.

Max's work, meanwhile, inhabits the corners and looms down from the walls. There is a white, meditative female in one crevice; an owl-like bird with a sharp beak and wide eyes poised on a wall. On the inside of the terrace is an unruly, dancing giant reminiscent of his 1937 master-piece *L'Ange du Foyer*, in which a wild beast dances with an unselfconscious joy. Go down to the basement and beneath your feet is a mosaic of a brown bat, wings unfurled, against an aquamarine floor. And then, outside the house on the wall that greets you as you arrive up the lane from the village, the pièce de résistance: a huge bas-relief which stands like an advertisement for the mission, the art and the love of Leonora Carrington and Max Ernst. It shows a tall figure with a beak-like nose: his arms are raised above his head as though in surrender. The game is up, it seems to say: the monster is tamed. Within the folds of his long, artist's gown is his alter ego Loplop; and the bird is dancing with joy and glee. Beside him stands a tall, young, naked female, her breasts like perfectly rounded apples on her smooth chest. These two figures represent Leonora and Max, and this is the lasting testament to the love that overtook them in that summer of 1939, in this remote and sunny corner of France that seemed too far from Paris to care about the storm-clouds of war that were gathering in the north.

At the beginning of their time in Saint-Martin the couple had seemed at pains to keep their whereabouts secret. In a letter to Man Ray from the inn, sent during their early days there, Leonora adds a PS: 'Please don't tell anyone where we are except Éluard and Nush [sic]'. Now, though, there were some guests, the first of whom was the artist Leonor Fini, whose stay was also to prove one of the most eventful. Ten years older than Leonora, and already well established in her career, the Argentinian Leonor – whose face, like her name, resembled the younger artist – had enjoyed a brief affair with Max a few years earlier, and he had inscribed a copy of his seminal collage novel *Une Semaine de Bonté* (1934) with the words: 'To Leonor Fini. The more I think of her, the more I forget the devil.' They had moved their love affair on into a warm friendship, and Leonor arrived at Les Alliberts with two male companions, the writer André Pieyre de Mandiargues and the painter Federico Veneziani. During her several weeks in Saint-Martin, Leonor painted two portraits of Leonora: one was subsequently destroyed, the other hangs today in the purple corridor at West Dean in Sussex. It shows Leonora as one of a female trio, playing the part of a Joan of Arc-style warrior, complete with armour breast-plate.

It was a prescient notion, because as it turned out the visit would end in a vengeful quarrel that saw Leonor take a knife to her other painting of Leonora, scraping off its surface before she flounced out of the house and went back to Paris. The two women later were reconciled, but it was a bitter blow for Leonora at the time; she confessed that when she realised Leonor had destroyed the painting, she felt as though Leonor wanted to destroy her; and she worried that this might be what was going to happen, that it was somehow portentous of her death.

Fini's visit partially overlapped with that of Lee Miller and Roland Penrose, who arrived at the end of July on their way to see Picasso and Dora Maar in Antibes. As in Cornwall, Lee's photographs are an evocative testimonial to the spirit of the set-up at Les Alliberts. They show the informality of the place, the lazy ease with which the hosts and their guests enjoyed the delightful playground Max and Leonora had created. There is Leonor in a high-necked white blouse, her hair piled up on her head, sitting against a wall looking pensive and beautiful, with a hint of the fierceness that would flare up during the row with Leonora. There is Leonora indoors, standing at a basin; this image has been interpreted as her doing the domestic work for Max, but look more closely and you realise it's not a kitchen sink, it's a bedroom or bathroom. There's a shawl hanging beside her, and a mirror to one side. There is Leonora with Max, his arm around her shoulders, his face still looking a little bit startled that she is his to be holding at all. In this collection of images, the best of all shows Leonora alone. She is wearing a dark, bolero-style matador's jacket, its edges fringed with tiny silver bells, and she is sitting with her hands behind her head, looking straight into the camera. She is unsmiling, and she looks steely and very sure of herself indeed.

The other guests that summer were the Powells: Joan, Leonora's friend from the Florence finishing school they had attended together in 1935 ('she was the first person I ever heard say the word "fuck",' Leonora told me) and her brothers Michael and Philip, who later in his life recalled the trip to the Ardèche. They motored down through France in Joan's Baby Austin, remembered Philip, and their stay in Saint-Martin felt 'frightfully grand'; he must have meant the bohemian company, because he was unlikely to have found the remote farmhouse, which had neither electricity nor mains water, anything other than primitive. Leonora he described as 'a terribly nice person, but totally outrageous; my sister was never totally outrageous'.

But with the guests came unsettling news of the brewing political storm. The visitors brought stories of how all the talk – not only in the Deux Magots and the Flore, but also in London – was now about what seemed the inevitability of war. Opinion was divided on how it would all pan out. It would be a brief war; no, it would be a drawn-out marathon. Hitler was poised to take over the whole of Europe; on the contrary, he would be quickly tamed. On a personal level, though, there was no doubt: Max's work had already been denounced by the Nazis at the Degenerate Art Exhibition in Munich in 1937, an event organised by the Nazis with the aim of declaring what Hitler called 'merciless war' on unacceptable art forms; in effect, that meant anything modern. The show, opened by a scathing Joseph Goebbels, Hitler's Head of Propaganda, had also included the works of, amongst others, Klee, Kandinsky and Chagall. If the worst happened and Hitler overran Europe, there was no question: Max Ernst was definitely one of the many millions who would no longer be safe. Perhaps anticipating the events that would follow, to him personally as well as to Europe, one of his paintings from this period in Saint-Martin is entitled simply: *A Moment of Calm*.

By the end of August the visitors were gone; and on 3 September came the announcement they had all been dreading: the declaration of Britain and France that they were now at war with Germany. As Leonora and Max had suspected, the political quickly became personal; and ironically, given the Nazi refusenik he was, it was being a

German citizen that was to cause Max difficulties. Within days he was informed that he would be interned because he was 'a citizen of the German Reich' who were now France's enemies. He was taken to a prison in Largentière, fifty kilometres to the north west of Saint-Martin, a frightening development for both him and Leonora; with Max gone, his twenty-two-year-old lover was alone. The only good news for them both was that she was able to move to stay in the inn near the prison and, even better, the camp commander granted Max three hours of freedom a day if he would use it to paint a souvenir for him, a landscape of Largentière. Leonora hurried back to Saint-Martin to collect the paints and canvas. It was a welcome diversion, and they were both grateful for the time they had together each day; but the situation was extremely stressful. On 16 September, Leonora wrote to Leonor Fini from the inn in Largentière, in response to a communication from her friend: 'Your letter was the first good thing to happen to me for a long time. I am deprived, tortured and half-mad ... ' Largentière, she reports, is 'a rather nice little town' but there is nothing to do except take walks, 'and you know how I detest walks'. She prefers, she says, to talk to the cats, but they are nervous and won't let her touch them.

Later in his life, in 1971, when the former prison commander asked him to authenticate the painting from Largentière, Ernst refused, saying he had 'the worst possible memory' of his time at the prison. But in fact life there was almost certainly better than the internment camp at Les Milles near Aix-en-Provence, to which he was moved just six weeks later. This camp was located in a former brick factory; it was littered with broken bricks and the air was thick with dust; the dust got everywhere, including into the meagre rations of food the internees were given, and its redness even crept into the pores of their skin. It felt to Max as though he was turning into a crumbling brick himself; the only consolation was that his cellmate was the painter Hans Bellmer, an old friend from Paris days, and another artist condemned by the Nazis as 'degenerate'. To pass the time, they made portraits of one another: Bellmer's depicts Max's face as a wall, the cracks between the bricks making up the lines of his skin. It's an inventive and thoughtful painting, but Max looks old, downcast and lonely; incarceration has hit him hard. The sparkling summer is over; the light in his eyes that Lee Miller captured so easily in the photographs at Saint-Martin a few months earlier has disappeared. His lids are hooded now, his face haggard. According to another of his fellow inmates, Max seemed 'like a phantom' at Les Milles; he hardly ever took part in activities or even in conversations.

Leonora was distraught at Max's predicament, and devoted herself to doing all she could do to get him released. She wrote to everyone she could think of who might be able to help: Paul Éluard, Erno Goldfinger, Roland Penrose. To Erno, from the Café des Voyageurs at Largentière where she was staying, she wrote, in typically understated fashion: 'Max is here in a concentration camp and things are not so cheerful as they might be.' At this stage (the letter is undated) she sees him 'twice a week for ten minutes'. She describes herself as 'very nervous and not too happy with all these miserable events' and says she is trying 'with a sinister and deliberate determination' to get Max out of prison. She's lonely and afraid ('I've been alone for 20 days so excuse this incoherence') and asks whether Erno could send the four pounds a month he is currently sending, as payment for an artwork he has purchased, to her instead of to Max, since all his goods are being confiscated, and anything addressed to her, as she is a British national, cannot be touched.

Erno's reply, dated 4 October 1939, is not everything she would have hoped for. He is, says Goldfinger, 'terribly upset about the happenings to Max' and he is looking around to see how he can help; later in the day he will be meeting Roland Penrose to talk about what can be done. But on the money front, 'It is most unfortunate that I got the letter about the installments for Max's picture only today, as the money for this month, which is the last, has gone already'. To a young woman now alone, and afraid, in a country at war, who has signalled that she is in need of money, it is not an overly generous response.

From Roland Penrose a few days later, though, came a more heartfelt missive. 'Prim darling,' he wrote from Hampstead; clearly the family nickname was still in occasional use with her friends. 'I have heard from Erno of your misfortunes. I am very anxious to do all I can to help. Yesterday I had a letter from Paul [Éluard] saying that he was already on the track and hoped to succeed, so I have written to him to ask what methods we should use. I can get together quite a lot of influential intellectuals with the help of Herbert Read and we could sign a letter together.'

He describes life now in England: 'London is all blacked out and what amusement we get is very limited. It's all in the dark. How unlike all we have known and enjoyed together.'

Roland's final thought is for Max. 'Give my love to Max when you see him. His nightmare can't go on for ever.' The letter ends 'with no end of love for you' from Roland, and Lee has signed in her own hand.

Meanwhile in Lancashire, Maurie was dreadfully worried about the situation her young daughter was in, and desperately wishing she could be persuaded to come home to the safety of Hazelwood Hall. She wrote the letters, but their tone suggests that Harold's attitude has softened, and he is also doing all he can. 'My darling Prim,' writes Maurie, '[I] Was delighted to get your letter, & am trying everything in my power to help you, when the Consul replies will send it on to you – it looks hopeful as he is taking his time. Pa increased your allowance to £5/10 a week. Let me know if it is getting through safely, & did you get a parcel of food from me just before war was declared – a plum cake, sardines, stockings, wool, black & white you asked for? Had a letter from Joan [Powell], she seems anxious to be with you. Would you like her? Let me know what kind of pub you are in & do they feed you well? Would you go back to your own house if Joan was with you, you could paint & work on the land, at times like these it is best to have plenty to do?' She herself, she continues, is looking after three young boys from the slums [evacuees from Manchester]. 'Most people think here that the war will be over very soon, I hope & pray they are right'. She is arranging to get newspapers sent from Smith's in Lancaster, and ends: 'Do write me full details of what you are doing & hope all will be well if you have patience, remember these jobs take time? All my love darling. Your loving Mother. Maurie.'

In another letter dated Monday 18th (probably October), Maurie reports that 'Pa had a spot of bother about getting your money to you, but the Bank is now in communication with France & you ought to be able to get it, let me know how things are going on'. She longs, she says, for Leonora to be back: 'Would you like to come home?' and has again sent provisions. She makes a reference to something she suggested on her trip to see the couple in Paris, probably that Max should be naturalized as a French citizen: 'What a pity M. didn't do what I told him to in Paris – but even now it might be managed?' There is plenty of family news – Leonora's brother Gerard, now in the army, is preparing to be sent overseas; Uncle Gerald (Moorhead) has also joined up; my grandmother Miriam has gone to stay with her mother in Staffordshire – and: 'No one could believe there was a war on, everything is very quiet TG & we all try to look happy & cheerful, but who is?'

And Maurie ends, in a heartbreaking line which suggests that she has put all their rows behind her, and now wants only to support her daughter: 'All our love darling & don't forget we will do everything in our power to help you. Your loving Mother.'

In December, it seemed that what Roland had called their 'nightmare' was at an end. Thanks to the intervention of

Paul Éluard, who had petitioned every powerful figure in France he could think of, Max was released, and returned to Les Alliberts. Leonora had hardly dared believe his freedom might be possible: now he was back, the rhythm of their life together was even more intense and precious than it had been before. Her letters from this period reflect the domesticity of their lives, with much emphasis – probably due to the privations of the prison camps – on food. In one letter to Leonor Fini, written in January 1940, Leonora reports that she has made a 'good dish' out of rice, chopped onion, black olives, two beaten eggs, black pepper and canned tuna and finished with a sauce made from tomatoes, small whole onions, olives and cream. Her mother, she says, 'has written and sent good things to eat (creamed mushrooms, peas, cake etc.) and a completely rotten pheasant (it was a voyage of two months).' In another letter, again to Leonor, in March of that year, she describes having made an 'exquisite' Bakewell tart, based on a recipe supplied by Maurie on her trip to Paris the previous year. She also reports that there is now an oven and stove installed at Les Alliberts, and says how much she enjoys cooking (indeed, it was a lifelong interest) and that she becomes 'like one possessed at five o'clock in the afternoon when I am preparing the dishes'.

In addition to cooking there was, of course, art, and that spring of 1940 saw the creation of two particularly poignant and important paintings: one of Leonora by Max, and one of Max by Leonora. His, entitled *Leonora in the Morning Light*, follows on from his series of forest paintings, and shows a composed and triumphant-looking

Leonora emerging into a turquoise dawn from a forest filled with fantastical plants and exquisitely bizarre creatures. She has had to battle through the undergrowth to reach this point; but her struggles, as she parts the branches of the undergrowth and steps into the clearing, seem to be at an end. If this is what Max thought to convey, he could hardly – as events would turn out – have been more wrong; but then again, a forest has many clearings. Perhaps Max knew what turned out to be correct: that this period when they were together again at Les Alliberts would turn out to be merely a hiatus, a lull in the tumult, and that after the clearing Leonora would have to plunge into the forest once more. Neither of them, though, could possibly have foreseen how thick and congested the branches and vegetation would be in this new patch of forest that lay ahead.

For now, though, she was safe; but her painting of him, *Portrait of Max Ernst*, hints at a doubt that had begun to seep into Leonora's mind about their relationship. The portrait shows him in a robe of rose-coloured fur that ends in a fish's tail; one long foot is visible, sheathed in a yellow and black striped sock. Max's snow white hair is echoed in the landscape around him, which is arctic: there are icy peaks behind him and icicles are dripping off the frozen island on which he stands. In the background is a white horse, but like the rocking horse in her self-portrait, this horse is static, and icicles hang from its frozen body. And just as in the self-portrait there is a second horse; but this one, in miniature, is enclosed within a lantern which Max is holding in his right hand.

Leonora knew Max loved her; she knew he cared for her; she knew he was educating her; she knew, also, that she loved him. Somewhere inside herself, though, she sensed that if she stayed with him the problems of her childhood would be repeated, and she would be stifled, ossified, petrified. The white horse in her painting is beautiful but inert; its eyes are glazed over, and it is going nowhere. This was the fear that had taken hold in her mind: if she stayed with Max, he would smother her. Around the same time as the painting, she wrote a short story called 'Pigeon Fly'; it told the story of a young female artist who is commissioned by a man who has recently been widowed to paint a portrait of his dead wife, now lying in her coffin. The artist completes the task, but is shocked to discover when it is finished that the face she has painted is in fact her own. She then finds the dead woman's diary, which describes her husband, Celestin, a man who wore a feather robe and striped stockings. Celestin is very full of himself – '"Am I beautiful?" he asked. "They say I am."' – and his wife, whose name is Agathe, begins to doubt him more and more ('The more I looked at Celestin, the lighter he seemed to me, light as a feather.'). At one point he tells her: '"You will always be a child, Agathe. I am terribly young, aren't I?"' Agathe's diary ends abruptly; the young artist turns back to the portrait, and finds the canvas empty. 'I didn't dare look for my face in the mirror. I knew what I would see: my hands were so cold!'

Although still only in her early twenties, Leonora had worked out an important and essential truth about being a woman who was also an artist: if she stayed with Max she would be dwarfed by him. She would be a bit-part in the painting of his life, like the petrified horse behind him in his portrait.

The key to how she saw herself is right there in her painting of Max, and it is the tiny horse in the lantern he is holding. That horse looks almost like a foal *in utero*; it is suspended in bluey-green amniotic fluid, and Max is its midwife. He has nurtured it in its womb, but Leonora has begun to suspect he will not be able to stay with it after its birth. The painting acknowledges her huge debt to him: his guidance, his care, his teaching, his rescue of her. But just as she absolutely needed him to bring her talents to birth, so she cannot risk remaining with him.

Spring was turning to summer when the gendarmes returned to Les Alliberts in May. Max had been accused by a deaf and dumb man in the village of sending light signals to the enemy, and General Henri Dentz himself had ordered his re-arrest and his return to the prison at Les Milles, via the jail in Loriol. This time he was handcuffed and escorted from the house by a gendarme with a rifle; Leonora was distraught. After he was gone she went down to the village where she wept for several hours; she then returned to the house where she drank orange blossom water, causing her to vomit. 'I had realized the injustice of society, I wanted first of all to cleanse myself, then go beyond its brutal ineptitude.'

A new spirit of defiance seemed to inhabit her, and for three weeks she remained alone at Les Alliberts. She ate sparingly, drank wine, worked on the land and refused to be daunted by the arrival of some Belgian soldiers who were staying in the village, and who came to the house to accuse her of being a spy after someone was seen with a lantern near the house at night (they were looking for snails, she said). They said she could be shot on the spot, but she wasn't afraid. 'Their threats impressed me very little indeed, for I knew that I was not destined to die.'

In mid-June there were more visitors: an English artist friend, Catherine Yarrow, and her lover, a Hungarian artist called Michel Lucas. Catherine had lived for a while in Zurich where she had met Carl Jung and been much influenced by him; now, at Les Alliberts, she applied what she knew of psychoanalysis to Leonora, and concluded that her friend needed for the second time in her life to get rid of her father figure. It was Max 'whom I had to eliminate if I wanted to live', Leonora wrote later. Catherine implored Leonora to stop punishing herself, begged her to take this opportunity to get away from this little corner of France that was no longer idyllic but increasingly dangerous by the day. She could make a new life somewhere else; she would find a new lover. It was madness, said Catherine, to remain.

Leonora procrastinated, genuinely torn. Despite her doubts about the wisdom of a long-term relationship with Max, she still loved him: and fiercely loyal, she couldn't imagine abandoning either him or the house into which they had both poured so much of themselves. On the other hand, if she stayed she would be alone; who knew when the Nazis would arrive, or what that would mean? The war was closing in, and this was a final chance of escape; it was not to be passed up lightly.

Eventually, after much soul-searching, she made her decision. She had Max's passport; what he would need, when he eventually got out of detention, was a visa so he could leave France, where he was clearly no longer safe. Leonora decided to go with Catherine, taking Max's passport with her, and to seek a visa for him in Madrid. His passport felt to her, she wrote later, like an entity: it was 'as if I was taking Max with me'.

It was imperative to go quickly. Leonora and Michel hurried to a nearby town, Bourg-Saint-Andéol, to get a travel permit. At the gendarmerie no-one was very interested – the police officers merely smoked their cigarettes and said there wasn't anything they could do to help. Back in Saint-Martin, there were more problems: where would she get money to take on her trip, and what could she do with Les Alliberts? She went to see the owner of the Hôtel les Touristes, Louis Jean Viano; she and Max had a tab with him, he had lent them money in the past, and she wanted to ask if he could lend her some money now for her journey. Viano said he could, but that he wanted the outstanding debts settled; if she wanted his help, she should make the house over to him. A solicitor was summoned; the deal was quickly done. On 18 June 1940 she signed a document giving Les Alliberts and all its contents over to Viano; the cost to him was twenty thousand francs, most of which she and Max already owed him. It was a tiny amount: the equivalent of around one thousand pounds, or one thousand four hundred dollars today. Leonora had been horribly, and shamefully, exploited. She knew it, but she also knew something else: she had no choice.

That night Leonora stayed up, going through the contents of the house, deciding what she could take in her suitcase; a case that bore, beneath her name, a small brass plate set into the leather, on which was written the word REVELATION. What to take, and what to leave, when you are packing your whole life into one small suitcase? One thing was clear: there was no space for art. Most of the paintings and sculpture at Les Alliberts were, in any case, part of the fabric of the house, and were not portable. But even her self-portrait, *The Inn of the Dawn Horse*, which was so emblematic of all she had gone through to escape from her past, as well as a manifesto for her future, was left behind. Perhaps it was as a message to Max: just as taking his passport meant she was keeping him at the centre of her journey, leaving behind her self-portrait meant she was leaving part of herself for him to find if and when he returned.

Early the next morning the schoolmistress of Saint-Martin gave Leonora papers that had been stamped at the town hall, giving her permission to travel. Catherine and Michel packed their tiny Fiat with the luggage, while Leonora struggled to come to terms with the idea that she was leaving the place that had been such an oasis for her and Max, and that she had sold it and all their work and was now leaving Max, her rescuer and lover, behind in prison.

When the car was packed, and Catherine and Michel were ready to go, Leonora closed the door of Les Alliberts for the final time. She walked into the garden in front of the house, opened the doors of the dovecote to release the birds, and stood for just a moment watching as they soared into the sky. Then she went down the lane to the Fiat, squeezed into the seat between her friends, and Catherine turned on the engine for the long drive south.

Leonora never returned to Saint-Martin, but almost seventy-one years after she left, I went there. I intended to see what I could find and report back to her; she was keen to have news of the village and wanted to know what had become of the house. An email correspondence with the owner revealed that he usually refused all requests for access to the property; but since I was Leonora's cousin, and would be able to take her news of the town where she had once been so happy, he would make an exception in my case.

And so, on an April day in 2011, soon after Leonora turned ninety-four, I walked into the house at Les Alliberts. The strange thing was that it felt almost as though the house was still waiting for her to return. Because the owner bought it much as Leonora sold it, contents intact, it is eerily almost exactly as it was when she left it in June 1940. The huge bas-relief, the lasting testament to her and Max's love, greeted me as I walked up the lane; the tall figure with the beak-like nose, and the willowy female with the rounded breasts, are still there on the big stone wall. Inside, on the terrace, the unruly giant in the style of *L'Ange du Foyer* is still dancing; in the cupboard, the she-figure in the purple dress is still standing, and the half-woman, half-horse is still resting peacefully inside another, her gaze as steely as ever. Through all the long years of Leonora's life this house stood here virtually untouched and, unknown to her, remained a silent witness to the love that shaped her life.

Most remarkable of all, perhaps, is that many of the possessions Leonora was unable to take with her when she left Saint-Martin are still there in the house. In the sitting room stands a bookcase full of her books: there are works by Aldous Huxley, Fyodor Dostoevsky; there is *Treasure Island*, and *A Century of Creepy Stories*. There is *Vile Bodies* by Evelyn Waugh, and *Can You Forgive Her?* by Anthony Trollope; Eric Gill's *Art Nouveau and Other Stories*, and *A Book of Ballads* by A. P. Herbert, which is inscribed 'from Pat [her brother], 1932'. On the wall is an old map of Europe, the Europe into whose war they had now been plunged; and in the basement, a set of golf clubs with the initials 'LC' embossed on their dusty covers.

In the room Leonora once shared with Max there is a writing desk, and in that desk the letters I have quoted in this chapter from Maurie, and from Roland Penrose, were still there in the drawer (the owner gave them to me to return to Leonora). And there was another letter, perhaps the most poignant of them all; a letter sent to Leonora from Max in prison. It is brief, but it manages to both acknowledge the happiness of their earlier lives, and to offer hope for a better future. Max describes the jail courtyard where at night, for a few minutes, he can see a few stars . . . lost horizons. He sends Leonora a kiss: he loves her. Just as he always did; perhaps more than ever.

6

Down Below

The Fiat was tiny: not much bigger than the coffee table around which we were sitting, said Leonora. Almost seven decades later, she could still remember exactly how it felt being squashed into the front seat of that little car, sandwiched between Catherine and Michel as they drove down the lane away from Les Alliberts, and turned towards the south. She remembered the speed with which they had to pack up the car. She remembered her fear, as the journey rumbled on, about the advancing Nazis: the Germans had broken through the Maginot line to the north, and were pushing on through France.

They drove all day, and then on through the night, passing trucks from which dangled arms and legs, and along roads lined with coffins. It all stank of death, Leonora remembered.

Every mile they travelled was taking her further away

from Max, and she was consumed by grief and guilt at leaving him. She could hardly bear to think of him, alone in the misery of the prison at Les Milles; and if he ever got out, and returned to Saint-Martin, she did not want to imagine how horrified he would be at her decision to sell the house and leave without him.

It was a frightening, perilous drive through the scorching summer heat of southern France. About fifteen miles from Saint-Martin, the car's brakes suddenly jammed. Catherine managed to free them, but they never worked properly again; to Leonora, the problem seemed emblematic of her own difficulties, and she wondered if she were somehow responsible for the mechanical malfunction.

By 7am they were in Perpignan, but there was no hotel room available and so they pressed on to Andorra. When Leonora got out of the car there, though, she realised she was unable to walk properly any more. She could not go straight, only sideways like a crab; once more she felt she had 'jammed'. 'I realised that my anguish – my mind, if you prefer – was painfully trying to unite itself with my body ... I was trying to understand this vertigo of mine: that my body no longer obeyed the formulas established in my mind, the formulas of old, limited Reason ... '

It was the beginning of a breakdown; or perhaps it was the continuation of a breakdown that had started when Max was taken away, the second time, by the armed gendarmes. In desperation, Leonora turned for solace where she had always turned: to animals. When they stopped for a walk on a mountain outside Andorra, Leonora noticed a herd of horses and ran eagerly towards them; when her companions caught up with her, the animals galloped away.

The plan was to cross from Andorra into Spain, but two attempts to get through the border failed, and Michel sent telegram after telegram to Harold Carrington in Lancashire, pleading with him to help get his daughter and her friends out of their predicament. Eventually Harold – whom Leonora once described as having more than a smidgen of mafioso about him – seems to have pulled some strings via the family's connections with the Jesuit order at whose school (Stonyhurst in Lancashire) her brother Arthur was still a pupil; one of its well-connected priests, Father Robert de Trafford, was also Harold's closest friend and fishing companion. His efforts seem to have paid off, because one day a mysterious Jesuit appeared with what Leonora remembered was a very dirty piece of paper. Whatever information it contained, that piece of paper did the trick: a third attempt to cross into Spain was successful, at least for Leonora and Catherine; Michel was not allowed to pass, so he remained in France.

Entering Spain was an emotional experience in more ways than one. Leonora felt relief, of course; but the country into which they entered was only just emerging from its own cataclysmic civil war, which she had heard discussed many times around the tables at the Deux Magots and the Café de Flore in Paris. The Surrealists abhorred the terrible war in Spain: the bombing of the republican village of Guernica by the Nazis, which had taken place a few months before Leonora's arrival in the French capital, had led Picasso to create his eponymous anti-war mural, and the civil war had inspired many other artworks by the

Surrealists. All of this was very clearly on Leonora's mind as she arrived in Spain: she felt, she later wrote, 'quite over-whelmed . . . I thought it was my kingdom, that the red earth was the dried blood of the Civil War. I was choked by the dead, by their thick presence in that lacerated countryside'. She and Catherine motored on to Barcelona, arriving there in the evening, and Leonora became convinced that they should get to Madrid as quickly as pos-sible. She persuaded Catherine to abandon the car, and they caught the train to the capital and checked into the Hotel Internacional, where they had their supper that first night in the rooftop restaurant; 'to be on a roof answered for me a profound need, for there I found myself in a euphoric state', she later wrote.

She had become convinced that she had been chosen to play a pivotal role in Europe's troubles, and that Spain was the place where she would realise it. 'I convinced myself that Madrid was the world's stomach and that I had been chosen for the task of restoring this digestive organ to health. I believed that all anguish had accumulated in me and would dissolve in the end, and this explained to me the force of my emotions. I believed that I was capable of bearing this dreadful weight and of drawing from it a solution for the world. The dysentery I suffered from later was nothing but the illness of Madrid taking shape in my intestinal tract.'

Leonora's memories of these days are contained in an autobiographical short story called *Down Below*, which charts two journeys: one, the flight from France to Spain; the other, the voyage from sanity to madness. It is a rare tract in English literature, the story from the inside of a psychological breakdown and serious mental illness; it sits alongside Sylvia Plath's *The Bell Jar*, and Antonia White's *Beyond the Glass* for its forensic examination of how it feels to lose one's grip on everyday reality.

Leonora and Catherine left the Internacional and moved to the Hotel Roma where they received a visit from a Dutchman called Van Ghent, whose son had business connections with Harold Carrington through ICI. The Dutchman showed Leonora his passport, which was 'infested with Swastikas'; this triggered a sudden desire in her to hand over all her papers, as well as Max's passport. Van Ghent refused to take them, but to Leonora this was another sign. 'I remember that I replied: "Ah! I understand, I must kill him myself," i.e. disconnect myself from Max.'

Leonora was now in the vortex of mental illness, and how much of the account she gives in *Down Below* is true, and how much is a result of being unbalanced, is unclear. In her story she says she attempted to divest herself of her belongings, giving the contents of her handbag to a group of soldiers. But Van Ghent disappeared, and she writes that the men pushed her into a car, took her to a house, which she remembered had wrought-iron balconies, and raped her. In *Down Below* she describes putting up a tremendous fight, and that afterwards they deposited her near El Retiro, the big park in central Madrid, where she wandered around with torn clothes until she was picked up by a policeman and deposited back at her hotel. She called Van Ghent; but instead of being sympathetic or helpful he insulted her. It seems to have been the final straw. 'I spent the rest of the night taking cold baths and putting on nightgowns, one after the other. One was of pale green silk, another pink.'

She was now convinced that Van Ghent was the evil master behind Spain's troubles. 'One night, having torn up and scattered in the streets a vast quantity of newspapers which I believed to be a hypnotic device resorted to by Van Ghent, I stood at the door of the hotel, horrified to see people in the Alameda go by who seemed to be made of wood. I rushed to the roof of the hotel and wept, looking at the chained city below at my feet, the city it was my duty to liberate.' She went to find Catherine, who like Van Ghent was now seriously worried by her state of mind; Catherine refused to listen to her and put her out of the room. Leonora went out on to the street, ran into a park and played in the grass; when an officer of the Falange took her back to the hotel, she again spent the night taking cold baths.

Now convinced that Van Ghent was 'my father, my enemy, and the enemy of mankind', and that the cigarettes he had given her were doped, Leonora decided to denounce him to the authorities. 'I therefore called at the British Embassy and saw the Consul there. I endeavoured to convince him that the World War was being waged hypnotically by a group of people – Hitler and Co. – who were represented in Spain by Van Ghent; that to vanquish him it would suffice to understand his hypnotic power; we would then stop the war and liberate the world, which was "jammed", like me and Catherine's Fiat . . . '

That day in August 1940, Leonora's freedom came to an end. A doctor was called; she was taken to another hotel, the Ritz, and locked in a room there. Frantic messages were no doubt being relayed to Lancashire, and to Harold and Maurie: their twenty-three-year-old daughter was now alone, and mad, in a foreign city. From being an inconvenience, Leonora had become an embarrassment and, more than that, a liability and a danger to herself. Presumably on the family's orders, and financed by them, she was admitted to a sanatorium run by nuns, who seem to have quickly realised they could not cope with her. 'It was impossible to lock me up,' Leonora later wrote. 'Keys and windows were no obstacles for me; I wandered all over the place, looking for the roof, which I believed my proper dwelling place.' Eventually, two doctors who had been involved in her care in Madrid arrived at the convent and told Leonora that a solution to her troubles had been found. They were going to take her away from the city to the north, to the beautiful seaside town of San Sebastian. There she would be able to walk along the sand and to enjoy the sunshine. She would be free.

That promise was a lie. The destination of the car that left Madrid bound for the north of Spain was not San Sebastian, but the neighbouring town of Santander, and a clinic for psychiatric patients. En route, Leonora was drugged; she was handed over 'like a cadaver' to the head of the clinic, Dr Morales. What lay ahead was a period of pain and suffering that would dwarf everything she had so far known.

She woke up in a tiny room with no windows on to the outside, just an opening into a room next door: the only furniture, apart from the bed in which she was lying, was a cheap-looking pine wardrobe, a matching table with a marble top and space below for a chamber pot, and a chair. There were two doors: one led to a bathroom; through the other, which was made of glass, she could see a corridor and another door of opaque glass through which she could make out sunshine. That gave her heart its first leap of hope; but her awakening was extremely painful: Luminal, the barbiturate with which she had been injected on her journey from Madrid, causes severe joint and muscle pain. Her initial thought, as she floated to consciousness, was that she had been involved in a car accident; after all, she was clearly in a hospital, and was being watched over by 'a repulsive-looking nurse who looked like an enormous bottle of Lysol'. But when she tried to move she realised that her hands and feet were bound by leather straps. It certainly was a hospital, but not a general hospital; this was a mental hospital, and she was now a prisoner.

Throughout the rest of her life Leonora referred to the clinic at Santander as 'the madhouse' or 'the asylum'; but those descriptions give a misleading impression of the institution to which she had been taken. Santander is today, as it was in the 1930s, a genteel seaside town that had been a favourite destination of the Spanish royal family; this patronage, combined with twelve square miles of bay, picturesque narrow streets and breathtaking views to the mountains, have long made it a fashionable destination. And the psychiatric clinic, called Villa Covadonga, run by Dr Mariano Morales was fashionable too in its own way: it was used by families with money who wanted somewhere discreet to deposit relatives who had become an embarrassment. It was certainly not unpleasant in itself, and was located on a spacious, grassy estate a couple of miles inland. There were gardens and an orchard and fields with horses; in fact knowing this was probably what led Maurie and Harold to agree to their daughter being admitted there, since they were undoubtedly paying the bills.

But what Maurie and Harold could not possibly have known, when they sanctioned Leonora's removal to what sounded like a pleasant sanatorium in agreeable surroundings, was that Dr Morales was an exponent of a brutal and experimental treatment for psychotic patients. It was a precursor to electroconvulsive therapy or electric shock treatment, and it involved administering a drug called Cardiazol to a patient who would usually have been strapped to a bed. The drug induced an epileptic fit, which doctors believed could restore lucidity; but it was an extremely frightening and unpleasant experience, and its lengthy list of possible side-effects included a heart attack, a dislocated jaw, spinal fracture, worsening depression, intense fear, hallucinations and memory loss. Patients who had been through it reported intense feelings of dread and panic once the treatment started; in fact, one theory about why it was successful was that the fear of the treatment became so overpowering in the patient's mind that it simply replaced whatever the original anxiety or problem had been. Even more damning was the fact that Cardiazol, particularly when given to patients whose symptoms did not merit such extreme intervention, could actually exacerbate, rather than improve, their condition.

The first few days at Covadonga were confusing and

humiliating for Leonora. Most of the time she was strapped
to a bed; at one point she reports in *Down Below* that she
was stripped and tied naked to the bed, and that she lay like
that for several days and nights 'lying in my own excre-
ment, urine, and sweat, tortured by mosquitoes whose
stings made my body hideous – I believed that they were
the spirits of all the crushed Spaniards who blamed me
for my internment, my lack of intelligence, and my sub-
missiveness'. At one point Dr Luis Morales – Mariano's
son – had all the furniture removed from her room other
than the bed; at another point, she was released and given a
bath. These moments brought hope: on both occasions, she
thought they meant she was about to be released from her
imprisonment. But she was wrong.

What Leonora called 'the most terrible and blackest day
in my life' began with the arrival in her room of a doctor
carrying a black leather physician's bag. The doctor said he
had come to take a blood test, but the room quickly filled
up with people. 'Each one of them got hold of a portion of
my body and I saw the centre of all eyes fixed upon me in
a ghastly stare,' wrote Leonora in *Down Below*. 'Don Luis's
eyes were tearing my brain apart, and I was sinking down
into a well . . . very far . . . The bottom of that well was the
stopping of my mind for all eternity in the essence of utter
anguish.'

Leonora 'learned later that my condition had lasted for
ten minutes; I was convulsed, pitiably hideous, I grimaced
and my grimaces were repeated all over my body'. When
she came to, she was lying naked on the floor of her room.
The first emotion she felt was defeat; she felt 'dominated,

ready to become the slave of the first comer, ready to die, it all mattered little to me'. They could do what they wanted to her now; 'I was as obedient as an ox'.

Over the next few days she was allowed to sit in the sun room she had first spied from her bedroom, and to go for walks in the grounds. She began to feel almost happy, because she believed the worst was behind her, and that she would soon be allowed to go to 'Down Below', the villa at Covadonga which was reserved for those who were almost cured, as a final staging-post before they headed back into the world. But there was to be a second episode with Cardiazol, and then a third. On the second dose she realised that closing her eyes meant she could avoid the most painful element, which for her was the staring eyes of the others in the room as she descended into a seizure. But on the third occasion, despite knowing that closing her eyes would help, Leonora decided to keep them open. 'I . . . felt again the atrocious experience of the original dose of Cardiazol: absence of motion, fixation, horrible reality. I did not want to close my eyes, thinking that the sacrificial moment had come and determined to oppose it with all my strength,' she wrote later.

What Leonora details in *Down Below* is a harrowing, and yet ultimately inspiring, combination of extreme vulnerability, and extraordinary resilience. She describes, in minute detail, where a human being has to go, and what she or he must cling on to, when there is absolutely nothing else left. In her most desperate moments in Covadonga, she can't even trust her own mind any more. All she has is her essence, and her will to survive.

Most striking of all in her story is the forensic way in which she explains her actions, making sense of 'mad' behaviour. Her description, for example, of how she took her food in a ritual way – first her milk, then her biscuits, then her fruit – show her finding a way to impose a kind of order on to a situation that had lost all reason. Her use of her few possessions – coins, eau de cologne, face cream, nail buff, mirror, lipstick – to represent the world she was trying to understand, sounds entirely and even admirably logical. The great irony of Leonora's situation was that madness and mental illness had long been a fascination of the Surrealists. In *Surrealism and the Treatment of Mental Illness* (1930), Breton argues that Surrealist works are designed to reveal the madness within normality, disturbing our understanding of sanity. In *Down Below*, Leonora seems almost to be providing the flip side to that: her recollections reveal the normality within the madness, and they disturb our understanding of what it is to be insane.

What Leonora endured in the asylum was to be the pivotal experience of her life, with ramifications that continued even into the long afternoons we shared together, many decades later, in another sunny, Spanish-speaking country thousands of miles away. Even in her nineties, Leonora was never comfortable with talking about what happened in Santander in 1940: a shadow would cross her face if it was mentioned, and she would quickly light another Marlboro, inhale deeply, and suggest a change of subject. The only things she ever said about that time were, firstly, that the Cardiazol 'did the trick ... it made me think, I'll never go mad again ...'; and secondly, that it made her realise, for the first time in her life, that she was vulnerable: 'What it mainly did for me in a conscious way was [to make me] suddenly become aware that I was both mortal and touchable, and I could be destroyed.' Because what happened to Leonora in Spain in 1941 was a kind of death; a death from which, against the odds, she would manage to be reborn. Seventy years on, during the long days we spent together in Mexico City, death was near again; and this time, there could be no escape.

In Santander, Leonora teetered between sanity and madness; it was one of those fluid boundaries, like so many fluid boundaries in her paintings. Was the creature in one of her artworks, with branches emerging from the neckline of her dress, a tree, or was she a woman? Were the birds submerged under the earth alive, or were they dead? Was Leonora Carrington sane, or was she mad? All her life, Leonora would be fascinated by boundaries and whether they could be penetrated or even removed; in Santander she lived out that fascination. It is this period in Leonora's life, this most gruelling part of her journey, that reveals her to be perhaps the truest of all the Surrealists. Because she did not simply study or debate or mull over the premises of Surrealism: she lived them. She once told me she had never tried to be a Surrealist. Of course she hadn't; she didn't have to try.

Some of the most Surreal elements of Leonora's life were provided not by her but by others: and now came one of those moments. One day Don Luis, Leonora's doctor, gave her what in other circumstances would have seemed an unbelievable piece of news: her nanny from England, Mary

Cavanaugh, was coming to stay at Covadonga. She had travelled to Santander from England on a warship; it had been, Leonora remembered, a terrible fifteen-day voyage in a narrow cabin. Nanny Carrington, as she was always known, had never travelled outside the British Isles before, and unsurprisingly she spoke no Spanish. Leonora was mistrustful ('she was sent to me by my hostile parents, and I knew that her intention was to take me back to them') and she also felt humiliated by the fact that Maurie and Harold had decided not to come themselves to their daughter in her hour of need, but had instead sent a paid employee. You would think, she said to me many years later, that my mother or father might have come to find me; but no, they sent Nanny.

Perhaps if Maurie or Harold had made the journey, the outcome would have been different. Perhaps; but probably not. With the arrival of Nanny Carrington, however, the future was sealed: Leonora would not be going home. She was cold and distant with the woman who had cared for her throughout her childhood; in turn, Mary was confused and shocked by what had happened to her former charge. Leonora's third Cardiazol injection took place during Mary's stay; Nanny wept by her bedside, crying out 'What have they done to you ... what have they done to you?' But far from being touched by it, Leonora later wrote, she felt exasperated, feeling that her parents were trying to pull her back through Mary. She sent her away.

As well as the story of *Down Below*, Leonora left two other tangible reminders of her time at Covadonga: a painting of the same name, and a map showing the park where

Dr Morales's clinic was located. The map has been interpreted by some art historians as a figurative representation
of the place where she met with the greatest challenges of
her life; in fact, when I travelled to Santander in 2011, I discovered the place almost exactly as Leonora drew it. Today
it's a public park on the outskirts of the town, surrounded
by high-rise flats and slightly ugly industrial buildings. But
you can still see the mountains, and you still get a sense of
it as an oasis of greenery and even calm. The fruit trees are
still there, and the footpaths along which she walked with
her nurse, Frau Asegurado. A little bower and cave at the
bottom of her map are exactly as she drew them, just inside
the perimeter fence of the park. 'Down Below', the villa
reserved for those patients who were on their way back to
health, would have been close by.

Leonora was dead by the time I went to Santander, but I
felt her spirit was very close as I wandered across the park.
In the centre of her map she has drawn a horse; it is kneel-
ing on its back legs, its head flung backwards, its front legs
kicking into the air. Its mouth is open as though it is neighing, and its mane is wild and flowing. At first this image
seems grotesque; what has happened to the horse? Why
does it look so disturbed? But look again, and the horse is
beautiful; and it has somehow remained composed despite
its struggles. Quite soon, it will rise up and gallop on to
new ground and fresh adventures.

Leonora's painting of *Down Below* is, unsurprisingly,
one of the most unsettling of all her paintings. The setting is a luscious-looking green garden which clearly
references the parkland at the Santander clinic; the two

horses that feature on the canvas are, again unsurprisingly, made of stone. There are four female figures clustered on the grass, and each one seems to represent a different facet of Leonora: one is a breastplate-wearing, moustached warrior; another a green Medusa; the third a masked, red-stockinged femme fatale; the last a white, beaked spectre with a bird-like face. Leonora, like all of us, was one individual made up of many instincts and personas; here she seems to be identifying the most important character-istics that shaped her personality and provided her raison d'être. She was a fighter, not afraid to take on behaviour generally associated with being male; she was a monster, shaped by terror; she was a sexual being, who needed the release of lovemaking and the haven of intimacy; and she was mortal, a woman whose fear of death never paralysed her, but made her brutally honest, and strangely free. And in a way, her experience of psychological breakdown, and the journey she had to make back to sanity, itself brought a kind of liberation. 'Well, at least being mad gets rid of all your fixed ideas about yourself,' she told a journalist many years later.

Leonora's rescue from the asylum came from an unlikely quarter: a distant cousin. His name was Guillermo Gil; he was related to her through the Bamfords, of JCB digger fame; one of Leonora's great-aunts, Jane Somers, had mar-ried Robert Bamford in 1893. Guillermo was a doctor, who was by chance based at the general hospital in Santander; he came to visit her, and told her he would help her get out. In *Down Below* Leonora says Guillermo wrote to the ambassador in Madrid; it seems more likely he would have been in contact with Harold and Maurie in Lancashire. In any event, he managed to secure Leonora's release, on one condition: she had to remain in the care of her nurse from Covadonga, the redoubtable Frau Asegurado. On 31 December 1940 Leonora left Santander for Madrid. It was a freezing day: they travelled by train, and at one point – near Avila, birthplace of St Teresa – the train was held up for a long time, and Leonora had to listen to the agonised cries of trucks of sheep who were perished by the cold. Their anguished lament seemed to echo her own desperation: she was now alone (save for Frau Asegurado, whom she would have preferred to have been without). She had no money, apart from the funds her father was making available for her accommodation. She had no friends: Nanny Carrington had gone back to England, and Guillermo was still in Santander. She had no lover: heaven only knew what had become of Max, from whom she had received no news for more than six months. It was the dawn of a new year, but Leonora was alone, afraid, penniless and friendless, in the middle of a continent that was being engulfed by a war that did not look as though it was going to end quickly. As she sat on the stationary train, looking out of the window at the frozen landscape and listening to the bleating sheep, she must surely have pondered how easy it would have been to have gone back home to Lancashire, back to the comfort and warmth of Hazelwood Hall, back to a life where she did not have to lurch from one heart-stopping crisis to another. Never in her long journey away from her family had her future looked quite so bleak as it did in that moment on the train outside Madrid.

They checked into a large and expensive hotel at Harold's expense, and a businessman who was a colleague of her father came to visit. One night he and his wife invited Leonora to supper at their house; she remembered with amusement that his wife was afraid of her 'because I'd just come out of the madhouse'. The woman hesitated before giving Leonora a knife and fork, and it was 'all I could do not to crack up, it was so funny'. Afterwards she didn't want to see Leonora again; 'I was much too alarming to have around in the social life of Madrid'.

One night the businessman took Leonora out to dinner alone, and told her that her family had decided her fate. She was to be sent by ship to South Africa, where she would be admitted to a sanatorium. 'He said ... "you'll be very happy because it's so lovely there". I said, "I'm not sure about that." Well then, said the businessman, there was another option ... a personal one. "I could give you a lovely apartment here, and I could see you very very often."' Under the table, his hand moved across to rest on Leonora's thigh.

It was, she remembered later, a huge dilemma. 'Either I was shipped to South Africa, or I was going to bed with this appalling man.' By the time they left the restaurant, she was still mulling over which would be less horrible; and then, as they were about to step into the street, a tremendous gust of wind blew the metal sign down in front of her; it landed at her feet. 'It could have killed me, and so I turned around to him, and I said, "No. It's no." And that's all I said. I didn't have to say any more than that. "It's going to be Portugal and then South Africa for you then," he said.'

She would sail to Cape Town from Lisbon; but first, there was paperwork to sort out. While it was being prepared, Leonora and Frau Asegurado remained in Madrid, and to while away the time they found the occasional diversion. One afternoon, this came in the shape of a tea dance. Leonora remembered that she wasn't allowed to join the dancers, but she could watch them; Frau Asegurado, of course, was there beside her.

And then, across the room, she noticed someone she had last seen two years ago when she was living in Paris with Max; someone who Picasso had brought to dinner at their flat on the Rue Jacob one evening. They had spent the evening together, the four of them, and she remembered liking this man very much indeed. He was dark-haired, well-dressed, handsome. He looked urbane, sophisticated, worldly wise; exactly the sort of man a young woman aged twenty-three, who was up against it on every possible front, might want on her side. His name was Renato Leduc; and when he smiled at her across that sea of strangers in the crowded room in Madrid, it seemed like the best thing that had happened to Leonora for a very long time indeed.

7

Le Grand Adieu

Everything about Renato Leduc seemed romantic. The first time they had met, back in Paris, Leonora had been struck by how handsome he was. She thought his dark features seemed Indian; in fact he was half Mexican, and had been raised in the Tlalpan area in the south of Mexico City. He had moved to Paris in 1935 at the age of thirty-eight, and once there he found himself increasingly drawn to the Surrealists, striking up friendships with André Breton and with Paul and Nusch Éluard. Through them he had met Picasso, and become close to him as well; and it was Picasso who had invited him to supper at Max Ernst's flat on the Rue Jacob on that evening in the spring of 1938 when he met Leonora for the first time. There had been a spark between them that night: Picasso and Max had been locked in conversation, and Renato had chatted to Leonora about her background in England, and about her new life in Paris. He was twenty years older than she was, but that didn't count against him in Leonora's eyes; quite the reverse, in fact.

Like Leonora, Renato had not expected to see anyone he recognised at the hotel in Madrid that January after-noon; but the moment he caught sight of her, he knew exactly who she was – there was something unforgettable about the wild black hair and the beautiful pale face. Soon they were chatting – in French, so as to confuse the ever present Frau Asegurado. Leonora outlined her predica-ment: she was alone and friendless, and her parents were about to have her shipped off to a sanatorium in South Africa. Renato realised immediately that he could help. He too was on his way to Lisbon, from where he intended to cross the ocean to New York. What Leonora should do, he suggested, was go along with her family's plan and journey on to the Portuguese capital with the nurse: but once they arrived there she must find some way of escape, and get herself to the Mexican embassy. Renato would meet her there, and he would help her leave Europe – if she could get to the US she would be free from both Hitler and Harold. ('Although of the two,' Leonora was fond of remarking, 'I was far more afraid of my father than I was of Hitler.')

Leonora and Frau Asegurado left Madrid a few days later. They caught a train to Lisbon, where they were met by a small delegation of friends of friends of Harold; business contacts who had agreed to oversee the arrangements that would culminate in Leonora's departure to South Africa. First, though, there was to be a sojourn in the upmarket seaside town of Estoril, a few miles outside the city, at the home of one of their contacts. By this stage, Lenora had learned not to argue; the trick, she said afterwards, was not to fight these people, but to think more quickly than they did.

In Estoril, Leonora remembered there was a surfeit of parrots, but a distinct lack of bathwater. She spent the first evening thinking up an excuse to go back into the city, and the next morning explained to her host that she had an urgent need for new gloves. '"The weather is going to be terrible for my hands," she told her. "I must have some gloves. And I haven't got a hat."'

It was an inspired ploy; the smart owner of the Estoril house understood immediately why it was essential for a young British woman to have gloves and a hat, and a trip into town was quickly arranged. When they arrived in the city, Leonora realised she had to act as soon as possible. 'I had to find a café that looked big enough, and then "Aargh!" I cried, clutching my stomach. "Got to go to the bathroom." "Yes, immediately," she [Asegurado] said. She conducted me inside. I had judged correctly: it was a café with two doors. I nipped out, got a taxi − I must have had a bit of money for buying the gloves − and I told the driver, in Spanish, "Mexican Embassy."'

At the embassy she asked for Renato, and was told he was expected in later. She would wait, she said. The officials protested: 'Señorita, you can't ...'. It was only when Leonora said: 'The police are after me' (which, she reasoned, was 'more or less true') that they agreed. 'Wink, wink. "You can wait for Renato."'

The ambassador then appeared and was wonderful, Leonora remembered; he assured her that in the Mexican embassy she was completely safe and even the British couldn't touch her. Eventually Renato turned up and a plan was hatched. 'He said, "We're going to have to get married. I know it's awful for both of us, as we don't believe in this sort of thing, but ... " As Leonora was over twenty-one she no longer needed her father's permission to marry, and as the wife of a Mexican she would have the right to enter the US.

Marriage to Renato was certainly convenient, but there was more to it than that. He was a charming man whose history as a revolutionary fighter made him even more irresistible. Renato had been fifteen when the Mexican Civil War broke out in 1910, and he had joined the forces of the most colourful of the rebel leaders, Francisco 'Pancho' Villa, whose troops were known for their daring and sometimes foolhardy assaults on the government militia who were desperately trying to keep order in the face of chaos. The Mexican Civil War featured a complicated medley of factions, of whom Villa's was one, which had joined forces to rebel against the seemingly interminable rule of an absolute dictator called Porfirio Diaz. Under Diaz's over thirty-year presidency, the poor – mostly people of Nahuatl, Mayan or other indigenous origins – had got poorer, while the rich – most the descendants of Spanish settlers – had got richer. By 1910 the top one per cent of Mexico's elite controlled eighty-five per cent of the country's wealth; and when in July that year Diaz was again 're-elected' to power, those opposed to his rule could stand it no longer. Diaz was deposed, and for the next ten years the country was mired in a series of chaotic battles and skirmishes that severely damaged its infrastructure and dominated daily life.

The civil war was bloody and brutal: it ended the lives of a million Mexicans, but not Renato's. He survived his adventures and went on to embrace the most passionate of occupations: he became a poet. He had studied law at university in Mexico City, but after graduation he turned to writing verse. And he was good at it.

Renato was still in Paris when the Nazis invaded in May 1940: Picasso was there too as were the Éluards. But by the end of that year, he decided to take the choice his Mexican nationality offered: he opted to leave this war, so different from the war he had known in Mexico, and return to his now more peaceful country. He left Paris after Christmas and paused in Madrid on his way across the Iberian Peninsula. Crossing Europe, and escaping from it, were a lot easier for Renato than they were for most people: the fact that he had been sponsored on his travels by the Mexican government, and had also been working for the Mexican embassy in Paris, gave him a quasi-diplomatic status.

He and Leonora found lodgings on the Trevassa de São Mamade in the Alfama district of Lisbon. It's the oldest part of the city; until the end of the Middle Ages it *was* the city, and it's full of tightly packed alleyways clustered on the hillside below the castle. Traditionally the merchant zone, in 1941 most of the buildings on the São Mamade would have been warehouses, with the merchants' living quarters above.

Number 13, the house in which Leonora and Renato lived, is a six-storey building clad with geometrically patterned blue and yellow tiles; the windows have wooden shutters, and there are balconies on the first floor. It's anonymous and neat: a house made for many residents rather than just one family. And there would certainly have been many residents here in 1941, because Lisbon was the World War Two refugee centre of Europe. In the movie *Casablanca* it's described as 'the great embarkation point' and is the city to which Ingrid Bergman and her screen husband depart in the final scene after Humphrey Bogart has insisted she should go with him and abandon their love affair. But in real life the place laced with all that on-screen glamour and intrigue, espionage and double-dealing was not Casablanca – it was Lisbon itself. As the capital of neutral Portugal, and the Atlantic-facing port from which beckoned a passage away from Nazi-run Europe and towards the free world, Lisbon was the bottle-neck, and also the melting-pot, of the continent. The refugees who made it there came from a huge range of backgrounds and walks of life: wealth and privilege brushed up against poverty and deprivation, but they all shared a common goal, which was to get across the Atlantic to the US, where they had the chance of a safe future in a continent that was not at war.

But it was not just refugees who were in abundance in Lisbon. The city was teeming with spies and secret agents: it was the hub through which the wires of intelligence were operated, and at least fifty separate intelligence agencies, including both the British and German secret services, ran operations from there. Add to this the casino tables of glitzy Estoril, and the champagne-swilling lifestyle there of the very wealthy among the migrants, and it's no wonder that when his work in naval intelligence brought the author Ian Fleming here, it helped inspire the central character of the novel that would come to fruition a few years later: James Bond, who made his debut in Fleming's first book, *Casino Royale*, which was set amidst a backdrop that was eerily reminiscent of war-time Lisbon.

By chance Fleming was in the city at precisely the same time as Leonora, and it was a particularly dangerous moment for Lisbon. A few months earlier, in October 1940, Hitler and Spain's fascist ruler Francisco Franco, victor of the Spanish Civil War, had met on a train in Hendaye in the Basque country and had talks that concluded with a pledge that Spain would, at some undecided future point, enter the war as Germany's ally. And once Spain was in, it could only be a question of time before Portugal was over-run; the Germans used to joke that Hitler would be able to take the country with a phone call. Years later, around the kitchen table, Leonora could still feel the tension of those times: in a Nazi-run Portugal, her future would have looked very grim indeed.

But amidst the fear and anxiety, Lisbon was also a place with a commodity that in the dark days of 1941 was in short supply in most of Europe: that commodity was hope. As the Lisbon correspondent of *The Times* newspaper, W. E. Lucas, wrote a few months earlier: 'Berlin may be the most depressing, London the most inspiring city in Europe. But Lisbon is the most extraordinary.' What made it extraordinary was that possibility of escape, an escape that was so near and yet so far, with the sounds and the sights of the ships in the port visible from across the hilly city. From her home in São Mamade, Leonora would have had constant reminders about the goal she and Renato were aiming for, their passage to the United States: whenever she turned right out of her front door and walked the short distance to the top of the hill, she would have seen the sea and the ships between the narrow buildings. She and Renato would doubtless, like all the refugees who had the means, have been enjoying the cafés and bars of the city – Lisbon was sometimes called the one place in Europe where the lights had not gone out – but the reason why they were there would never have been far from their thoughts.

Like all those who were passing through the city, they had plenty of time on their hands. These were weeks of waiting: waiting for the papers to be in order, waiting for places on a ship, and in their case, waiting for a date when they could be married at the British Embassy. Hours passed sitting in cafés on sunny squares, drinking endless cups of black coffee from tiny cups, smoking cigarettes, and discussing with other foreigners the chance of getting a place on a boat this month, or next month, or in another three or four months. Renato spent a lot of time at the Mexican embassy; when he was there Leonora would roam around the city, enjoying the views across the terracotta rooftops to the castle of St Jorge on the hillside, and the open sea. Now she was with Renato her father's spies didn't bother her any more.

As the days turned to weeks, she often came across

people she had begun to recognise. Lisbon was small enough that you chanced upon people you had come to recognise the whole time. Arthur Koestler, another writer who spent time there in the early 1940s and was himself a refugee from Hungary, later wrote a book called *Arrivals and Departure*: it's the story of K, who like Koestler is a former Communist; he describes Neutralia, the country to which he has escaped, and says the dominant conversation there is the threat of invasion, which hangs in the air, 'a constant threat'. Everyone in Lisbon bumped into everyone else at regular intervals: 'in this town we all run into each other at least once a day,' remarks a woman in the novel.

So it was inevitable that, when a man she hadn't seen for almost a year arrived in the city towards the end of April, it would only be a matter of days before they would meet up. Leonora believed Max was still in France; she had just sent a telegram to mutual friends, in fact, in the hope that they would be able to pass on to him the news that she was safe. Instead, she glanced across a market place in the middle of the town as she was buying the food for supper: and there he was, right there in the square.

He was as stunned to see her as she was to see him. By now, he was well aware that Leonora had left Saint-Martin the previous summer. He would have guessed she was making her way to the US, but he probably expected she had already sailed. If anywhere, his hope would have been that he would find her on the other side of the Atlantic; he had not imagined she was not only still in Europe, but right here in Lisbon.

The time since they had last seen one another had been

adventure-packed for Max, just as it had for Leonora. He had remained in the prison at Les Milles until the Germans reached Andance-sur-Rhône one hundred and fifty miles away, at which point the camp commander announced that inmates whose lives would be in danger once the Nazis arrived would be offered places on a train to Marseilles. Max was one of two and a half thousand who got seats on the train; but the soldiers guarding them soon disappeared, and they made slow and erratic progress until eventually they reached Nîmes and another camp. From there, Max managed to escape and return to Saint-Martin, where he was horrified to discover that Leonora had left, and that Les Alliberts was no longer theirs. He rescued what work he could from the house, at one point even returning under cover of night to retrieve not only pieces of his own work, but also Leonora's; but then the gendarmes again arrived to escort him back to the camp. By this time rather good at it, he escaped again; but on this occasion he need not have bothered, as his release papers came through at almost precisely the same moment: they are dated 29 July 1940. Max was now legally free, but in the most agonising of circumstances: he had no idea what had become of Leonora, and the house to which he had dreamt of returning was no longer his to return to. In a letter to the then minister of the interior, Albert Sarraut, petitioning for his release, Paul Éluard had given a personal assurance that Max, 'a simple, proud, loyal man . . . [who is] my best friend' would not leave Saint-Martin, if he could only be allowed to return there. In different circumstances, Éluard would have been correct; but now, with Leonora gone and the house sold, there was nothing to keep him there. He did return, but only to collect as many paintings as he could realistically carry in his bags; and then he left for Marseilles. Among the work he chose to take were pieces by Leonora: her self-portrait, and her portrait of him. If it hadn't been for this action on his part, Leonora's paintings might easily have been destroyed, her reputation being nothing like as established as his own.

In Marseilles he was given a bed at the Villa Air-Bel, the chateau used by the American writer Varian Fry, who ran a rescue network designed to help artists and intellectuals whose lives were in danger to escape from Europe. Already there was André Breton; the two had quarrelled before Max left Paris with Leonora, but now they attempted a reconciliation.

Breton and his family left France for the United States in March 1941. A few weeks later, Peggy Guggenheim arrived in Marseilles, and on her very first evening in town she had supper with Max and a mutual friend from Paris, the artist Victor Brauner. Over the meal Max invited Peggy to call in at Air-Bel to see the work he had managed to rescue from Saint-Martin; this she did a few days afterwards, and agreed to buy some of his paintings. As a celebration, after they had done the deal, they drank together a bottle of wine that Max had brought from Saint-Martin. It was the eve of his fiftieth birthday, 1 April 1941.

The next night Max and Peggy, again accompanied by Brauner, dined on seafood in a restaurant in the old port; but by now the straight-talking, sexually upfront Peggy had realised that she was interested in more than Max's art. As they said goodnight she slipped him the key to her hotel room; after saying farewell to Brauner he went to find her, and the two began an affair. At this stage, Peggy later confessed, she was not really serious about Max; and he was certainly not serious about her, since he was still in love with Leonora. But he had always found it easy to fall into casual sexual relationships with women, and he liked Peggy, finding her interesting as well as useful.

Within a fortnight, however, the relationship was becoming more serious; or at least, it certainly was for Peggy. When she left to visit her ex-husband Laurence Vail, his wife Kay Sage, and their children for Easter she convinced herself that Max had tears in his eyes when he bid her farewell at the station. And on the train journey to the Alpine village of Megève, where the Vails were staying, Peggy read the books Max had given her for her suitcase – and realised she had fallen in love with him. Oddly, these books included Leonora's stories written in Paris and illustrated by him, as well as a book he had given to her that was inscribed, in his hand: 'To Leonora: real, beautiful, and naked.' From the start, Leonora's presence was to loom large in their relationship.

Peggy, though, was not deterred; when a few days later Max sent a telegram to say he was on his way to Megève she hurried back from Lyons, where she had been meeting Marcel Duchamp, to see him again. But Max arrived before her, in a flurry of snow, wearing a long, black cape. 'The children thought he was a very romantic figure,' Peggy recalled in her memoirs. 'It seems he spent the whole evening telling them tales about himself and Leonora, about her departure and his troubles.' It seems fairly obvious which woman was on Max's mind, although it definitely didn't seem obvious to the love-struck Peggy; and when the couple were together again they began to make plans in earnest for their departure, together with the Vails and the children, to New York via the Pan-Am Clipper, a seaplane with regular, if expensive, flights from Lisbon. Peggy, needless to say, would be footing the bill.

First, though, they had to get to Lisbon. Max set off first; but when he reached the Spanish border he came up against a problem with his visa. When he opened his case and showed the officials his canvases, however, their attitude changed. The stationmaster at the railway station, who had previously halted his journey, now told him he respected his artistic talent, and returned his documents. He warned him that, as his visa was not in order, he should board the train back into France; but he added, emphatically, that there was a train coming in that went to Spain. 'Be careful not to board the wrong train,' he said. Max took the hint: when the 'wrong' train arrived ten minutes later he boarded it, and was soon on his way to Madrid. From there it was easy to journey on to Lisbon where, within a few days, he ran into Leonora.

In a letter to some friends dated 9 May he has good news: Leonora is now staying in Lisbon and despite suffering terrible horrors she has made a full recovery. He then goes on to say that he himself is due to leave Lisbon by Clipper; Leonora will follow by ship. There is no hint in the letter that anything has changed between them, no inkling that Leonora is about to marry someone else, or that he has a new lover. He describes how elated he is to be reunited with her, and says he believes there's a strong likelihood that the two of them will one day return to Saint-Martin, and he looks forward to seeing them again.

For Max the new circumstances in both his own and Leonora's life seem to have felt like a blip rather than a seismic shift in their love story. He was aware, of course, that Peggy's patronage was incredibly useful at a difficult time – she was his passport to America, after all, just as Renato was Leonora's. But he seems to have wanted to be straight with Peggy – or at least, as straight as possible – about how he felt. Here is Peggy on what happened when she herself arrived at the railway station in Lisbon in early May of 1941, having travelled across Spain. 'Max looked strange and, taking me by the arm, he said: "I have something awful to tell you". He walked me down the platform and surprised me by saying, "I have found Leonora. She is in Lisbon." I felt a dagger go through my heart, but I pulled myself together and said, "I am very happy for you." By this time I knew how much he loved her. Max was overcome by my reply.' Later Max spoke again at length about finding Leonora; Peggy says she 'felt as though I had been stunned and wandered around in an agonized daze.' Her children, Sinbad and Pegeen – who were with her by this stage – were very worried; Sinbad in particular, Peggy says, thought his mother was 'getting a dirty deal'.

The next few weeks were to prove, as Leonora described them seventy years later in her kitchen in Mexico City, 'very strange indeed', for everyone involved: Leonora, Renato, Max, Peggy, Laurence, Kay, Sinbad and Pegeen, and the four daughters of Laurence and Kay's marriage; so many relationships, so many complications, so many permutations. An ex-husband, an ex-wife, a new wife, an is-he-or-isn't-he new lover, an are-they-or-aren't-they new couple. Four children of one couple, and another two half-siblings whose mother was also there, sharing meals around the dining table with her ex-husband with his now wife. And behind it all, one person was paying most of the bills: only Leonora and Renato were funding themselves.

Max was clearly very unhappy about the fact that Leonora was about to marry Renato; he tried to talk her out of it, but he also understood that it was going to help her get to America. In any case, plans were quite well advanced for the ceremony by the time Max appeared in Lisbon; so it went ahead, on 26 May 1941 at the British Consulate General, which at the time was situated alongside the ambassador's residence on the Rua de São Francisco Borja. It was a civil ceremony carried out under the provisions of the Foreign Marriage Act of 1892. On the marriage certificate the bride's name is given as Leonora Mary Carrington, 24, a spinster, daughter of Harold Wylde Carrington, a cotton manufacturer. The bridegroom is Renato Leduc, 43, whose occupation is secretary at the Mexican Legation in Lisbon, son of Alberto Leduc, a government official. The witnesses are Leopoldo Urrea and Jose Dominguez; later in her life Leonora had no recollection of who these people were, and thought they were probably embassy employees. There was nothing a wedding usually entails: no guests, no reception, no speeches, no fuss, and definitely no family; but in Leonora's heart there must surely have been a sense of celebration as she headed off back to the São Mamade as Renato's wife. She was one step closer to the new life that she craved; one step further away from the life in Lancashire that had stifled her. And once again, she had outwitted her father who had thought that, even from hundreds of miles away, he could control and corral her.

The big question, though, was this: was it a marriage of convenience, or was it a love match? And the truth is that everyone involved, from the bride and groom to the people closest to them, seems to have been confused as to the answer. In her memoirs, Peggy says she couldn't make head or tail of what was going on between Leonora and the man they all called 'the Mexican'. What was obvious to her was how much Max despised him: he called him *un homme inférieur* and made fun of him whenever he could. He felt bitter about the fact that Renato, whom he had regarded as a friend in Paris, had now become the partner of his great love. In a role reversal from the days in Saint-Martin when Max had oscillated between Leonora and Marie-Berthe, Leonora now oscillated between Max and Renato. 'Leonora could not make up her mind whether to go back to Max or to remain with her husband,' says Peggy. But when they were together, Leonora and Max appeared to be 'in perfect harmony'. They spent whole days reading and doing drawings together; Max 'was completely happy when he was with her, and miserable the rest of the time'. At one point Leonora needed a minor operation, and Peggy went to visit. '[She] was beautiful; I realised it more than ever in the hospital when I saw her in bed. Her skin was like alabaster and her hair was rich in its black waviness: it swept all over her shoulders. She had enormous, mad, dark eyes with thick black brows and a tip-tilted nose. Her figure was lovely but she always dressed very badly, on purpose.'

When Leonora was discharged Max begged her not to return to Renato, but she told him she had to stay with him until they reached New York. Max had asked Peggy to reserve a seat for Leonora on the Clipper, and to keep him happy the ever generous Peggy had agreed, even offering to pay for the ticket. But, probably wanting not to be beholden to Max and Peggy, Leonora was determined to stick with Renato. Max, when he heard this, was upset and decided he couldn't stay in the city near Leonora any longer, so the entire Guggenheim gang upped and left for Estoril a few miles out of town by the sea, where they spent the next five weeks. Max and Peggy started sleeping together again in Estoril, she reports in her memoirs, but 'Max was constantly waiting for Leonora to phone him. She often came and spent the day with him and I felt so let down that I wouldn't speak to him for days.'

The hub of the Guggenheim party's life in Lisbon was the Leão d'Ouro, an unpretentious restaurant in the centre, founded in 1842. It's still there today, looking almost exactly as it did in their day: high ceilinged, cavernous, festooned with dry hams hanging from the rafters, and decorated with blue and white tiles which depict scenes from Lisbon's history. During their stay in the city, Leonora, Peggy, Max and the rest of their retinue were regular diners, with the twists and turns of their complicated existence often thrashed out around its tables; or else ignored completely, with everyone concentrating steadfastly on the delicious seafood and the excellent wine, which was another way of dealing with all the difficulties. Peggy remembered being in there one night with Laurence when Leonora was also there; the two chatted and had 'a terrible scene' in which Peggy begged her either to go back to Max, who 'wanted nothing more than that', or to leave him 'in peace' with her. Leonora, apparently, told Peggy that she was only seeing Max out of pity and had no idea he was with her (this last point seems unlikely). When Peggy relayed the conversation to Max he was so upset that she wrote to Leonora and asked her not to end her visits to him; but she never came out to Estoril again.

Eventually, on 11 July, Leonora and Renato left Lisbon, aboard the SS *Exeter*. On the passenger list her name is given as 'Leonora Leduc'; under 'calling or occupation' is a single word that could not have been more wrong: 'none'. Two days later, on 13 July, the Guggenheim caravan followed, piling on to a Pan-Am Clipper, which was the exclusive means of transport to the United States – a flying hotel with a bar and dining room on board, and a real bed for each passenger. The Clipper took just twenty-four hours to reach New York, with a stop-over in the Azores; the plane was notorious for causing airsickness, and in her memoirs Peggy says her party were badly affected, especially the four Vail girls who were aged between two and fourteen. One of the only excitements in the long journey – although Peggy could probably have done without it – was the moment when 'we passed over the boat that was carrying Leonora and her husband to New York'.

For all of them, a new life beckoned in the United States. But the central question in the minds of Leonora and Renato on their ship, and Peggy and Max in their luxury plane, was this: was the Leduc marriage going to hold out, or was it going to flounder? Everything, for all four of them, rested on that.

It all hinged on what one person was going to decide to do: and that person was Leonora Carrington, who was at last free; or, as she would say, as free as any of us ever can be in this life.

8

Cat Woman

By the time Leonora reached New York, Max had endured another spell of incarceration. Photographs show Peggy and her party newly disembarked from their plane and making their way through La Guardia Airport after landing there on 13 July 1941; they are surrounded by journalists, with flashbulbs popping and questions being fired about their decision to quit Europe, and their plans for a new life in the US. There to meet them were Jimmy Ernst (Max's son with Luise Straus) and Howard Putzel, Peggy's art adviser, who had come with the good news that her collection of paintings, which had travelled by sea, had arrived safely. But, just as Max was about to greet Jimmy, 'he was seized by the officials, and not allowed to talk to him', as Peggy explains in her memoirs. 'This made a marvellous photograph for the Press and appeared in the papers. It seems the Pan-American Airways could not accept the responsibility of admitting a German into the United States without a hearing. I offered bail, but to no avail. Poor Max was whisked away.'

Jimmy was disappointed that his mother had been unable to get to the US with his father; he was right to be concerned because Luise, who was the first woman ever to get a PhD in art history from Bonn University, would not survive the war – she was on the penultimate train to Auschwitz from Paris, and died there in 1944. For the moment, though, the anxiety was about Max and whether he would be allowed to remain in the US; although Jimmy was 'not too worried about Max's finding himself in those historically sad surroundings. He had a unique way of extracting sardonic humour and novel insights from just about any unexpected situation.'

While Max was being detained on Ellis Island, Peggy went to see André Breton who had arrived in New York a couple of months ahead of them. He wanted to know all that had happened in Lisbon, and was particularly keen to know what was going on between Max and Leonora. 'The report had gone round New York that Max would not leave Leonora in Lisbon, and that was why we had remained there so long. Breton did not gather that I was in love with Max. We talked a lot about Leonora and Max, and Breton confirmed my opinion that she was the only woman Max had ever loved,' recalled Peggy.

After being held for three days, Max was released and reunited with Peggy and Jimmy. Within a week, on 21 July, the SS *Exeter* sailed in, and Leonora got her first glimpse of the Statue of Liberty and the skyscrapers of New York

City. It must have been quite a moment: after four years of running away, of outwitting her father and her family, of hiding from them and escaping from their clutches, she was finally free. Harold's tentacles, through his business connections, extended to Paris, Madrid and Lisbon, but they did not stretch across the Atlantic. Quite what she was going to do next she didn't yet know, but what she now had was something she had not felt she had before: choices.

She and Renato moved into a flat on West 74th Street in Manhattan; Renato was given work at the Mexican embassy, and Leonora began to pick up her connections with the Surrealists, many of whom were now in the US. Just as in Lisbon, it was only a matter of time before she would see Max; but first, by chance, she bumped into Jimmy. 'One night Jimmy met Leonora in a drugstore in Columbus Circle, and was in a terrific state of excitement about it,' reports Peggy. 'He hadn't seen her for years. He had been alternately in love with her and jealous of her because of his abnormal attachment to Max. Max couldn't wait until he saw Leonora. She had brought all his paintings with her. When he got them, he hung them up in Julien Levy's gallery and invited Breton, Putzel, Laurence and a few other people to see them. They were greatly admired.'

But getting his paintings back wasn't the only reason Max had been so keen to see Leonora. As summer gave way to autumn, the two of them began to spend more and more time together. Peggy, not unreasonably, was annoyed. According to her memoirs, Leonora would frequently phone up and ask Max if he would take her out to lunch; he would then often spend the rest of the day with her, something Peggy felt he never did with her. It was the familiar pattern all over again – just as in Lisbon, where Leonora and Max had spent hours horse-riding together, something else Peggy said Max never wanted to do with her. 'It made me wildly jealous and I suffered agonies,' confesses Peggy.

Jimmy was also acutely aware of the effect Leonora's presence was having on his father. 'I don't recall ever again seeing such a strange mixture of desolation and euphoria in my father's face as when he returned from his first meeting with Leonora in New York,' he wrote. 'One moment he was the man I remembered from Paris – alive, glowing, witty and at peace and then I saw in his face the dreadful nightmare that so often comes with waking. Each day that he saw her, and it was often, ended the same way. I hoped never to experience such pain myself, and I was at a loss of how to help him.'

But for all the time that she was happy to spend with him, Max's feelings were not reciprocated by Leonora. She was now using Max to fill a gap in her life: and the gap was Renato, who was spending lots of time away from her. They were living together as husband and wife but he was hardly ever around, especially during the evenings; he was a loner who went in search of his own entertainment, and enjoyed nights in clubs and bars with other men. Leonora was frequently by herself; she would stand by the window waiting for him, looking to passers-by on the Manhattan street 'like a familiar ghost [though] strange looking, her clothes were too long and her hair much too untidy, like those of a person barely saved from drowning'.

This description is taken from a short story called 'Waiting', published in 1941, in which Leonora describes the heartache of Margaret, a woman who is waiting, always waiting, for her lover to return. The story has often been presumed to be about her feelings for Max, but it seems much more likely to be about her relationship with Renato; Margaret's partner even has a Latino name, Fernando, and is a similar age to Renato. When Margaret describes him she says: 'His hair is so long and straight and almost blue, blue grey, I love it so much,' echoing what Leonora said about Renato's hair after she first met him in Paris.

And the truth was, Leonora was no longer in love with Max. They shared a history, but the doubts that had started to creep into her mind in Saint-Martin had solidified and taken shape, and where Max once represented liberation and opportunity, he was now equated in her mind with trouble.

He was too needy; he would be too demanding; he would take up too much of her; and she would end up being subsumed into his genius. It is Peggy, in fact, who spells out this side of Max's personality in her memoirs. In many ways, she says, he was like a small child, and she always felt like his mother. 'Max, like all babies, always wanted to be the centre of attention,' she explains. 'He tried to bring all conversations around to himself, no matter what they were about.'

As well as Max's neediness, there was his fame to contend with. He was now fifty, his work was well known in Europe, and his reputation had gone ahead of him to New York; Peggy said she had 'no idea how famous Max was' until they got across the Atlantic and she realised he was already a big name there. Surrealism was in the process of relocating from Paris to the US; as well as Breton others were gathering: Salvador Dalí, André Masson, Yves Tanguy, Kurt Seligmann, Roberto Matta, Gordon Onslow Ford, Wolfgang Paalen and Stanley William Hayter were either there already or in the process of arriving, and Breton was attempting to pick up the threads of the movement and reignite its fire for an American future. Almost as soon as Max was released from detention, plans began for a show of his work; Pierre Matisse, son of Henri and a leading New York gallerist, was immediately interested in showing his paintings alongside the work of Masson, Tanguy and Matta. The problem for the still only twenty-four-year-old Leonora was that next to Max she was almost invisible. As a girlfriend who was also a practitioner, she was almost unique among the Surrealist women: avant-garde the movement may have liked to think it was, but when it came to women the Surrealists' views and expectations were depressingly narrow and conventional. She now felt very strongly that if she went back to him, her life as an artist would be for ever overshadowed by his work, by his story and by his fame.

So it was in New York that she made her decision to finally leave him. It was the moment of reckoning, and all four of them realised it; none more than Max. His relationship with Peggy, by contrast, had come about because of what he called a 'misunderstanding' between them in Lisbon (a rather convenient misunderstanding at the time, one is tempted to think). Max never did love Peggy: he never had loved her and he never would love her. Even as she lay dying in her Venetian palazzo nearly forty years later, reports Jimmy in his memoirs, Peggy asked him plaintively, on every night of his stay: 'Max must have loved me at one time. Didn't he?'. Certainly he didn't seem to during those months in New York, when his every waking moment seems to have been filled with thoughts of Leonora, and how to win her back.

Two of Max's paintings tell the story of the Max-Leonora-Peggy triangle; both, poignantly, are today in Peggy's collection at the Guggenheim Palazzo in Venice where she spent the last thirty years of her life. The first, and in some ways the most significant, is *The Robing of the Bride* (1940), which dates from the period when Max was with Peggy in France and not yet reunited with Leonora. It is one of the finest of all Max's works, an extraordinary piece executed, as most of his paintings were in this period, using the method he had invented a few years earlier, decalcomania; the strange effect this pressed paint gives the long, dark hair of the naked female figure to the right of the painting makes it look like a butterfly's wing. She is, of course, Leonora, and she is being pushed ostentatiously to one side by the central figure, another female with bird-like eyes and a beak who is dressed in a bright orange cape. Peggy, apparently, had an orange cape. To the left is Loplop holding a spear, but the spear is broken: he is powerless, unable to dictate the course of events. The Peggy creature is in control, and Leonora is literally being pushed out of the picture.

The other painting in the Guggenheim collection in

Venice is even sadder. It is called *The Antipope* (1941–2); it features again the beaked woman, this time in a red dress. She is standing next to a horse, and the horse is looking forlornly at four other figures that seem all to represent Leonora. One is totem-like and has her back turned to him; another is a partially clothed woman who is nestling up to a rather elegant, black-maned horse. Another female figure, with long dark hair, is turning her head away.

Max continued to pour his agonies out in his work, and every painting he produced around this time contained the same haunting image, a female figure with her face turned away. The most desolate of all is *Europe After the Rain* (1940–42), which shows a strange and post-apocalyptic landscape filled with twisted vegetation, torn and ragged structures, and the detritus of a lost civilisation. It's clearly connected with the impact of the war on the continent he had recently left; but there is another narrative to this painting. The lush and promising landscape Max and Leonora had inhabited together, and that he would like to go on inhabiting with her by his side, has gone for ever. He is coming to terms with its ruins, and in the midst of them is the bird-like warrior who must now battle on alone, looking forlornly at the departing woman who has turned her back on him.

What, though, for Leonora? Should she remain in New York, or should she travel with her husband to his home in Mexico, 2500 miles away? The longer she remained in Manhattan, the more tempting staying must have seemed. From being the quintessential *femme-enfant* of the Paris days, the young beauty whose worth was seen far more as a muse than as an artist in her own right, in New York was claiming a different, and autonomous, status. When André Breton decided the city needed its own dedicated magazine of Surrealism, his idea for funding it involved getting the leading artists of the movement to each contribute a work that could be reproduced in a special limited edition. Of the nine he asked, Leonora was by far the youngest, and the only woman; the others were Max Ernst, Alexander Calder, Marc Chagall, André Masson, Kurt Seligmann, Yves Tanguy, David Hare and André Breton himself. And in early 1942, when an exhibition was held on Madison Avenue to raise funds for French victims of the war, Leonora again found herself in good company: her work was exhibited alongside the likes of Ernst, Chagall, Miró and Picasso.

New York began to be a productive place for her: she had soon finished at least eight paintings, as well as a commission – her first – from Manka Rubinstein, sister of Helena, for which she received two hundred dollars, more than she had ever been paid before for a painting. The commission was an exciting moment for Leonora, even though for a while it seemed as though it might not be possible: she could not afford to pay for the large canvas required. The only artist she knew who was making much money from his work was Marc Chagall, so she asked him for a loan. He refused, but after seeing one of her canvases he nodded patronisingly and said: 'Continue painting, my little one, continue painting.' Eventually Breton saved the day, giving Leonora one of his bed sheets; and Leonora completed the mural with Max Ernst, Marcel Duchamp and Roberto Matta as assistants. Manka loved it.

When one day early in 1942 Peggy decided to get the most important figures of Surrealism together for a group photograph – an image entitled *Artists in Exile* – Leonora was clearly one of the essential invitees. There are only three women in the line-up of fourteen – the others are Peggy herself, and the photographer Berenice Abbott; the men are Max Ernst, Leonora's former teacher Amédée Ozenfant, André Breton, Marcel Duchamp, Piet Mondrian, Stanley William Hayter, Friedrich Kiesler, Kurt Seligmann, Fernand Léger, Jimmy Ernst and John Ferren. Leonora is sitting in the front row on the floor: cross-legged, composed and cool. She looks comfortable, sure of herself and perhaps even faintly amused.

She seems also to have been experimenting during her time in New York with that other intrinsic aspect of her life as an artist: performance art. How else to explain the curious incident recalled by the film director Luis Buñuel, who met her during this period? Buñuel describes being with Leonora at the house of a Mr Reiss when she 'suddenly got up, went into the bathroom, and took a shower – fully dressed. Afterward, dripping wet, she came back into the living room, sat down in an armchair, and stared at me. "You're a handsome man," she said to me in Spanish, seizing my arm. "You look exactly like my warden."'

Or there is the memory of André Breton, who recalled that while in an elegant restaurant 'she had removed her shoes and was slathering her feet with mustard'. Breton recalled too visits to Leonora's house where he was invited to partake of extraordinary culinary feasts which had taken 'hours and hours of meticulous preparation', following recipes emanating from a sixteenth-century English cook-book; one such, he remembered, featured a hare stuffed with oysters. Her intention, he opines, was to save herself from what he calls 'the hostility of conformism'; her curiosity was so ardent that its only outlet was what was forbidden.

What is clear is that Leonora, newly free and at last removed from the influence of her family, is living life on the edge. As an artist in the heady and charged atmosphere of New York's flirtation with Surrealism, she is again refus-ing to conform to anyone's expectations of how she should behave. Performance art will not be categorised for another twenty years, but this is what Leonora is already explor-ing in Manhattan in 1942. A canvas is not big enough; the art that is bubbling up inside her and must find an outlet is not limited to one dimension or defined by one single medium. Art and life are interchangeable, inseparable; she had a constant need to challenge boundaries; and right now, the boundary she was most keen to explore was that between life and art. Like all her boundaries, it was fluid and malleable and penetrable. There were no absolutes in Leonora's world.

And so, when it came to it, staying in New York was just too easy; not edgy enough, not boundary-breaking, too conformist, too obvious. At some point during 1942 Renato's thoughts began to turn to his home in Mexico City, and he started to make plans for his return. There was no pragmatic or moral or practical reason why Leonora had to go too. She could have settled into life as an artist in an art-hungry city; all the early indications, in terms of her reputation, invitations to exhibit and patronage, were good.

But she had got used to rejecting the easy path, and she decided to reject it now. At the end of 1942, Renato left New York for Mexico, and he had Leonora by his side. Perhaps there was already a stirring within her, roused by the descriptions she had heard from her husband, for his wild and exotic country. No doubt she was relying, as she did throughout her life, on her strong and almost spiritual instinct. What her instinct was telling her now was: go to the edge. Take a leap into the dark, and see what the future there might hold.

Neither Leonora nor Max documented a farewell meeting between the two of them, and reading between the lines of Peggy's autobiography, it seems likely that Leonora left New York while Max was out of town. Max, says Peggy in her book, 'saw a lot of Leonora and, just when I told Jimmy I couldn't stand it any longer and I was going to leave Max, we were all invited to California by my sister Hazel'. Max was keen to see the West Coast; Jimmy went too, as did Peggy's teenage daughter Pegeen. In Peggy's book, there are no further mentions of Leonora after the California trip, suggesting that by the time they returned, she had left.

It was towards the end of the year when Max and Peggy flew back to New York; a few weeks later the Japanese bombed Pearl Harbor, triggering America's declaration of war on the Axis powers including Germany. 'I did not want to live in sin with an enemy alien,' says Peggy in her book. Instead, she and Max were married; but sadly for Peggy, the disappearance of Leonora to Mexico did not magically fix things in the Guggenheim–Ernst relationship.

The following year, 1942, Peggy had the ground-breaking idea of holding an exhibition at her new gallery, The Art of This Century, showing the work of women artists. *Thirty Women*, as it was to be called, included the work of Frida Kahlo, Leonor Fini, Méret Oppenheim and Leonora; throughout the complicated tangle over Max, Peggy was always able to separate her views on Leonora's merits as an artist, which she had been convinced about from the first time she saw her work in the studio on the Rue Jacob in Paris in the spring of 1938.

In her autobiography, Peggy notes that she entrusted to Max the task of organising the *Thirty Women* exhibition, but that it was a decision she later came to regret. Max found a thirty-first woman to include – 'a pretty girl from the Middle West', as Peggy describes her. Dorothea Tanning was her name, and before long she and Max were very friendly, playing chess together while Peggy was at the gallery and complimenting one another on their work. 'Soon they became more than friendly,' reports Peggy wryly, 'and I realised I should only have had thirty women in the show.' Within a few months Peggy and Max were divorced, and in October 1946 Max married Dorothea, in a double ceremony with Man Ray and his new partner, a dancer called Juliet Browner. Both these marriages would survive the rest of the bridegrooms' lives. Max and Dorothea moved to live in Sedona, Arizona, and in the 1950s they went back across the Atlantic to Paris, where Max would eventually die in 1976 aged eighty-four. But after New York in 1942, he and Leonora would never meet again.

Leonora left New York with Max's parting gift to her in her suitcase: *Leonora in the Morning Light*, the painting he had done in Saint-Martin. Her gift to Max was her portrait of him wearing the bird-like cape and holding the lamp containing the embryonic foal, her acknowledgement that all she would be in her life would be influenced by his role in helping to form her. The bride of the wind was moving on: painful and seismic though it was, Loplop would have to learn to live without her.

Since Leonora's death, both paintings have been sold. Max's painting of her, sold at auction in New York in 2012, went for just shy of eight million dollars; her painting of him, sold in New York in May 2016, realised 490,000 dollars.

Leonora's final tribute to Max came in a short story entitled 'The Bird Superior', published in the March–April 1942 issue of the New York magazine *View*, which was devoted to Max. In it, for the last time, Leonora brought together their two alter egos, the horse and the bird, in a story that seems like a literary rejoinder to Max's 1926 *Bride of the Wind*, the painting of the two entwined horses hurtling headlong through a moment in time.

Her story takes place in the magical, alchemical, subterranean kitchen of the Bird Superior, who is in the process of being transformed into a bird when a horse arrives; she 'leaps into the kitchen throwing up a shower of sparks under her hooves, the sparks turn into white bats and flit blindly and desperately around the kitchen upsetting pots, tins, bottles and phials of astrological cooking ingredients which crash to the floor in pools of colour'.

But the horse's name is Fear; she is a wild, untamed creature, and what she is afraid of is herself, her own power, her own destiny. The Bird Superior ties her to the flames of the fire and works his magic on her: he shows her how to paint, and he shows her how to evoke trees and plants out of the surroundings. The horse is reborn – 'memory races back to the birth of time, whips the infant away from the nipple of an erupting volcano, and tosses it playfully into space' – before the Bird Superior unties Fear from the fire and ties himself on to her back with her mane; the two then 'escape through the four winds which leap out of the pot like smoke, like hair, like wind'.

In a spiritual sense, the story suggests, Leonora and Max will be united for ever. What they have given one another, what they have done for one another, is woven into the very fabric of their beings. Neither of them, to their dying days, will ever underestimate the difference the other has made. But their moment in time is over. The dancing, coupling horses have separated.

9

El Mundo Mágico de los Mayas

The Mexico into which Leonora arrived in 1942 unfolded a landscape that managed to be strangely familiar and exquisitely alien at the very same time. This was a country that was now hauling itself into the twentieth century. The revolution in which Renato had played his part had eventually delivered and there were new roads, schools for the poor, and millions of acres of land had been redistributed to previously landless labourers. New business opportunities were opening up, both for 'gringos' from North America, and for Mexicans. The most fashionable streets of Mexico City now featured Western-style shops, and the women walking along them wore the same fashions, high heels, nylon stockings and make-up Leonora was used to seeing on women in New York, Paris and London. The novelist Graham Greene, who had visited the country four years earlier, had been struck by how European Mexico

City seemed, and how it felt completely divorced from the surrounding rural regions. There was nothing to connect it, he said, with the farmers he had encountered in the hills; the capital was 'like Luxembourg – a luxury town'. He described 'the white skyscraper of an insurance office, the Palace of Arts, white and domed and dignified, the great tame trees of the Alameda, a park which is said to date back to Montezuma, expensive jewellers' and antique shops, libraries ...' There were American tea bars, the original Sanborns restaurant in its beautifully tiled courtyard, the Avenida Juarez full of tourist shops, hawkers and little confectionery stalls. Marimba players were everywhere – 'the marimba, gentle sentimental, with the pleasing tinkle of a music-box,' said Greene – as well as the lottery-ticket sellers, peddling a quick way to what everyone now wanted: wealth.

Mexico City was and is the oldest conurbation in the Americas, founded by the Aztecs on what was then an island in the middle of a lake; and 1940s modernity sliced sharply into thousands of years of indigenous history. There is a painting by Frida Kahlo from 1929, in which she depicts in her immediate and intimate style the stereotypes of Mexican society, lined up on a bench on a bus. In it, a bourgeois lady sits alongside a moneybag-grasping gringo, and between them and an overall-clad manual worker and a mestizo matron is a bare-footed Indian mother, Madonna-like, suckling her rebozo-wrapped child. These were the new characters in the crowd scenes in Leonora's story, as she and Renato settled into an apartment in Mixcoac to the south of the city; she must have loved its native name, which derives from the Aztec language, Nahuatl, and means 'the place of the serpent cloud'.

Everything, for Leonora, was new: from the appearance and demeanour of the people, she said later, to the variety of foods, plants and animals, to the landscape and the contact with the dead. 'One of the activities that I liked the best was going to market: it was fantastic to discover chipotle chilli or the maguey worms.' A few streets from the house there was 'a popular, colourful market', and she soon realised this was her favourite place to be. There was something about the buzz of human life, the crush of old and young, the knowledge that the market was the most ancient gathering-place in human history, an umbilical cord linking human beings back to their need for interdependence and the exchange not only of goods and gifts, but also of friendship and ideas. Visually, and crucially for an artist, the market places were stunning: vast crowns of blooms like the lilies in Diego Rivera's 1941 painting *The Flower Seller*; walls of avocados, tomatoes and corn piled alongside mangoes, papayas and melons. Sacks of herbs, beans, spices and chillis brushed up against stalls selling brightly coloured hand-woven fabrics, and clay pots made the way they had been made since pre-Colombian times. For Leonora, the market place was an explosion of all that was new, exciting and enticing about Mexico: her senses were bombarded by unfamiliar sounds, sights and smells. This was a country of dazzling colours and bright sunlight; of rapid Spanish and impenetrable Nahuatl; of centuries of history and ancient traditions; of people who were often open and friendly, and yet also magical and mysterious.

It was a place of contradictions, of frictions; layers of history, of indigenous people with their ancient traditions up-ended by the sixteenth-century Spanish invaders, had left a trail of fault-lines that were never far below the surface of Mexican life. On one of his mornings there, Graham Greene noticed in his newspaper two reports of murders: one, he said, was a few hundred miles north in the border town of Ciudad Juárez; the other was just three minutes' walk from his hotel. 'Riddled with bullets', he pointed out, was a stock phrase in this country; and also, the two deaths in question were only in the paper because the victims were both senators. Death, whether as an idea or in reality, was never far away in Mexico. Leonora was fascinated, entranced, excited and amazed by this extraordinary new country, the country André Breton had, when he visited a few years earlier, called the most surreal nation on earth.

But if Leonora felt at home in her new surroundings, she felt dislocated in her new marriage. Back in his homeland after several years in Europe, Renato was keen to rekindle old friendships and to enjoy his native city again. As in New York, he was often out alone and late into the night. Leonora felt neglected and disappointed: but she had not cut herself off from her family and travelled halfway round the world to be defeated by one man's shortcomings, or the inadequacies of a relationship. Instead of feeling victimised or hopeless, she saw that Renato's ambivalence towards her meant not disaster but opportunity. The marriage had been more than merely convenience, but it did not have enough to ground it for the long-term. Leonora realised that if her life was going to move on in Mexico, she would have to turn her attention outwards.

She had to be a pioneer, because Mexican women in the 1940s did not have independent social lives. The revolution had begun to change the female lot, much as the First World War changed it in Europe: through the 1920s and 1930s women began to work outside the home, in factories and offices, and Mexico City even instituted a female police corps. These changes in turn undermined the traditional system of chaperonage: but it did not do away with it entirely, and while Mexico was considered by the 1930s US commentator Carleton Beals to be the most advanced country for women in Latin America, its advancement was relative. Frida Kahlo, who was born in Mexico City in 1907, never enjoyed across a lifetime the kind of freedom Leonora managed to procure for herself, as she looked up old contacts from Paris and began to go to parties and even to cantinas in the city centre on her own. Now she was safely thousands of miles from home, coming from England had its advantages: her background gave her the confidence and independence to strike out on her own terms.

One of those she looked up from their Paris days together was Benjamin Péret, a French poet who had been friendly with Éluard and close to Breton. Péret and his lover, a Spanish painter called Remedios Varo, had escaped from Europe via the Villa Air-Bel; they had arrived there soon after Max departed. Like him, the couple were helped by the American journalist Varian Fry, and they eventually sailed across the Atlantic on the *Serpa Pinto*, the cruise liner known as *Le Navio da Amizade*, or 'friendship boat' that, sailing under the neutral Portuguese flag, transported thousands of retreating refugees to a new life in the US, and Central and South America. Benjamin and Remedios disembarked at the Mexican port of Veracruz, from where they made their way to Mexico City, arriving at the end of 1941. Across the five years of war they and more than fifteen thousand other refugees were given a warm welcome: Lázaro Cárdenas, Mexico's president between 1934 and 1940, had instigated an open-door policy towards European refugees, especially people with Spanish ancestry who were intellectuals and artists. It was a positive example of international neighbourliness, and it had hugely advantageous long-term implications, bolstering the country's intellectual middle-classes with a largely Spanish-speaking cohort who went on to play their part in post-war Mexico, helping it emerge through the following decades to be a player on the world stage.

Benjamin and Remedios rented an apartment in the *colonia* (or district) of San Rafael in the centre of old Mexico City, on a street called Gabino Barreda. It was a ramshackle dwelling space: the plumbing was primitive, there were holes in the bricks and occasional rat invasions; but on the walls were pinned original drawings by artists like Picasso, Tanguy and Ernst – pieces of work the couple had brought with them from France.

As well as extraordinary art, the place was crawling with cats, Remedios' favourite animals, and filled with birds in cages. Dotted around the rooms, meanwhile, was an extensive collection of treasures picked up on her travels: talismans, shells, quartz crystals and pieces of wood;

Remedios loved to surround herself with objects she believed contained a kind of magical power.

The first time Leonora stepped into the apartment – via a window, since it had no proper door – she felt at home. Remedios, nine years her senior, was a kindred spirit, and both of them seem to have recognised that from the outset. Neither had grown up with a sister, and the almost conspiratorial friendship they fell into quickly felt sibling-like. When, a few months after meeting them, Leonora decided to leave Renato, it seemed entirely natural that she would move into the bohemian apartment on Gabino Barreda.

She seems to have left Renato without any misgivings or soul-searching; there had been affection between them, but not the highs of ecstasy and lows of agony that she had known with Max. Staying with Remedios gave her an immediate distraction and meant she was never lonely or at a loose end: as more emigrés poured into Mexico City, the Gabino Barreda apartment became the central point of the European group, with parties and gatherings happening almost nightly; as in Paris, regular meetings and get-togethers were the lifeblood of the group. As well as Benjamin, Remedios and Leonora, the circle included Remedios' former husband, the Spanish painter Gerardo Lizarraga; the painter Esteban Francés, who stayed in Mexico for the next few years but eventually relocated to New York; a writer called Miriam Wolf; and a Hungarian photographer called Kati Horna who arrived in Mexico with her sculptor husband José, another Spanish artist whom Remedios had known in Madrid.

Gunther Gerszo, a Mexican-born but European-educated

painter, was another frequent caller, and in his painting *The Days of Gabino Barreda Street* (1944) he depicts in smoky greens and blues the wild surreality of the days and evenings when they all gathered amidst the creative chaos to talk, drink, smoke and to eat. Leonora is depicted in two separate but entwined forms: both female, naked and tangled up in red roots, one is sitting on the floor holding the torso of the other up towards the sky. Remedios is in the centre, surrounded by cats and looking distinctly feline herself; Benjamin is sitting on a box but his head and arms have separated from the rest of his body and are up in the clouds; and Gerszo's self-portrait is also disembodied, peering out of a box on the floor. In the background is Esteban Francés, playing his guitar and surrounded by paintings of nudes.

Behind the figures is what looks like the sea, and on the horizon is a fire. Perhaps it represents the emigrés' burned boats, because by the mid-1940s almost all of them were committed to remaining in Mexico, even as the war in Europe drew to a close. 'Home' had once been Europe, but now that Europe had been completely changed. Not only was it scarred by bombs and the aftermath of fighting, but the people the emigrés had loved, their friends and families, were often displaced or dead. Mexico provided the space for a fresh start.

In Mexico Leonora also had a new canvas, an empty canvas, and she felt something in her heart that she had not felt for a long time: hope. And part of that hope centred on a man she was becoming close to, a man who was a childhood friend of Kati Horna and through her connected to the Gabino Barreda Street circle. He, like Remedios and Benjamin, had made the journey across the Atlantic aboard the *Serpa Pinto*, arriving in Mexico in October 1942. The two had met at a party in San Ángel; Kati met Leonora for the first time at the same party, and remembered she was wearing a cape, and was strikingly beautiful. 'I thought she was just like a glittering star, she seemed like a life force,' Kati recalled.

His name was Imre Emerico Weisz Schwartz, but like Leonora he had been known from childhood by a nickname: 'Cziki', later Anglicised to 'Chiki', which means 'tickle'. He looks in photographs like a man who enjoyed fun and laughter: his face is usually lit up by a huge smile, and he has a brightly impish air about him. But behind this light-hearted and relaxed exterior there was a hinterland of suffering and tragedy; difficulties Chiki, like Leonora, would struggle all his life to bury, and never quite manage to do so.

He had been born on 21 October 1911 in Hungary's capital Budapest, that grand and imposing city that straddles the wide, blue waters of the Danube. His childhood was overshadowed by difficulty and deprivation: it was a time of economic stagnation and fierce anti-Semitism, and Chiki's family were Jewish. He was one of four children: his father, a saddle-maker called Abraham Armin Weisz, died in an accident at the end of the First World War, forcing his impoverished mother to make a heart-breaking choice. She could not afford to raise all her children, and she decided she would have to send one to the Jewish boys' orphanage. Chiki was the child she opted to send: he was only four years old, and would have been the youngest child at the Pesti Izraelita Hitközség Fiúárvaháza. Life at the orphanage was tough and harsh, especially for such a young child. Leonora later made it the basis for one of her longest stories, 'The Stone Door'. In the story, Chiki is represented as Zacharias, a tiny boy whose mother tells him, before she takes him to the orphanage, that he must always remember his Judaism 'with pride and dignity, no matter what the world outside may do or say', and who then kisses him once, between the eyes, before he is taken away, shorn of his hair, dressed in trousers made of harsh wool and a jacket buttoned up to the chin, and given a new identity. No name, just a number: 105. A little boy called 105 with no mother to hold him or family to cherish him, cast adrift in a world of harsh discipline and few comforts.

But in the story Zacharias/Chiki is transported to another place, a metaphysical dream landscape where his future is laid out before him. Lying in his hard, narrow dormitory bed, 105 has a dream; a dream that unites him with a little girl who is growing up in very different circumstances in England. Like Chiki, the girl is sleeping. She had expected to dream about a horse, she explains to the Hungarian boy she is surprised to have instead encountered. Chiki is twelve, which makes Leonora six. Together they walk to a pond – the big pond that the gardener says has no bottom. It's a dangerous place, the girl explains: it's haunted, which is why she and her younger brother, Gerard, love to visit it. She starts to complain, not about Gerard but about her older brother, Pat; but the Hungarian visitor admonishes her, telling her to stop moaning because that is a waste of their time together. 'Don't you realise,' he says, 'we have to wake up?' The girl becomes quiet and afraid. 'We won't go back, we'll refuse,' she tells him. 'Can't we escape now that we're together?'

In the real world, as in the dream, their backgrounds could hardly have been more different. Chiki was from a different country; he had been raised as a member of a different religion; he spoke a different language; and while she came from wealth and privilege, he came from poverty and deprivation. But like her he had a fierce spirit, and subversion and rebellion burned within him. Like Leonora, he was no conformist; like her, he was not afraid. The Hungarian painter Endre Bálint, a contemporary at the orphanage, relates in his memoirs the story of their last day there. Chiki, he says, was a popular boy, liked by everyone. As he was preparing to leave, the cruel mistress of the orphanage, Mrs Ida, who often slapped the children, asked him: 'Why is your face so sad?' Chiki replied: 'My face can only be the way it is.' 'It's so I can slap it, like this,' said Mrs Ida, hitting Chiki one last time. And in response, writes Bálint, Chiki raised his hand and hit her back. '[He] gave this beautiful and good slap as a gift to the pupils who were leaving, and to those who had to stay in the orphanage.'

It was the act of a young man who cared deeply about justice, and who understood the importance of protest. And there was plenty to protest about in Hungary, especially for a Jew; there was a strong anti-Semitic undercurrent in Budapest, and Jews were often targeted, sometimes dragged off buses, and there were even rumours that they were taken into the woods and beaten up or shot.

As he approached the end of his teens Chiki's closest friend was a young man called Endre Ernő Friedmann, two years his junior and every bit as intent on changing the world for the better. Together they became disciples of a left-wing, anti-fascist writer called Lajos Kassák, a thinker whose philosophy 'attracted many of Budapest's brightest and most radical minds between the ages of fourteen and fifty'. Chiki and Endre, whose nickname was 'Bandi', made Kassak's values their own – and they were going to find an extraordinarily effective vehicle to help them; one that would at times allow them to bring the whole world to pause and reflect on what they had witnessed.

By the summer of 1933 Bandi and Chiki had decided to go to Paris, the centre of the ideas they valued, and the most exciting city in Europe in which to seek a meaningful life. Chiki had no money, but Bandi had enough for two fares; not much more, though, so the two young men who pitched up at the Gare de l'Est on a rainy September morning had almost nothing in their pockets, spoke no French and had no contacts in or knowledge of the city. Their experience could hardly have been more different from Leonora's introduction to Paris, by chance the same year, when she arrived with her mother to be installed in a finishing school.

For the next few months Chiki and Bandi rented a tiny room in the Latin Quarter on the Rue Lhomond. They survived on potatoes and eggs; if they couldn't get these they begged a bar of chocolate from a Hungarian chocolate-seller; and if even this wasn't forthcoming they fell back on surviving on sugar dissolved in water.

For both men, their most prized possessions were their cameras; however difficult life got, these could never be sold. Bandi had already started to get his pictures published in magazines; so when in the summer of 1936 civil war broke out in Spain, it was an obvious next step for him to go there to document the fighting. This was a clash of ideologies in which Bandi and Chiki could be very clear about which side they were on. It was a war against fascism, a war in aid of freedom for the ordinary people, a war against corruption and power that was concentrated in the hands of too few, making life a misery for too many. Bandi had a girlfriend called Gerda Taro, and the two decided to travel together to Spain. Chiki would stay behind in Paris; Bandi would send his negatives back to him for processing, and Chiki would sell them to magazines. In effect, Chiki was now his business partner. But somehow 'Endre Friedmann' did not seem like a great by-line for an up-and-coming snapper who hoped to one day see his work in publications like *Life* and *Picture Post*. Weren't all the best photographers American, and wouldn't an American name stand more chance of success? Bandi had a think, and came up with a new moniker. From now on, he would be known as Robert Capa.

The war was only a few months old when, on 5 September 1936, Capa pressed the shutter on the image that would make him the most famous war photographer of all time. His picture, titled *The Falling Soldier*, shows a soldier on the point of death; his heart has just been pierced by a bullet, and he is falling backwards, his rifle still in his hand. The impact of the image is all about its timing; Capa has captured a young human being at that instant when he is poised between a healthy life and an untimely death. The picture is about mortality as much as it is about war; its power is about death more than about a battle.

He sent it back to Paris to be developed, and Chiki spotted its potential, and sold it to the French magazine *Vu*. But its real moment came the following year, when it was republished in *Life* magazine alongside an editorial on the futility of the war. For the next few decades *The Falling Soldier* was regarded as the quintessential war photograph, although during the 1970s it became mired in controversy, and some said it had been faked, a charge fuelled by the fact that the negative was missing. So when one day in 2007 Leonora asked me if I wanted to look at the images in Chiki's darkroom in her home in Mexico City, I couldn't help wondering: is this where the negative of *The Falling Soldier* could have been, all these years?

Two years later, in 2009 – after Chiki's death – there was a strange discovery. A collection of Capa's negatives came to light in Mexico City, where it seemed to have been stored for many decades. Precisely how 'the Mexican suitcase', as it became known, got there has never been clear.

By the end of the Second World War, Robert Capa was probably the most famous photographer on the planet, and along with others including Henri Cartier-Bresson he founded the Magnum photographic agency in New York. Gerdo Taro had died in the Spanish Civil War, and Capa's many subsequent lovers included Ingrid Bergman. Capa is one of the most romantic figures of twentieth-century journalism; when news came in May 1954 that he had been blown up and killed while photographing a French advance during the first Indochina War, his oldest friend Chiki was devastated.

For Chiki and Capa friendship was everything. And so it became for Leonora, Remedios and Benjamin Péret, Kati and José Horna, and for all those for whom Gabina Barredo Street in Mexico City in 1944 was the hub. Most of the artists in the Gabino Barreda Street circle would never see their families again; many of them would never return to their homelands. What they were laying down in those early days in Mexico City were connections that would take the place of all they had left behind in Europe. For Leonora, who had not so much lost as deserted her first family, this chance of a second was an opportunity. For the first time in her life, she was somewhere she felt she fitted in. The fact that it was a tumble-down apartment with rats, cats and broken walls, peopled by inhabitants with no money, could not have mattered less. Five thousand miles from Lancashire and her family, in a city founded by Aztecs in the middle of what was once a lake 7000 feet above sea-level, she had found what she had been looking for all her life: a home where she felt she fitted in.

The growing friendship between Leonora and Chiki was a welcome development for the entire group. Chiki was popular with everyone, funny and clever; he was in his early thirties by this stage but, with his hair already receding prematurely above his long forehead, he could easily have passed for an older man. Everyone knew that Leonora, six years his junior, had endured harrowing experiences in Spain, and that she needed someone steady, loving and caring. It wasn't a bright, burning flame of a relationship like the one that had consumed her and Max; it wasn't the passing infatuation she had felt for Renato. Chiki was kind and understanding; and he would never threaten her sense of herself, or her art. He would not take up, as Max had, too much of her; he would never eclipse her. He would support her and humour her, cherish and admire her. And he would give her children. When in early 1946 she found she was pregnant, Leonora was pleased. She and Renato had already divorced; now, she married Chiki, and the two settled into their own apartment off Avenida Álvaro Obregón in the Colonia Roma area of the city. Kati Horna's photographs of the group on Leonora's wedding day capture the sense of hope and confidence they suddenly all had in the future, a future none of them would once have even dared might be possible. Leonora and Chiki's union, and the baby who was on the way, signalled a new life and a new beginning.

Leonora explored her own feelings on all this, unsurprisingly, in a painting; and it is a magnificent, wide-ranging, colourful and complex canvas, as rich and full of promise as every young person's future should be. The work is called *Chiki, Ton Pays* (Chiki, Your Country); but really it ought to be called *Leonora and Chiki, Your Country*, because it represents what is ahead for both. The couple are being conveyed on a wheeled vehicle through a fantastic and hybrid universe. All around are entwined figures, faces, creatures and Hieronymus Bosch-style concoctions; below the earth are symbols and signs, and in the background are buildings and church spires that could have come from one of the medieval masterpieces Leonora had seen in Florence. The transport inhabited by her and Chiki is travelling through the landscape, but it is clearly separate from it; swathed in a crimson curtain, it is topped by the tiny trees and grounds of that other country, those two other countries, that Leonora and Chiki will always bring with them, wherever they end up. Chiki is looking intently ahead, steering their ship; Leonora, her dress billowing with the child she was carrying, is looking out of the canvas directly at the viewer. Here it is, she seems to be saying: this is my new lot. Here is the new world I have created for myself; here is the man I now have by my side; and now I intend to go on moving through my new landscape, to discover what adventures lie ahead.

In March 1946, just after her wedding, Leonora wrote in buoyant mood to the gallerist Pierre Matisse in New York, full of promise for both her personal and her professional future. 'I am painting a good deal and hoping to open lucrative possibilities towards next year perhaps with Julien Levy – I'm not sure – However my responsibilities thicken owing to being in the 5th month of pregnancy, so if it turns out alive & with the normal numbers of hands and feet etc & looking more or less like the ordinary human animal I shall treat it to the rich possibilities of an exhibition of paintings. As you no doubt know I am married again & entirely happy & perhaps for the first time in my life living in peace.'

The baby arrived on 14 July after an easy labour; it was a son, a boy in whose genetic make-up Lancashire and Ireland had been mixed with Hungary, and Roman

Catholicism with Judaism. For him there would be no boarding schools, no requirement to conform to a predetermined set of values and expectations.

From her new vantage-point as a wife and mother in Mexico City Leonora took the rare step of looking back at her past. She had spent so long railing against her father for his inability to bend and his bloody-mindedness; but were these not the very traits of character that had seen her through the last seven turbulent years? To whom did she owe her strength of spirit, her utter determination to go on in the face of any adversity, her constant quest for something bigger, better and more ambitious than the hand she had been dealt?

What must Harold Carrington have made of it, standing by the fire at Hazelwood Hall in Lancashire on a winter's day, when he heard the news of the arrival of his first grandchild in Mexico? From across the world, his only daughter had decided to make a powerful and heartfelt gesture, a gesture of forgiveness. She had called her new baby Harold: Harold Gabriel Weisz Carrington.

10

The House Opposite

Objective chance, that intriguing quality of life so beloved of the Surrealists, had catapulted Leonora into a country with a particularly vibrant and exciting art scene; but the irony was that she never entirely connected with it. Her long life in Mexico was to be lived out in her own artistic tributary: she steered clear of the main river, and if by the end of her days she had become the darling of her adopted country then that was because of talent and accident, rather than design. She had as little as possible to do with the so-called experts of galleries and museums, art historians. She was a democratic artist who was interested in enabling others rather than confusing or overwhelming them. 'Your view is as important as anyone else's,' she told me. 'You have as much right to say what you feel about a painting as anyone has.' Art historians lay down the laws, she told the distinguished US art historian Whitney Chadwick in front of a TV camera, 'but I don't go along with the laws'. When Chadwick remarked that it must be difficult when art historians came along to critique her work, Leonora retorted, in a tone that was at the same time amused and resolutely honest: 'It's not hard, because I ignore what they are saying.'

Ignoring what the art world said about her was something she had done from her earliest days in Mexico; she was regarded as an interloper, and trying to gain acceptance held no attraction for her. In the 1940s Mexican art was dominated, as it had been in the two preceding decades, by the artists known as *Los Tres Grandes*: Diego Rivera, José Clemente Orozco, and David Siqueiros. Their art was very different from one another, but connected in the sense that all were muralists, and all were heavily influenced by the events of the revolution earlier in the century. All three were left wing, and interested in tracing the history of Mexico and examining the place of the indigenous Mexican, and the damaging influence of the sixteenth-century Spanish invaders. Today is it hard to go to Mexico City and not encounter the work of the Big Three: their huge and complicated, but at the same time accessible, paintings cover the walls of important buildings like the National Palace in the main square or Zócalo, the Palace of Fine Arts and the ancient Jesuit headquarters – the Colegio San Ildefonso. These works, especially those of the best known of the three, Rivera, provide a succinct and colourful résumé of the history of Mexico, its people and the historic injustices they suffered.

The rich contribution of muralism in the middle of the

twentieth century sparked the careers of many other artists, and helped create the country that is today known
for its rich diversity of visual art. Back then, though, the
great boast of *Los Tres* was that they were operating outside of the European 'bubble': they wanted to create art
in the Mexican tradition, and for inspiration they looked
to the prehistoric art of their own country rather than the
traditions of another continent. Given all this, it is not
surprising that no close relationships were forged between
the emigré artists, whose sensibilities had been formed in
Europe, and the established Mexican ones. Gunter Gerzso,
the artist whose painting captured the early days of the
group on Gabino Barreda Street, remembered that the
friends would meet every Saturday. 'It was a very exclusive
group, they never went out, they never interacted with
any Mexicans, and their feelings of friendship amongst the
members of their group were very close,' he remembered.

And yet, almost inevitably, there were a few links. Diego
Rivera's wife was Frida Kahlo, another artist who revelled
in her Mexican roots; she had never fully recovered from
the serious injuries she sustained in the bus accident in
which she was involved in the 1920s, and by the 1940s her
health was increasingly precarious, and she often painted
at an easel propped up in her bed. Her works, which since
her death in 1954 have made her the most famous artist
in Mexican history (not a situation any of her contemporaries would have predicted, since in her lifetime she was
overshadowed in every way by Rivera), focus resolutely
on herself and her own colourful story, which included
many lovers, much personal anguish, and a complicated

and fascinating relationship with her history and her country. She and Diego had been friendly with André Breton;
indeed, it was to visit the couple, and their famous lodger
Leon Trotsky, that Breton had gone to Mexico in the late
1930s. Now, though, Trotsky was dead, executed on Stalin's
orders. Frida, increasingly housebound, undoubtedly heard
stories of the new arrivals from Europe, and she was not
enamoured of them; during a stay in Paris in 1939, she had
written to her then lover Nickolas Muray: 'You have no
idea the kind of bitches these people are. They make me
vomit. They are so damn "intellectual" and rotten that I
can't stand them any more. It is really too much for my
character. I [would] rather sit on the floor in the market of
Toluca and sell tortillas, than to have anything to do with
those "artistic" bitches of Paris . . . '

The women she had encountered in Paris were, to Frida's
mind, overprivileged and pretentious; so when some of
their number pitched up in Mexico City during the early
1940s, she was far from keen to connect with them. But
Leonora was neither intellectual nor rotten, and Frida
seems to have made her an exception. Leonora visited
Frida, by then bedridden, several times in the Blue House
where the older artist was born, and where she died. She
remembered chatting to Diego too at a party: it was a long
conversation, full of gossip, and Diego was lots of fun,
very animated and full of life. In general, though, Leonora
liked Frida better than her husband; and she admired her
work, in general so different from her own although in one
respect very similar: both artists were determined to reflect
life through the prism of female experience.

For Leonora, the overwhelming female experience of this period of her life was motherhood; and it was a revelation to her. She had had no expectations of it, but it had opened up a part of her she had not realised existed. After Gabriel's birth in 1946 she was soon pregnant again and a second son, Pablo, followed just sixteen months after his brother. Motherhood, she said, 'certainly was a grand commotion', and 'I had no idea what maternal instinct was until I had my children'. As someone who had always been grounded in her instinct, she adapted easily to being a parent; and she also seems to have taken effortlessly to that essential requirement of motherhood, multitasking. She would certainly have agreed with this sentiment from the sculptor Barbara Hepworth, herself a mother of four including triplets: 'A woman artist is not deprived by cooking and having children, nor by nursing children with measles (even in triplicate) – one is in fact nourished by this rich life, provided one always does some work each day; even a single half hour, so that the images grow in one's mind.' This seems to have been very much Leonora's approach: she was a natural at muddling through, and provided her family was safe, she seems always to have been able to focus on her work and, like Hepworth, to keep it going. 'I paint,' she wrote, a few months after Gabriel's birth, 'with the baby in one hand, and the paintbrush in the other.'

The person to whom she addressed that sentence was a new friend who would go on to become one of the greatest confidantes of her lifetime. They had met on the beach in Acapulco in 1944; he said later that 'she struck me as a haughty, brittle, witty, but slightly arrogant woman … a ruthless English intellectual in revolt against all the hypocrisies of her homeland, against the bourgeois fears and false moralities of her conventional background and sheltered upbringing'. He was Edward James, a member of an Anglo-American family. He had grown up in Sussex and had inherited two large fortunes, part of which he used to collect Surrealist art. An important patron of the Belgian René Magritte, Edward's biggest claim to fame is probably that he was the model for the artist's work *Not To Be Reproduced* (1937), which shows the back of a man's head; he is looking into a mirror, but the image in the mirror has been reversed so that instead of seeing his face, we see an impossible reflection – the back of his head in duplicate. Edward had allowed Magritte to live in his London house rent-free so he could paint; he had extended similar assistance to the Spanish Salvador Dalí, buying everything the artist produced across an entire year.

Edward was a complex and tortured character whose early life, notwithstanding his wealth, had been difficult. He was the youngest child, and first boy, in a family with five children. His mother was rumoured to be either the daughter or the lover of King Edward VII, who was a regular visitor to West Dean, the family's vast, flint-faced pile in the midst of the rolling countryside of the South Downs near Chichester. The connection meant the junior Edward was either the monarch's son or his grandson; he favoured the latter explanation, and there is clearly a physical resemblance to the famously philandering king.

By 1944 Edward VII was dead, his legitimate grandson

George VI was on the throne, and Edward James's life had been blighted by a disastrous marriage in his twenties to a ballerina called Tilly Losch. What started as an infatuation petered into a relationship in which Edward, who was almost certainly homosexual, seems to have become resentful at having to prop up Tilly's career financially, by funding theatrical productions in which she had major parts. In the end Tilly had an affair and a horribly acrimonious divorce case, with plenty of accompanying bad publicity, followed in 1934. When it was all over, Edward left England and began a series of lengthy trips first to the US and then to Mexico where, in the early 1940s, he met a Post Office manager called Plutarco Gastalum, with whom he set out on an expedition to find the perfect place for his next pet project, which was to be an orchid garden. They eventually settled on a picturesque mountainside in the tropical jungle outside Tampico, just outside a small town called Xilitla (pronounced Hill-eetla); Plutarco would spend the rest of his life there, while Edward would flit in and out of the place for the rest of his life too. In the early 1960s a hurricane destroyed the orchids, and Edward and Plutarco decided not to re-plant another crop that would be vulnerable to inclement weather: instead, they used concrete to create a Surrealist sculpture garden which is today fêted as one of the must-see landmarks in the tourist guides to modern Mexico.

Both Leonora and Edward seem to have realised the potential and importance of their friendship straight away. He quickly revised his initial impressions, he wrote later, realising that 'she is not arrogant at all when you know her. She is shy. That is what it is. And she has great inward humility. Nearly always short of money herself, she and her husband are nevertheless invariably ready to help out other artists of their acquaintance whenever these are in trouble.'

Introduced to Leonora's wider circle of artist friends on a visit to Mexico City, he quickly became friendly with the others too, especially Kati Horna. Edward was a larger-than-life and colourful character: noisy, and given to gestures of extravagant and eccentric largesse. On 1 December 1947, Leonora wrote to Pierre Matisse to tell him about Pablo's birth: 'Edward wired me & is supposed to be arriving in Mexico today. He always turns up with a lot of loud laughter & general upheaval but I shall be glad to see him again although I might slip some bromide in his beer to make things more peaceful.'

Leonora and Edward had much in common. Both were products of wealthy, upper-class homes in England; both had felt, from their earliest times, that they didn't quite fit the mould. Both had ended up in exile from their families and their wealth, and in the same place: Mexico, where both struggled to make their Englishness understood. Their sense of humour, their wryness, their honesty that bordered on rudeness – all these attributes they completely understood about one another, while most Mexicans were completely mystified.

If Edward was an ally, and a wisp of shared Englishness a long way from home, he was also very welcome for his enthusiastic championing of her painting. From the beginning of their friendship he was enchanted by her work – and not only what she produced, but her holistic approach to her art. As a patron he had always noticed, he said, that there was what he described as 'an inverse ratio' between the luxuriousness of an artist's studio and the worth of her or his work. In this regard Leonora's chaotic studio seemed an utter delight. It 'had everything most conducive to make it the true matrix of true art. Small in the extreme, it was an ill-furnished and not very well lighted room. It had nothing to endow it with the title of studio at all, save a few almost worn-out paint brushes and a number of gesso panels, set on a dog-and-cat populated floor, leaning face-averted against a white-washed and peeling wall. The place was a combined kitchen, nursery, bedroom, kennel and junk-store. The disorder was apocalyptic: the appurtenances of the poorest.' Edward could hardly contain his excitement: 'My hopes and expectations,' he wrote, 'began to swell.'

From a financial point of view too Edward's arrival on the scene in the mid-1940s was opportune: his interest in buying her work could not have come at a better moment. Because life in Mexico with first one and then, quickly, two small children made life even more financially precarious. There was no money from England; Chiki was working as a jobbing photographer, picking up work where he could; and the family needed to sell Leonora's work to make ends meet. In November 1946 Leonora wrote to Edward to say that she and Chiki hoped to move to a new apartment. Their current apartment, she describes thus: 'There are no panes hardly left in the windows as the pelota enthusiasts in the street have broken them all. I can hardly move in the studio & have to jump over things as I bought another easel for 2 pesos (!!!) rather rickety but works . . . it [the studio] is so full of things that one would have to be an acrobat to be able to paint.' In a postscript, she says 'Chiki has just returned and there isn't much hope for the [. . .] apartment as they want 450 pesos rent [she doesn't say for what period]'. But then, a few days later, she wrote again, 'with terror & hope & delight' because they have rented the apartment for 425 pesos. A couple of months earlier, she had written to Edward to report that she had 'started your big seascape [probably *Seascape over Manzanilla*] & I think it will be good'. But he should not, she emphasises, think of paying for the piece until it is finished and he has seen it.

The letters that passed between Leonora and Edward are the most complete correspondence, largely because Edward kept copies of the letters he mailed, and all the letters he received; Leonora, by contrast, destroyed her mail. The archive at West Dean, the house Edward inherited from his parents and where towards the end of his life he established an arts college, has eleven boxes of correspondence between the two of them, mostly dating from the 1940s and early 1950s; they were friends until Edward's death in 1984, but maybe through the 1960s and beyond they spoke by telephone rather than mailing letters, and perhaps they saw one another more often in later years too. Their correspondence is revealing: for both, it was a close and lifelong friendship. In September 1946 Edward wrote from Hollywood to say he had been sick, 'a partial nervous breakdown', news he said he would not be sharing with anyone else. Leonora's response was revealing about her own experience, as well as his. It was, she reminded him, 'far more difficult to be kind to oneself than to other people'. She sympathised with his difficulties, but suggested that the solution 'is cold clear reason – not lying on one's back & screaming for a mother or nanny who isn't there any more. That, I should think, sums up your nervous breakdown and my own six months in a mad house'.

As well as being her confidante, Edward had become her patron, a role he held for the rest of his life. The good fortune in this situation worked in both directions, since Edward had chanced upon her at a time when her work was becoming better known, a situation he helped encourage. Pierre Matisse seems to have guarded her jealously, wanting her to sell work only through him: but in a letter dated 12 April (probably 1948) to Matisse's assistant Miss Vivano, Leonora wrote: 'I have had to sell the picture called *Tuesday* to Edward James for six hundred dollars because I had to have this money to be able to take a Nanny for the baby otherwise I wouldn't have time to work during the summer. Up til now I've looked after him myself and it doesn't leave much time for anything else . . . ' She ended in an apologetic tone: 'I hope he will understand and I won't sell any others unless there is a major catastrophe which I hope there won't be.' In another letter, though, she mentioned she has sold *The Giantess* to Edward for five hundred dollars, 'being in need at the time'. (The painting was a good investment; when it was auctioned on the open market at Christie's in New York in 2009, it fetched $1,483,500. When I read the news on the internet the next day and phoned Leonora she hadn't heard about it, and was convinced I was joking.)

Having two babies in such a short space of time turned life upside down for Leonora, as it would have done for any woman; but she embraced the changes, and always with her inimitable sense of humour. In a letter to Pierre Matisse dated 28 December 1947 she promises to paint more pictures, but says it's difficult because 'with 2 babies I am very busy & my life is very disorganised. I always seem to be washing bottles, changing diapers and making baby food – except for once when I went out with Edward I haven't been out of these four walls for about 2 years & have become so intimidated by the outside world that I might have grown a hare-lip, a long grey beard & three cauliflower ears, bow legs, a hump, gall stones & cross eyes. You might well imagine that in this state of mind I'm not likely to be in New York for the exhibition so you'll have to have it without me ... ' She ends with a thought that shows how she folded her pressing domestic concerns into her burgeoning fame: 'I want to buy a washing machine so try & sell some more paintings if you can'.

The exhibition she was referring to was an important milestone: her first substantial one-person show, at Pierre's gallery on East 57th Street in New York. It included twenty-seven works, *The House Opposite* and *Tuesday* among them, and it took place between 24 February and 13 March 1948, garnering favourable reviews, including one in *Time* magazine, whose correspondent noted that the walls of the gallery seemed to be almost hopping with demons. Creatures with hair and horns and half-luminous bodies were merged into birds, animals and plants. The reviewer commented on the precision and intricacy of the pieces, and marvelled at how

The Giantess, 1947, by Leonora Carrington

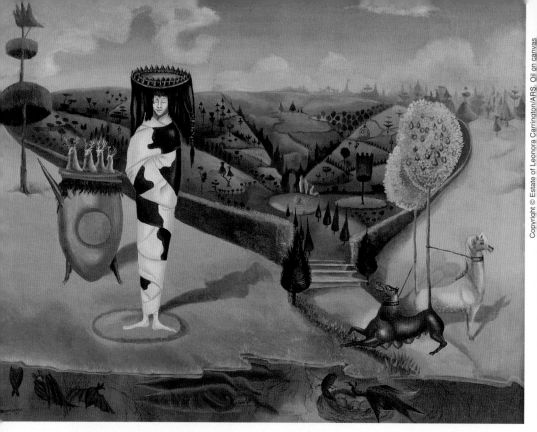

Green Tea, 1942, by Leonora Carrington

Leonora in the Morning Light, 1940, by Max Ernst

Portrait of Max Ernst, 1939, by Leonora Carrington

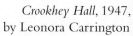

The House Opposite, 1945,
by Leonora Carrington

Crookhey Hall, 1947,
by Leonora Carrington

The Robing of the Bride, 1940, by Max Ernst

Chiki, Ton Pays, 1947, by Leonora Carrington

Grandmother Moorhead's Aromatic Kitchen, 1975, by Leonora Carrington

the creations danced against misty landscapes and dark skies. And each painting, he said, had two things in common: the signature, *Leonora Carrington*, and an all-embracing feeling of melancholy.

While it was crucial to Leonora to carry on working through pregnancy (she once said she felt she had done some of her best work while pregnant, possibly because she was able to indulge herself with the food she liked, and she believed she worked best on a full stomach) and while the children were young, she was very clear about her priority: it was the boys. So there was no chance that she would leave them in Chiki's care and go to New York, even though this was a huge milestone, her first solo show. Instead Edward was sent to deputise for her, liaising with Matisse and sending a running commentary via his letters back to Mexico City. The show's opening, he reported, was a tremendous success. 'I have never seen more enthusiasm at any "vernissage" among the crowd ... To give Pierre his due, he did a wonderful job of hanging – for which I must give him almost the entire credit as I did not want to butt in ... he [also] did a wonderful job of lighting ... your pictures ... shone like jewels from the wall ...'

As for many women, becoming a mother herself brought Leonora closer to her own mother. Her relationship with Maurie had certainly had its fractured moments, and there had been times when Maurie had seemed to side with Harold against her; but in general, Leonora's issues with her family were not with her mother. And now there was a new grandchild; and when news came that a second baby was on the way, Maurie decided to undertake the long and arduous journey from Lancashire to Mexico City so she could be there for the baby's arrival in November 1947. As her due date neared, Leonora told Pierre Matisse how relieved she was that her mother would soon be there. '[It] takes a heavy weight off my mind as I was desperate to know who would look after Gabriel while I was in the Sanatorio.'

She wrote in similar vein to Edward, making the surprising admission that she was even tempted by the idea of going home, at least for a visit: 'I have a hankering to return to England next year – the family have bought Hazelwood [Hall – until this point, they had been renting it] & only my mother and father live there now – it tempts me beyond reason to rest in an organised household.' In the next breath the confession was dismissed – 'this will probably blow over as most of my England nostalgias do' – but even to voice it showed that she, at least, had moved on from the difficult relationship she had endured with her parents in her final years and months in England.

And life in Mexico was hard: it was very tempting to think about how much easier things would be in Lancashire. In 1947, as Edward packed up in Mexico to make another trip back across the Atlantic, Leonora implored him to 'let me know how you find England ... Apparently I have quite a lot of money [there] & tell me how far that helps for living conditions? What would be the possibilities of Chiki finding work?' But then, at the end of the letter, there is a final sentence that is perhaps more of a plea: 'Don't hesitate to say if you advise staying in Mexico.'

Rapprochement with the Carringtons, combined with becoming a mother herself, naturally reminded Leonora of her own childhood, and some of her paintings from this time draw on those memories: her mother, dressed to go out for the evening, coming in the night nursery at Crookhey to say goodnight to her children, was the inspiration for *Night Nursery Everything* (1947); recollections of her unhappy schooldays form the basis for *The Hour of the Angelus* (1949), in which teenage girls play while being spied on by menacing creatures.

Another sign of the new closeness between Leonora and Maurie came at the end of her New York show, when she told Pierre Matisse – who had written to enquire whether he could sell one of her finest works from the exhibition, *The Temptation of St Anthony* – that he could not, because she had made a present of it and wanted it shipped to her mother in Lancashire. In December Maurie wrote to Matisse to arrange the transit of the work. Having thanked him for some catalogues and books he had sent, she continued: 'We are always delighted to learn of what Leonora is doing, we miss her desperately and long for the time when she can come home again. Could you let me know what the cost is of getting her *St. Anthony* over here will be, & I'll get permission from this side?'

There is no direct mention of Harold, and the 'we' was probably more a figure of speech than a sign that Leonora's father was having a change of heart. The improved relationship with Maurie could, given time, have perhaps opened up a thaw with Harold: but fate was to intervene. In May 1950, while he and Maurie were on a fishing holiday in Bundoran in Donegal, Ireland with my father and grandparents, Harold was suddenly taken ill. He died, aged sixty-nine, in the Great Northern Hotel where the family were staying; he had been deemed too ill to be taken to hospital, and my father remembered the consternation of the hotel manager, who had a large banquet booked for the following evening; just as he was about to reluctantly cancel the event, Harold conveniently breathed his last.

It was an unexpected death, probably the result of pneumonia after he caught a chill; and if Leonora ever wondered if a reconciliation might be possible, it certainly never could be now. Five thousand miles away, she was stunned by the news. To Edward she wrote: 'My father died & this gave me a shock probably stronger than I thought at the time, anyhow I seem to be going through a kind of metamorphosis with a certain amount of agony & a giving up of old customs. I would like to see my mother & she is expecting me to return to England & I keep on miss-ing boats so that I can first get myself together – I feel very peculiar . . . ' The pull to return to England was stronger than it had ever been since her departure in 1937, but she continued to be haunted by the old fears that she would be pulled into a life she did not want and never had wanted. Could Edward, she asked, make the journey with her? 'I need you urgently – I am so terrified of all my awful family (except my mother!) I thought we might go to Hazelwood together & this would make an entirely macabre situation into something which would provide us food for amuse-ment for years to come.' She goes on: 'My sinister brother Pat has telegraphed me that he will pay for the trip out of the "Estate" whatever that is & I imagine they now await my final & eventual capitulation into a respectable cocoon of fox terriers, Hazelwood & hunt balls & balls . . . '

It was not until 1952 that Leonora made the journey back to Europe. She took Gabriel and Pablo, then aged six and five, with her: they arrived in Southampton on 14 April. Though it was a long trip lasting several months, and included time in France as well as in England, Chiki remained in Mexico: perhaps doing things that way gave Leonora the guarantee that she would definitely return. She spent a few weeks at Hazelwood with Maurie, and no doubt she enjoyed very much the luxury of the family's mansion with its comfortable sitting rooms and terraces, its views of the sea and its ever helpful staff. There was tennis on the lawn and walks in the woods; there were trips to see other members of the family and old friends. There was even her old nanny, Mary Cavanaugh, now in her seventies but still living at Hazelwood and happy to help with the boys. So it must have been a wrench for Leonora to pull herself away from this easy life and return to the tribulations of survival in Mexico; and from papers in the Edward James archive, it seems that perhaps the Carringtons did all they could to dissuade her from going back.

According to these documents it appears Leonora had opted to pay her own way for the journey home, despite Pat's offer of the fare. When the time came to return, however, she had run out of funds. 'Her mother,' said Edward in a memorandum, 'had given her an emerald ring, which was supposed to be very valuable. She hoped to sell this to pay for her journey. But the emerald – like her relations' assurances of affection – proved to be false. Her [Leonora's] husband could not send her enough money for the journey home.'

Edward went on to describe a tangled set of events that

culminated in a stand-off between Leonora and Maurie. At issue were some paintings she had left at Hazelwood ('as collateral', according to Edward) and a 'loan' of £300 from her mother which Leonora later, in what Edward calls 'the thoughtlessness and rather childish impetuosity of a moment of pride and humiliation', covered by signing a blank cheque. Suffice to say that it is clear from Edward's account that the trip to England ended extremely badly, with Leonora locked in a dispute with Maurie – fuelled by her brothers – from which they would never recover.

Under the terms of Harold's will Leonora was provided for by a trust, but effectively she had been cut out of her inheritance, as her only way of accessing the family's money would be to do something she could never do, which was kow-tow to her relatives. According to Edward's account, Leonora's brothers had used her visit to Lancashire to remind her that they now held all the cards as far as money was concerned. In a memorandum about the events, which Edward seems to have left for posterity because of a situation he felt was grossly unfair, he wrote about his resentment for Pat, Gerard and Arthur Carrington 'because they have behaved particularly badly towards a close relation of theirs, who is living in great poverty in Mexico and who is unable to get the major part of the small income which she inherited from her father out of England ... I have every reason to suppose that this little income, which she requires for the support of her two children and which only amounts to £300 per annum for each child, is being held up by the machinations of these brothers and their influence on her trustees'.

The contrast between the life she had given up in England, and the life she had embraced in Mexico, must never have seemed sharper when Leonora and her sons arrived back from their visit to Europe. They were by now living in a new house in Colonia Roma, a Bauhaus-style building which, though much bigger than their previous dwellings, was in poor repair and would need lots of work. Leonora, though, was thrilled with it; in a letter to another friend, Pablo O'Higgins – like her an artist outsider who had gravitated to Mexico, in his case from Utah – Leonora described it as 'absolutely perfect'. It was on 'a quiet street with trees on each side. The house is very old & was built by campesinos who were intelligent enough not to get an architect . . . there are 3 floors – the third floor has 3 rooms only they haven't got doors or windows, these communicate with the top by a wooden ladder. There is another terrace which communicates with the kitchen & below by another ladder. The studio is beautiful & we are putting in a fireplace. This room will be divided by [a] blue curtain . . . there are two yards which will be gardens includ- ing a large sand heap . . . ' She hoped, she said, to plant grass, orange trees and geraniums, and there would be enough room for the family to have four or five cats and a dog.

Returning from Hazelwood to the house in Colonia Roma felt like the final act in Leonora's separation from her family. With the return to England she had allowed herself to taste again the benefits of wealth and splendour as afforded by the Carrington millions, and once again they had proved nugatory. The row Edward described ended any chance of reconciliation with her family, and she would never return to Hazelwood (though she did see her mother on one final occasion, on a trip back to Britain in the 1960s with Edward, when the two went to visit a Buddhist retreat in Scotland).

In Mexico Leonora would again, she knew, be plunged into all kinds of financial and domestic difficulties; and it would be hard, as she had realised it was going to be hard, raising her boys without the practical and emotional support of her mother and extended family. She turned her face to the future, a Mexican future, and she closed the door even more firmly on Lancashire, her past and the Carringtons.

Back in Mexico her life was firmly anchored in the new house, and in the small but tightly knit group that had formed in Gabino Barreda Street. At its centre were three women: Leonora, Remedios and Kati. All of them had a hinterland that, though unrelated, was similar: each had gone through a long, exhausting and emotionally draining journey to get to Mexico. Now they were here, their journeys mostly took place in their kitchens, in their minds and, especially, in their conversations: and the fruit of these exchanges was their art. Domesticity seemed not to limit their lives; their outsider status, as Europeans, meant they were not bound by the usual rules ascribed to women in macho Mexican society, and in a country in which labour was cheap even impoverished artists could afford maids.

In this outpost of Surrealism, an art movement that had in its Parisian heyday been dominated by men who had seen women merely as their muses, Leonora and her friends had made a radical departure: this was Surrealism as it had never been practised before. For all its avant-garde ambitions, the architects of Surrealism had not been forward-looking when it came to women and their place in the world, and in the world of art; Leonora had rejected the role of muse, but that was very much how the Surrealists saw the women who were close to them. Now, though, in a hidden corner of Mexico City, Leonora, Remedios and Kati took Surrealism to a new place, a place where it was women-centred and instinctive. It was a kind of hermetic surrealism, almost entirely divorced from what remained of the art movement that had spawned them. Indeed, Leonora made quite clear in this letter to Edward in 1946 that she would not want to be part of the 'mainstream' Surrealist movement any longer. An acquaintance in Mexico, she reported, had just returned from Paris '& gives a rather dreary account of the Surrealist Brethren in St Germain de Pres. Apparently Breton is back in the Holy See of Les 2 Magots – Picasso has left Dora Maar for a younger woman of 20 odd years who he keeps cloistered away from the roving eyes ... They all paint like mad, Paul Éluard, poet Extraordinaire of the new whatever it is, communism or something – etc. etc. Nothing really interesting or amusing.'

But if Paris had lost its sparkle, Leonora had found new glitter in her rundown neighbourhood in Mexico City, which was now the centre of the universe for her new extended family, the other European emigrés, all of whom lived close by. The year after Pablo was born, Kati gave birth to a daughter, Norah, named after Leonora. Remedios, meanwhile, had parted company with Péret when he returned to Paris, and had a new partner called Walter Gruen, although he was never part of the circle of the 'Surreal Friends' in the way Péret had been. There were others too in the group, or on its periphery: the painter Esteban Francés, the South American poet César

Moro, and the writer Octavio Paz, who would go on to win the Nobel Prize for Literature in 1990.

The house in Colonia Roma, which hosted so many meetings of the Surreal Friends group, gave Leonora what she had been searching for all her life: a safe base from which she could thrive as an artist. It looked nothing from the outside, but just as in her painting *The House Opposite* (1946), once one stripped away the surface, all sorts of fantastical, exciting and experimental pursuits opened up. It was the hub of Leonora's creativity. She had not come to Mexico in search of adventure: there had been enough of those already. What mattered now was unpacking her adventures and exploring them again in her paintings.

Leonora's friendship with Remedios deepened, and became one of the most precious of her life. The women felt a level of communication with one another that neither had felt with anyone else. When, some years later, Leonora wrote her novella *The Hearing Trumpet*, Remedios was the model for the Spanish character Carmella Velasquez, and Leonora described the friendship between her own character, Marian, and Carmella thus: 'I often feel like Joan of Arc so dreadfully misunderstood ... I feel I am being burned at the stake just because I am different from everybody else because I have always refused to give up that wonderful strange power I have inside me and it becomes manifested when I am in harmonious communication with some other inspired being like myself.' The flamboyant, dark-haired Englishwoman and the red-headed Spaniard fused their strange powers and their extraordinarily fertile imaginations, and together they egged one another on to increasingly outlandish and bizarre projects. Both had got away from countries laced with restrictions: in Mexico they could be free – and they made the most of every minute of that freedom. One of Remedios' favourite pastimes, sometimes aided by Leonora, was to write to complete strangers, chosen at random from the phone directory, inviting them to visit: 'Dear Stranger, I am totally unaware if you are a solitary man or a father of a family, if you are a timid introvert or a bright extrovert, but one way or another perhaps you are bored and wish to fling yourself intrepidly into the middle of a group of unknown persons with the hope of seeing something that interests or amuses you ...'

With Kati too Leonora had a relationship that made her more like a sibling than a friend; indeed, one of their contemporaries once dubbed them 'psychic twins'. The two women would talk for hours; Kati once described how 'we would get together several times a day. Our houses were close, and we would start walking around 8 at night, and walk until 1 in the morning as we continued talking. We talked about an endless number of things, from our creative activities to our children and our lives.'

Cooking was another preoccupation: a task that has so often been burdensome to women was, to Leonora, Remedios and Kati, an exciting vista of endless possibilities and potential experiments. As with everything else, they refused resolutely to accept society's limitations: meals were simply another landscape in which to celebrate the ridiculousness of rules, and to break them. Their most spectacular culinary endeavour came at a dinner party where they served pearl tapioca coloured with squid ink to friends claiming it was a rare and expensive caviar; other outlandish meals included

dishes claiming aphrodisiac qualities, and another that promised to stimulate dreams of being the king of England.

The kitchen was a laboratory: for Leonora, cookery
and painting were closely intertwined: she once said that
'the real work is done when you are alone in your studio.
First it becomes a sense of something and then it becomes
something that you can see and then it becomes something
that you can do. It's like cooking, but cooking isn't that
easy either.' Her paint of choice was egg tempera, which
involved separating the yolk from the white and using it
as a binder with pigments. This was the painting material favoured by the Italian Renaissance artists, and she
would have been acquainted with it from her time at Miss
Penrose's finishing school in Florence when she was fifteen;
her year-long stay there was an introduction to painters
like Paolo Uccello, Giuseppe Arcimboldo and Pisanello,
and she loved and admired the works of these and other
Italian Renaissance artists all her life. Uccello was one of
her favourites: she was already familiar with his work from
trips to the National Gallery in London, and central to his
Battle of San Romano, which she would have seen, is a white
horse that bears a more than passing resemblance to the
horses in her self-portrait. Uccello painted in egg tempera;
in terms of the lasting quality of the colours it could not be
bettered, and it also has the ability to reflect and capture
the light. When Edward reported that her paintings 'shone
like jewels from the wall' at the 1948 show in New York,
egg tempera would have been the reason why.

Leonora loved what might be called the artisanship of art:
she loved technique, of which mixing egg tempera colours

was but part, and it mattered to her throughout her life to improve on the essential skills. It was the message Amédée Ozenfant had drilled into her in his tiny Kensington art school: technique, technique, technique. To her, painting was a craft 'like that of carpenters ... it's a craft, and that sort of process is falling into oblivion'. Surrealist artists were very good at the craft, she said, especially Picasso, who had been a great artisan. And her own work, particularly through the 1940s and 1950s, was painstaking, complex, detailed, laborious. She would work for hours at one tiny section of the canvas: works like *Chiki, Ton Pays, The Giantess* and *The Elements* are testaments to the extraordinary attention she took to detail, especially at this stage of her career.

Her son Gaby has written about his memory of seeing her at work when he was a young child; he remembers her painting, he says, with 'a cigarette on the ashtray sending up a long smoke signal. An assortment of paint tubes rest over a stained wooden table, bleeding colorations. Leonora holds a paint brush and guides her strokes with a mahl stick or rest stick, a wooden stick with a round head at one of its ends that can be placed against any of the canvas frames; she is tracing a thin straight line that becomes the solid wall of a room. Different beings come to life as if they'd always been there, inhabiting these realms with their own passions, myths and legends, a place where each one of our imaginal bodies can finally exist, far from our mortal frames and in a place invented by the painting itself...'

Leonora very rarely collaborated with other artists; she was always very clear about that. In fact poor Edward James was almost banished from the magic circle when he made the mistake of thinking he could 'improve' one of her paintings by daubing some paint on it. He soon realised what a huge faux pas he had committed, as his contrite letter to her afterwards revealed. 'I should have specifically asked your permission, before touching it – and I was wrong to go ahead, just because I had a sudden burst of inspiration and a lot of orange and white paint left over from the other picture,' he told her. But what made the episode 'take on a more serious aspect' was that, according to Edward, Leonora had in the past allowed him to touch other canvases. 'Your words the night before last were 'I was wrong to let you do it, but you were even more wrong to do it. You ought to have known that it wasn't right.'

The exchange of ideas with Remedios led to paintings that seem to be based on similar ideas – Leonora's *Syssigy* and Remedios' *Women's Tailor*, both 1957, share the same scene, and figures who are reminiscent of one another. Look more closely at these and other paintings by both artists, though, and it's clear they are very different practitioners. When they explored the same theme, as they do in Remedios' *Creation of the Birds* (1957) and Leonora's *Bird Birthing* (1962), the contrast is obvious: even the titles they have given their works hint at their disparate approaches. In Remedios' painting, an ordered and carefully planned operation is taking place: a feathered creator sits neatly at a table, painting implements to hand, as a bird emerges from her parchment and prepares to fly off the page. It is a beautiful, thought-provoking work. But Leonora's more elusive painting is perhaps truer to life: a whole flock of birds is emerging from a process that seems to resemble cooking.

There are two creators, but neither seems particularly confident about what is happening or what they are doing. A fully formed bird is emerging from what might be an invisible cauldron. The message of this work seems to be that the process of life is messy and complicated, and most of the time we human beings can only stumble through. But somehow birds are being created, and they are flying away. There is hope.

Leonora's work is instinctive, organic and flowing; Remedios' work is about structure, form and precision. Leonora's paintings often feel as though they have erupted on to the canvas from somewhere very deep inside herself; Remedios' work has been pre-ordained, considered, planned. Leonora's work is about letting go and giving oneself over to elements beyond human power: Remedios' is more controlled and the work of an artist who seems to want to remain in charge. That was never Leonora's ambition: she saw herself as a conduit, a channel. Where Remedios was an illustrator, an interpreter, a painter of reality – albeit at times a magical reality – Leonora was unbridled, free from rules, and her work reflected the chaos, complications, paradoxes and contradictions of the widest reaches of the universe.

Just occasionally, Leonora did collaborate with another artist from the Surreal Friends group, though never with Remedios. In 1949 she worked with José Horna on a cradle (*The Cuna*, now in a museum in Mexico City) for his young daughter Norah, painting a sequence of images of moons, women and transports: the result was a charming, wooden boat on a rocker, a bed that could float a child off to the world of dreams. Another collaboration that came much later, in 1962, saw Leonora take the role of model in a series of surreal photographs taken by Kati and entitled *Ode to Necrophilia*: Leonora was photographed naked, from behind, crouched over a bed on whose pillow lay a candlelit death-mask.

By 1957 when she turned forty, Leonora was becoming increasingly well known in Mexico. Her first solo show there had been in 1950; it took place in the rather incongruous surroundings of a furniture showroom, but led to a great deal of positive press, and to a friendship with the doyenne of the Mexican art scene, Ines Amor. Amor was the owner of the country's most prestigious gallery, the Galería de Arte Mexicano, and when she took Leonora on as a client her future as an artist seemed starred. With Gaby and Pablo growing up, professional success seemed to beckon at last. But over the next few years a series of calamitous events would throw Leonora into a very different, and unexpected, way of life.

11

The Naked Truth

Early in the 1960s the circle of the Surreal Friends was shaken by two unexpected deaths. In April 1963 José Horna died; the same year, apparently of a heart attack and aged only fifty-five, Remedios also died. With the loss of José, Leonora grieved a great friend and occasional collaborator, someone she had valued highly as both a fellow artist and a personal ally; but the death of Remedios felt like losing a sister. For twenty years, Remedios had been part of the framework of Leonora's life. The two women saw one another almost every day, sharing their thoughts on everything from domestic goings-on to their esoteric interests, to their art and events in Mexico. They were often together, and their work seemed to many to be linked. Octavio Paz called them *Dos Transuentes* (two passers-by) and described them as a pair of beautiful Surrealists who shared the same inner vision for living and creating work in a kind of vacuum untouched by worldly ambition, wealth or social constraint. 'There are in Mexico two admirable artists,' he wrote, 'two bewitched witches: they have never heard the voices of praise or disapproval from schools and parties ... Unaware of social morals, of aesthetics and price, Leonora Carrington and Remedios Varo go through our city ... Where are they going? Where imagination and passion call them.'

Leonora herself never regarded her relationship with Remedios as collaborative or twin-like: for her, it was about sharing ideas, and she revelled in their common way of looking at the world and dealing with it. Supportive friendships are common among male artists – the Paris Surrealist group was an extended version of exactly that – but there are fewer examples of it amongst women artists. Leonora and Remedios fed ideas back and forth across their kitchen tables, as well as while walking around the markets and sitting in cafés and bars; they were engaged in a constant and energetic conversation that had begun in the dilapidated surroundings of Gabino Barreda Street, and ended with their last get-together the day before Remedios complained of chest pains, and died a short while later.

As much as shared ideas, the pair had a common vision of how life could be. And what that came down to, more than anything, was a belief in their own autonomy: Leonora and Remedios each had an independence of spirit that is as unusual for women now as it was in the middle of the twentieth century. Their marriages, though an important part of both their lives, never overwhelmed them: neither the high points or the low points, the romance or the rows, were ever allowed to become too absorbing or distracting. They saw marriage in a way that is more common among men than women: it was part of their lives, but it had its discrete space, and it could not and would not impinge on the part of them that was dedicated to ideas and art.

Motherhood, though, was different: for Leonora, being the mother of sons was a consuming passion. Having rejected her first family, she seemed determined to do all she could to safeguard her second. She had no expectations of parenthood, she told me: she had been surprised, from the day she gave birth to Gabriel, by how much it overwhelmed her emotionally. So whereas art had trumped her ties with her parents and brothers, there was no possibility that it could do the same where her children were concerned. The fierceness with which she cast herself out of the Carrington family was now redirected towards establishing her new family, the Weisz Carrington family, in Mexico. She adored her sons, revelled in their childhood, fussed over their education, worried about their futures. They were the centre of her world, and to the end of her life they were absolutely her priority.

But being surrounded by men all her life shaped who she was, and she was well aware of that. Just as the nursery at Crookhey Hall had been dominated by her brothers, so the house in Colonia Roma was a testosterone-charged zone. This time around, though, she softened: she was sensitive to her sons and their needs in a way she had never been with her brothers. As a woman she was even more alone in her second family than in her first: in Lancashire and London there had always been Maurie, the most successful of her relationships in her birth family. Having no sisters and no daughters, and having cut herself off from her aunts and female cousins, made her friendships with women particularly important, especially those with Remedios and Kati.

Towards the end of her life Remedios' work had blossomed beyond her studio, a process that continued after her death: the following year, 1964, there was a major retrospective at the Palacio de Bellas Artes, the chalk-white cathedral of the arts in the centre of Mexico City, and a book about her life. In one sense Remedios' death, which ended her career so prematurely and so long ahead of Leonora's own death, enabled Leonora to be seen again as a separate artistic entity, rather than one who was often linked with her friend and fellow European.

Her work too was becoming more widely known. In October 1960 *The Times* of London carried an article about the work of three British women artists living in Mexico 'who, because of distance, remain unknown to their fellow countrymen'. Leonora, one of the three, was described as 'a deeply imaginative surrealist artist who has worked hard to achieve a technique so sound and careful it might belong to some early Renaissance or Dutch master. She builds her pictures layer by layer, rubbing down constantly with sand-paper and leaving nothing to chance in the final effect. Out of this technical virtuosity she builds a world of fantasy that is all her own. Beasts and men such as never were on land or sea wander ethereally on to her canvases and gaze at the spectator with mild surprise to think they were invented at all. There is much that is macabre and ghoulish, and yet, in spite of Miss Carrington's apparent desire to shock she gives the impression that in her heart of hearts it is sheer beauty that matters most.' The review ends: 'So masterly is [her work] that one can look for hours at the variety in a few square inches of paint. It is the kind of quality that makes many other modern canvases seem as if their perpetrators had done them between urgent appointments elsewhere.'

Of one thing, *The Times* was certain: there was nothing Mexican about her work at all, which in the main was true, and this militated against her becoming better known. To achieve success as an artist, it helps to live in the surroundings that inspire you: one of Frida Kahlo's big advantages was that her work was rooted in the Mexico where she was born, and where she spent most of her life. Being Mexican was part of Frida's brand; whereas for Leonora, there was no clear brand at all. She often seemed determined to sabotage or undermine any attempts to define or unravel her art. 'What's that?' she asked me sharply, when I produced my notebook a couple of days into my 2006 visit to meet her. When I reminded her that I was a journalist and intending to write an article about her, she looked horrified. 'Journalists! I don't want them in here.' I was there as her cousin, she reminded me. In an undated letter in his archive, to someone he is trying to interest in Leonora's work, Edward James wrote something similar: 'Unlike so many of her contemporaries she has no gift for publicity and no apparent desire for fame. But her work [the word 'work' is in red] deserves to be more famous.'

Leonora refused to co-operate with journalists, and with publicity opportunities, in much the same way that she had refused, according to one of her reports from the nuns at her convent, to co-operate at school. She often used to quote a rhyme her nanny had instilled in her in the nursery at Crookhey Hall: 'Fools' names, like their faces, always appear in public places.' Another favourite verse, also remembered from her childhood, was this:

The codfish lays a million eggs
The little hen but one.
The codfish never cackles when her lowly task is done.
And so we praise the little hen;
The codfish we despise.
Which proves, my friends and countrymen –
It pays to advertise.

Worse, from the point of view of the media exposure that might have made her better known, was that her paintings were inspired by events and memories that had no resonance in her surroundings, making an already esoteric artist even less accessible. It meant, for example, that art historians, writers and journalists in her adopted country knew little or nothing of the Celtic legends of her Irish family, or the traditions of the English upper classes, that infected and invaded her canvases.

There was, though, one significant exception. In the early 1960s Mexico opened its National Museum of Anthropology in Chapultepec Park in the capital: in a city that today has more museums per capita than any other city except Paris, this museum would grow to become the jewel in its crown. Leonora was asked to produce a mural for it, which she decided to base on the beliefs of the Chiapas Indians, descendants of the Mayans, whose homeland is the forests and highlands of central Mexico and Guatemala. She travelled there by bus and mule, staying with a Swiss anthropologist called Gertrude Blom, who lived in San Cristobal de las Casas and was a pioneer against the destruction of rainforests. Together they trekked around the countryside meeting villagers, and learning about the way traditional Mayan beliefs had been intertwined with the Catholicism of the sixteenth-century Spanish invaders, creating a kind of hybrid belief system that seemed to precisely embody Leonora's instinctive conviction that the world needs to be seen as a layering of experiences and events. Her art had always been about exploring boundaries, looking always at the fluidity and blurred edges rather than the impenetrable barriers (she didn't think there were impenetrable barriers, anyway); and the way the Mayans had layered their traditional beliefs into Christianity was exciting to her.

The resulting mural, a huge work that stands seven feet by fifteen feet, was painted in the sitting room of her house on three large panels and remains in the museum in Mexico City to this day. It's a vivid panorama that sets a Catholic church in an ochre-floored village where the sheep are sacred and a turquoise serpent floats across a blood-red sky, undisturbed by a flock of swooping owls and a one-eyed watchful cat. Like so many of Leonora's works, *El Mundo Mágico de los Mayas* encompasses the world of sky, earth and underworld, and meshes together the spirit world with the here and now, the dead with the living, and the ancient with the new. There is no value judgement:

Leonora gives no creed, no theory, no belief system pre-
cedence or advantage. Who is to say that the Mayan belief
system was any more, or any less, true than the Christianity
with which it was later blended? Who can say whether it
is better to be a human being than a serpent? Who knows
whether it is better to be alive than dead?

In the Mayan mural, and in many of the works that
followed through the 1960s and 1970s, Leonora drew heavily on the Catholicism of her youth. As strongly as she
fought against the Church's petty restrictions, its inherent
misogyny and its top-heavy power, she had been formed
in its magic and theatre, both in England and on holidays
with her grandparents in Moate in County Westmeath.
She had grown up in a church that was still several decades
away from the reforms of the Second Vatican Council:
Mass was an event recited in Latin, with a priest who
had his back turned to the congregation, and it had at its
heart a miracle, the moment when the bread and wine was
transformed into the body and blood of Christ. This process, transubstantiation, was something Maurie believed
in (Harold was not a Catholic) and the nuns at school
believed in; it made the ephemeral and the inexplicable
a part of the everyday, and this sense that the spirit world
was right here in the midst of everything was fundamental
to Leonora's thought process. Her work is infused with
images borrowed from Catholicism: there are tabernacles
and altars, altar boys and nuns, priests in skull-caps and
compositions that seem to evince the scene of the nativity,
or of a Eucharistic celebration. Tables reminiscent of altars
occupy the central space in several of her paintings; figures

play ecclesiastical-looking organs; hands are extended in gestures that seem to evoke the moment of an offering. Sometimes, as in *The Naked Truth* (1962), there are characters who are clearly high priests, in this case presiding over a hearing in which a nude woman is standing in a dock-like cage, reading what the title suggests is more true than the creed the men of God have invented. Perhaps in that painting Leonora was remembering the conversations she used to have with Father Robert de Trafford, her father's Jesuit friend, on his frequent visits to Crookhey and later Hazelwood. She used to say she found him intelligent, and that she relished the chance to talk to someone else whose life, like hers, was rooted in a belief that reality was wider than the here and now.

Catholicism was a heavy influence on Leonora's work throughout her career, but it was far from her only spiritual reference. She was drawn, from her early years in Mexico, to the study and understanding of different belief systems, sinking her energy variously into Tibetan Buddhism, Gnosticism, Kabbala and the occult, as well as the Celtic traditions of her youth and the ancient Mexican customs such as the Day of the Dead. Among the authors and thinkers whose work heavily influenced her were the psychotherapist Carl Jung, the mystic G. I. Gurdjieff and his follower P. D. Ouspensky, and Robert Graves, author of *I, Claudius* but more important in Leonora's eyes for his 1948 *The White Goddess*. This book, which draws on Celtic mythology to advance the idea of a matriarchal religion centred on a goddess, was described by Leonora as perhaps the most important single book she ever read.

The basic idea Leonora was drawn to, and this was threaded through all the belief systems that caught her interest, was that the systems and structures of other worlds – previous worlds, the celestial world, the underworld – are accessible in our present universe. If her work has a unifying feature, that is perhaps it. Equally important was her belief that liberation came from within: and there is an irony in the fact that she turned her back on her family, and travelled halfway round the world, in order to delve into what she had had inside herself all along.

Leonora mined deep, and many of her ideas were way ahead of their time. She was an eco-feminist and a New Ager long before these terms were even invented: and since she had a vehement aversion to labels, that was fortunate. But her views put her squarely into that camp: she was instinctively and adamantly feminist, and had a natural concern for the environment and an anxiety that the planet was being abused because the so-called 'intelligent' species, human beings, were damaging it. She once remarked that what women needed was what men so often had – a wife – and when I talked to her about feminism, she shrugged her shoulders and said equality between women and men was something she regarded as a given, something she couldn't quite believe we were still, in the early twenty-first century, having to fight for. Many of her paintings feature figures that are neither obviously female nor obviously male, or have characteristics of both; and almost all her work has echoes of the natural world: birds, the sky, trees, animals. Her painting *The Giantess* (1950) has an alternative title, *The Guardian of the Egg*: it shows a cloaked female figure, her tiny face surrounded by a wheat-field halo, towering over an earth featuring farmers, animals, trees, boats and fishes. Amidst swooping birds and against a thunderous sky, the outsize female is holding something very precious and very small: an egg, which seems to represent the future.

US academic Gloria Orenstein, who became a friend, has called Leonora's art 'a modern woman's codex' for a kind of joined-up world, a world which 'speaks of past ages, of cycles of matriarchy and patriarchy, and of lost continents that once possessed matristic cultures. Through a meditation upon her work, the viewer is induced into a new formulation of both reality and identity, of space, time, self and cosmic history'.

Nowhere in her work was this codex better expanded on than in a novel Leonora wrote in mid-life, although it was not published until many years later, 1977, when she was sixty. The book is called *The Hearing Trumpet* and it is still in print. In 2009 the *Guardian* included it in its list of '1000 novels everyone should read'; when I called Leonora to let her know, she thought I was joking.

It's a story about old age, and specifically female old age; but it's also a story that revisits many received wisdoms of our age and every other modern age, and refashions them in a completely new light.

The protagonist of the tale is Marian Leatherby, a ninety-two-year-old British woman who has somehow been transported, earlier in her life, to a Spanish-speaking land on the other side of the world. For many years she has longed to escape and return to Europe, but it has never been the right moment to go back, and now she has accepted that she never will. Instead, she is living with her son Galahad and his wife Muriel: but everything changes when her friend Carmella, a flame-haired Spaniard who writes letters to people she has never met, gives her a hearing trumpet. Marian uses it to eavesdrop on her son and his family, and discovers they are plotting to dispatch her to an old people's home. Galahad preserves a modicum of civility ('There's no desperate hurry ... she will have to be told') but for Muriel the gloves are off ('Remember Galahad, those old people do not have feelings like you or I') and to Robert, their son, Marian is 'a drooling sack of decomposing flesh' who would be better off dead.

Robert is a youthful, motorbike-riding male: he believes the world is constructed around him, and people like him. His grandmother represents his polar opposite: as an elderly female, he believes she has nothing to contribute, nothing to offer, no purpose to live out and no excitements ahead.

He could hardly be more wrong. Marian knows she has no choice but to go to the care home. She gives a lot of thought to what to pack, because 'one has to be very careful what one takes when one goes away for ever'. Into her suitcase goes a screwdriver, a hammer, nails, birdseed, ropes, an alarm clock, a bag of sugar and matches. Finally, she throws in a few clothes 'to prevent things rattling about inside the trunk'.

The institution in which she finds herself sounds like a cross between Leonora's boarding schools and the asylum: at its centre is a castle, around which is parkland dotted with pavilions. And on the dining room wall, an eighteenth-century portrait of a nun (done by a Spaniard, because 'an Italian could never have done anything so enchantingly sinister') with a leering smile, and who seems to be winking.

Lightsome Hall is about as far removed from a sleepy geriatric outpost as it is possible to imagine, and the old ladies who inhabit it turn out to be the front-line army in the world's most vital and enduring quest. They are in search of the Holy Grail, whose true secret is a collection of documents that discredit the Gospels, overturn millennia of patriarchy, and restore the position of the great goddess whose existence is the fount of a new and energising life force. Mary Magdalene, it turns out, was executed for selling her secrets to one Jesus of Nazareth; half a century before Dan Brown, Leonora was setting out the tale that became the bestselling *Da Vinci Code*, and coming up with an even racier storyline.

One of the most striking elements of *The Hearing Trumpet* is the way it reworks not just the purpose, but also the condition, of being a later-life female. Robert believes Marian is living a kind of half-life, locked inside a body that doesn't function properly any more. In fact, she is perfectly poised to uncover the deepest wisdom humanity can access, and it is the very attributes Robert sees as weaknesses that make her so receptive to that wisdom. Older women, far from being superfluous to humanity, turn out to hold the keys to its salvation; and the truths they will uncover are ones no-one else, and certainly not young men like Robert, can get anywhere near.

Later-life women combine female intuition, lived wisdom and insightful logic: they are perhaps the only human creatures to bring these elements together, which is why Leonora believed they are pivotal in the human story. This is revolutionary feminism, and like all the best revolutionary feminism it is as liberating for men as it is for women.

All her life, Leonora was a searcher; and she believed that searching effectively meant discounting nothing and no-one. 'There are so many questions,' she wrote, 'and so much Dogmaturd to clear aside before anything makes sense, and we are on the point of destroying the Earth before we know anything at all. Perhaps a great virtue, curiosity can only be satisfied if the millennia of accumulated false data are turned upside down. Which means turning oneself inside out and to begin by despising no thing, ignoring no thing – and make some interior space for digestive purposes.' At another point, she wrote that: 'A nameless, unknown force operates in the soul, or a pre-form of life that perhaps effects miracles, if miracles are allowed ... and the only thing that I can allow myself is to be myself. Awareness liberates permission and permits the miracle.'

For a quarter of a century after 1943, when she arrived there with Renato Leduc, Leonora's searching took place in Mexico. But then a horrific and shocking event took place that changed her relationship with her adopted home, and meant that for the next twenty-five years she would base herself elsewhere.

It was 1968, and like everyone else in Mexico Leonora was keenly aware of the preparations being made for the country's first-ever hosting of the Olympic games, due to open that October. The government had sunk millions of dollars into the preparations for the games, and President Gustavo Díaz Ordaz was desperate for his country to appear united and organised in the glare of the world's spotlight. But as in other cities across the globe, it had been a summer of unrest: there had been student demonstrations and strikes across the city, and the protests culminated in a stand-off on 2 October in the square in the mainly poor neighbourhood of Tlatelolco. Ten thousand were gathered there, and tanks and troops were surrounding them; at first, the mood was friendly. But then, suddenly, the government forces opened fire; the exact number killed has always been the subject of controversy, but it is likely the dead numbered around three hundred and fifty. As athletes from around the world began to pour into the country for the opening ceremony a few days later, the scene of the massacre was sealed off, bodies were hurriedly disposed of and the whole thing was hushed up as far as possible.

Leonora was appalled: her sons Gabriel and Pablo were students at the university, which exacerbated how keenly she felt the fall-out from the violence. Like most left-leaning intellectuals in Mexico she was well aware of heavy-handedness in the country's government, but this took things to a new, and shocking, level. Her close friend Octavio Paz put what happened into the wider context of the country's troubled history. 'The deeper meaning of the protest movement,' he wrote, was 'the revelation of that dark half of man that has been humiliated and buried by the morality of progress: the half that reveals itself in the images of art and love.' The student protestors had

been stunned into silence by the severity of the government's strike and the horrific outcome; now, in the days
and weeks following, the older generation took back the
torch and began to mobilise, holding meetings to plan the
next move against a government that had become mesmerised with Western success, and deaf to the cries of its
own people. Leonora, who had never got involved with
politics in Mexico before, attended meetings at which a
fight-back was being discussed; but government spies were
out, and she had enemies in Mexico as well as friends. One
of these denounced her to the authorities and, having been
alerted to the fact that she was now in danger and might be
arrested, she decided to flee the country. Chiki had never
left Mexico since arriving there in 1942, and he never had a
passport; and in any case, he was not in danger. As so often
in her life, Leonora did her running away alone.

In a letter written in January 1969 to Norah Horna, Kati
and José Horna's daughter, Edward James described what
happened next. Leonora had, he told Norah, many influential friends in Mexico, including the actress Maria Felix,
a good friend who was close to the president. But even
these well-connected friends 'could not save her completely
from the mess' and 'when she heard that she was in danger
of being arrested as a political agitator, she leaped on to a
plane and flew at first to Louisiana; she got off in fact at
the first stop on Pan American airlines north from Mexico.
This is New Orleans, where she stayed – waiting to hear
how things developed in Mexico. In New Orleans she thus
remained waiting for one month and a half ... she seems
to have ... waited to hear if things would blow over and if

it would be safe for her to return to Mexico. But evidently the news she got from Mexico City was not reassuring enough; so – instead of returning after that month and a half in New Orleans – she flew on to New York.'

Leonora did eventually return to Mexico City later that year, but only to visit: for the next twenty-five years she would base herself in the United States, living first in New York and later in Chicago. Now in her early fifties, she was hungry for new experiences and a new vantage-point from which to observe life.

It was not an easy existence. She lived in rented apartments, always alone. There were basement flats and upstairs flats; one condominium she inhabited for a while was on the edge of New York's Gramercy Square, home of the eponymous hotel that would later become the base for musicians including the Beatles, Bob Marley and the Rolling Stones; it amused Leonora that she had been a trail-blazer, frequenting it long before any of them. 'I went there before any of them,' she boasted to me on one occasion as we sat chatting over our tea in her kitchen in Mexico City. 'No-one else was there when I started to go there. I just loved the place. I loved the park. There were lots of old ladies living there at the time.'

Gloria Orenstein, who encountered Leonora for the first time in New York in 1971, called her 'the most magical friend I ever had', and the most intelligent and multi-talented woman she ever met. As in Mexico, Leonora spent her time in New York, and later in Chicago, exploring esoteric interests that included alchemy and Tibetan Buddhism. She was also, Orenstein remembered when we met at Leonora's house on one of my visits, fascinated by the women's liberation movement, then in its heyday: the two friends attended rallies together, meeting, among others, Betty Friedan. Leonora was always aware that, though her own existence in Mexico was relatively unencumbered by misogyny, the country around her was one in which women were frequently oppressed, and she wanted to pass on the ideas she was getting in America to friends in Mexico, which she did on her visits there. In 1972, she designed a poster for the Mexican women's liberation movement called Mujeres Conciencia (Women of Conscience).

The growth of feminism brought, in the 1970s, a reappraisal of the place of women in the Surrealist movement, led by the Californian art historian Whitney Chadwick: there were articles in journals and conferences, and a feeling that the experiences of women like Leonora, and Leonor Fini, and Lee Miller – the reluctant muses – needed to be re-evaluated, with far more emphasis on the work they produced and less on the effect their lives had on the great men of art. But what much of this academic searching failed to recognise was that Leonora was still living out her response to having escaped being a *femme-enfant* in the 1930s: she was on a surreal journey all her life, and her solo wanderings across North America through the 1970s and 1980s were as much a part of that as anything that had gone before. As always in her life, Leonora's decision to base herself in the US in her fifties and sixties was a rejection of a more materially attractive, but less challenging, path: she had an almost pathological aversion to anything resembling a comfort zone, and that instinct was as strong in mid-life as in her youth. Just as in her twenties and thirties, taking the uphill option brought hardships; just as in those earlier decades, they were difficulties Leonora recognised as the price she had to pay for autonomy. So her New York years were a time of poverty, perhaps the greatest poverty in a lifetime of rejected wealth. One of the many books on her shelves in her house in Mexico City was called *How to Survive in New York on a Dollar a Day*, and she told me she used to eat ice cream because it was the cheapest way to get some calories inside her.

Throughout Leonora's long sojourn in the United States she and Chiki remained married; indeed they were still married when he died in 2007 (he was alive the first time I went to visit Leonora). But like so much in Leonora's life, the boundaries were blurred. She felt very strongly that it was best for her children that she had stayed with their father; but she was, as she had always been, a woman of passion, and there were love affairs, some with prominent figures in Mexican society, others with people she encountered in her daily life in Colonia Roma. She believed her romantic attachments were her own business, nothing to do with anyone else; she believed in love, but she did not believe in marriage break-up at any price. In many ways, there was no reason to dismantle her marriage to Chiki: they accommodated one another, they were fond of one another and they were respectful of one another. Leonora was far too much of a Surrealist to allow bourgeois ideas about marriage to dominate her choices; she was never exactly a proponent of free love, but she was certainly not someone who could or would have allowed herself to be shackled by the conventions of marriage. Her extra-marital relationships inspired her in her art; some were with intellectuals whose opinions she valued highly. She had an affair with the Nobel prize-winning author Octavio Paz in the 1950s, during a period in which the two worked on a play together, him writing and her designing the costumes and stage sets.

As usual, Leonora managed through these years to sabotage the possibility of becoming more widely known. After a quarter of a century in Mexico, she was at last being taken seriously by the art world there; her move to New York was spectacularly unhelpful. She had no gallery in the US, although she did eventually persuade the Brewster Gallery to represent her; and in fact, she was at times so badly off that the owner of the gallery paid the rent on her apartment.

Despite being almost entirely estranged from our family during these decades, Leonora continued to return to her roots in her art. Sitting alone in her flat in New York she remembered her childhood holidays at Moate in County Westmeath, Ireland, with her grandparents: it might have been half a century later, and she might have been thousands of miles away in New York, but she could still remember Granny's vast, cavernous kitchen with its huge range, and she could still smell the wafting scent of her cooking. The room was mysterious and magical; in her memories it was bathed in a crimson glow, but rather than symbolising warmth and safety, the colour seems to have been linked more to a blood-red warning of underworld currents and dangers that lurked in the shadows. That, certainly, seems to be the message of the painting that resulted: *Grandmother Moorhead's Aromatic Kitchen* (1975), a work that is both humorous and ominous, with a trinity of hooded cooks waiting at the table, and an outsize white goose strolling into the scene. One of the cooks is wielding a knife: but is the goose their prey, or are they his? The painting has all the ambiguities that are the hallmark of Leonora's work; and also, it straddles the two halves of her life, since she has placed the staple ingredients of Mexican cuisine – corn, peppers, garlic – on the table of a kitchen in rural Ireland. Surviving members of my father's generation remember the kitchen; but the only person who could have put those ingredients there was Leonora. She might have left our family, but they never left her; and more importantly, there was part of herself that was still very firmly anchored there, and wanted, if not to return, then certainly to be acknowledged in our family story.

Leonora's peripatetic lifestyle was not anchored to existing friendships, as many people's wanderings are: instead of seeking out people she knew, her irrepressible sense of adventure led her to pitch up in cities where she knew no-one, and to look for new friends once she arrived. She met fellow artist Karena Karras when the two found themselves having a cigarette outside an exhibition opening in Chicago; Karras told me she became Leonora's closest friend in the city. This was the late 1980s and at this point, Leonora told her she did not miss Chiki and was not planning to return to Mexico. She was living at the time in a small apartment in a three-storey building in the Oak Park area of the city; there was little sense, remembered Karras, of her having spent much time or effort on the decoration or look of her living space. Since she was lonely, and never precious about her talents, Leonora even joined the Oak Park Art League – although this ended badly when the teacher at the drawing class made the mistake of thinking she could improve on her work. 'Leonora said, if you touch my pencil I'll poke your eye out,' remembered Karras.

In the end it was Chiki, the man who had been in the shadows of her life for so long, who influenced Leonora's return to Mexico. His health was deteriorating; they were both getting older, and she made the decision to return. Maybe she would have gone back anyway, eventually: she had never really missed Mexico, but she needed some-where more permanent than a series of glorified bed-sits in which to live out the last decades of her life; decades which, Leonora knew, were going to be as much of an adventure as her earlier years, and every bit as much on her own terms.

12

Kron Flower

The morning of 19 September 1985 brought one of the most terrifying and shocking events of Leonora's life. She was in Mexico City when the ground began to shake violently beneath her feet; it felt, she said later, as though the planet itself was in rebellion. It was a massive earthquake with a magnitude of 8.0; and it churned up the capital, leaving at least five thousand dead and the city devastated. Cuauhtémoc (pronounced 'Kwowtemoc'), the borough in which Leonora lived, was one of the most severely affected: her own house was unscathed, but Kati Horna's in a nearby street was badly damaged and many other friends were left with their homes in ruins.

Repairing Mexico's wrecked buildings and shattered pavements would take many years; when I walked down her road to meet Leonora in 2006, one of the first things I noticed was the jagged edges of the concrete slabs underfoot, and the dilapidated building opposite Leonora's house, which she later told me had been ripped apart by the earthquake and never rebuilt. The city was left crumbling, its walls and pavements cracked. To Leonora, over the years that followed, those lines etched into the concrete and bricks seemed to mirror her own condition. Her friend Remedios Varo, like many women, had feared old age; in the end, she died without experiencing it. Leonora, though, was different: she was not afraid, in mid-life, of the years ahead of her, or even of the physical and psychological changes they would bring. They were an equal part of the adventure that was life; and as someone who had always had an intrinsic fear of anything resembling a comfort zone, she intended to go on making challenging choices, as long as she had the ability to choose.

There was another reason too why later life was appealing. Being a great beauty had often felt more of a burden than a blessing, and part of Leonora felt relieved to cast off the discomforting role of femme fatale. Her looks had singled her out, drawing eyes to her when she would rather have been anonymous. She had an effortless sex appeal, and men were mesmerised by her well into her sixties and beyond. Beauty, she wrote, had been 'a responsibility like anything else, beautiful women have special lives like prime ministers but that is not what I really want, there must be something else ...'

Now she was free to pursue that something else: the liberation of a later life uncomplicated by love affairs. It felt like a relief, she told me: although her affairs had brought inspiration and passion right through her life, she felt the weight of being in love as well as the headiness of it. Love affairs were consuming, demanding, distracting; sometimes they inspired her, at other times they contained her. And at some point in her late sixties, or early seventies, she realised, without regret, that this part of her life was behind her. Now she could be her protagonist Marian Leatherby, with adventures to come that would not be complicated by the existence of men who were in love with her. For a woman who had always sought the adventure of being free, there was a new frisson to the excitement of this stage of the journey.

She took up the themes of later-life womanhood on her canvases. *Kron Flower* (1987) shows three elderly women standing on a street, their cracked faces matching the earthquake-shaken paving stones. They are wearing black, and they are studying intently a red flower that has pushed its way up through the concrete. Meanwhile in *The Magdalen* (1986), a crone (Leonora loved that word) is placing a pill into the outstretched palm of a younger woman. Unusually, Leonora broke her own rules, and explained this to me: the tablet she is handing over, she said, is a contraceptive pill. In a matriarchal world, a woman's right to control her fertility would be sacramental.

Our history has been so skewed that we can hardly imagine anything different from the patriarchal world in which we live: and yet Leonora determined to try. Her painting *Tell The Bees* (1986), is a sunbeam of a work that reminds us there are some creatures who do live in a female-centred world. Stories about threats to the survival of bees were one of the many warning signs, to Leonora, of an era that was dangerously out of touch with whole swathes of its history, ecology and psyche.

The Leonora I knew in Mexico City in the last five years of her life was Marian Leatherby, on a personal and passionate quest for the Holy Grail. She was also the crone of her painting, trying to make sense of the new bloom. And she was the sage old Magdalen too: standing at the entrance to her cave, passing on her wisdom to the younger woman who had come to visit.

Alongside her wisdom there was a fragility that she sometimes acknowledged, but was not comfortable with; she had been used to hiding weakness for many years, and it was difficult for her now to have to accept it in any form. Around the time I got to know her, she was moving into that category of person who is truly ancient. The skin on her face was etched with deep lines, the notches of many years: she had looked out of that face for tens of thousands of days. Having rejected the idea of being a *femme-enfant* in Paris in the 1930s, she was having to accept in Mexico in the first decade of the twenty-first century that she was a different kind of *enfant*; a *vielle-enfant*. Just occasionally I catch that look in her face that my children had when they were tiny, when they needed protecting. And Leonora sometimes needed, sought protection. 'There's a journalist coming to interview me,' she told me one day. 'I wish I'd never agreed to it. Don't leave me, will you?' I reminded her that I, too, was a journalist, but she brushed that aside, as she always did: I was her *prima*, her cousin. Even when her memory was failing towards the end of her life and she forgot my name sometimes, she never forgot I was her cousin.

Leonora lived very much as Marian Leatherby had, in a house with a bedroom that 'looks on to the nice back yard ... I merely have to open the door in order to enjoy the stars at night or the early morning sun'. Marian's maid, Rosina, bears more than a passing resemblance to Yolanda, Leonora's housekeeper, and the two seemed to have a similar way of rubbing along together. 'I do not believe she puts me in a human category so our relationship is not disagreeable,' says Marian of Rosina.

Like Marian, Leonora saw old age as the culmination of her journey, rather than a slow decline into the twilight. She didn't claim to have all the answers; indeed, like Marian, she didn't believe she had even assembled all the questions. There were very few certainties in her life; but there were a few. One was that she had never been a muse, and that women should not allow themselves to be the handmaidens of men: and in surviving into her tenth decade, she was able to live out what amounted to a complete reversal of the earlier rejected role of Surrealist *femme-enfant*. In *The Hearing Trumpet*, she positively revels in the visual elements of later life that are so often seen as distasteful: Marian has a short, grey beard 'which many conventional people would find repulsive. Personally I find it rather gallant'. Like Frida Kahlo, who painted herself with a moustache of fine, dark hair, Leonora was never afraid to grasp a taboo and have fun with it.

While *The Hearing Trumpet* is on one level a preposterous romp, it's also a deadly serious reappraisal of a male-centric, youth-obsessed world; and it's a cri de coeur too from one of life's least explored, and yet universal, margins. In Leonora's hands, and in her living out of it, old age became a write-up rather than a write-off. Like Marian, Leonora not only survived old age but flourished in its wild and unpredictable landscape; as for Marian, it was as surreal and interesting as her earlier years.

A casual visitor to Leonora's house (not that there were many of those) might have thought its inhabitant's life, in her dark, chilly cave, was rather uneventful: it seemed, on first impression, like a house where life had already happened and was now wound down. In so many ways, Leonora's house was a throwback to other eras. The old black range from St Louis, reminiscent of the huge range that dominated her grand-mother's kitchen in Moate in County Westmeath, served as the telephone point in the hall-cum-dining room and was covered in yellow and pink Post-it notes on which she had written the important telephone numbers: doctor, dentist, handyman, friends. There were maquettes of her sculptures: a half-moon-shaped face at the top of the staircase, a miniature of the crocodile sculpture that stands in the centre of Mexico City, a monk-like figure, its face masked by its hood. And there were paintings, but mostly these were studies: most of her work had been sold, and her best pieces were not there. Family snaps, with pictures of her sons and five grandchildren, some of whom lived in America and weren't in Mexico very often, were arranged on shelves. And everywhere, in the public rooms and in Leonora's bedroom too, there were books: shelves and shelves of them, from art catalogues to shows long gone, to the latest novels by her favourite writers, Ian McEwan and Doris Lessing. Being a voracious reader set Leonora apart in our family, where book-lined rooms were not a common trait.

She had lived there for more than six decades, and every object, every item, had a past, and a place in her past. The table in the kitchen was the handiwork of José Horna; it was covered with a Liberty print tablecloth, on whose green peacock feath-ers sat a couple of boxes of biscuits and a packet of Twining's tea. With its brown enamel gas cooker and its big, rattling old fridge, the kitchen belonged in 1950s England: there were even picture magnets of the Manchester to Liverpool railway on the fridge door, reminders of the origins of the enigmatic woman who sat at its table. Taped to the wooden cupboard doors were postcards, including an image of the seventeenth-century portrait of the Cholmondeley Ladies, and two of her own paintings, *Bird Bath* and *The Magical World of the Mayans*.

Old age had not blunted Leonora's edge: she sat in her chair at that table like a hawk poised for its kill: ever-vigilant, ever-watchful, always on her guard. If she looked from the outside like an old lady fading into the twilight, that impression could not have been more wrong. Leonora in her eighties and nineties, when I knew her, was the warrior she had always been; and the battle she was facing now was the most demanding of her life. Death was near: it had seemed near once before, back in Santander; but then the risk had receded. With age came the certainty, the sure knowledge that she could not escape; and that knowledge coloured every day, every moment. Most of the time I spent with her we didn't do anything much at all: mostly we sat in the usual spot, at her kitchen table, our lunches and suppers interspersed with endless cups of tea.

Sometimes, for a change of scene, we moved to the book-lined upstairs sitting room where two battered sofas faced one another across the coffee table, and maquettes of her sculptures were dotted around the room. In the time I knew her she had all but stopped painting, although she did spend a few hours each week in her garage making sculptures, many of which seemed like 3-D versions of the creatures that inhabited her canvases.

Not many visitors breached the threshold to Leonora's kingdom, but there were some. One evening, on one of my early visits, Leonora announced that 'a young man' would be joining us for supper, and that I should arrive early. But when the doorbell rang, the person Yolanda showed into the kitchen was in his late seventies. I couldn't hide my amused surprise. 'Well,' said Leonora, 'everything is relative. To me, he *is* a young man.' He was a fellow artist, a French Canadian called Alan Glass. He lived round the corner and had been a friend of Leonora's for decades; every Saturday night he brought her a batch of his home-made fudge.

Her direct contemporaries were all dead by the time I knew her. The only other surviving member of the Surrealist circle, living in New York, was Max's widow Dorothea Tanning; but Leonora had never known Dorothea, and they had not been members of the Paris group at the same time. Edward James had died in 1984; more than twenty years later, Leonora told me that she missed him still. Kati died in 2000; and in 2007, a blow probably greater than Leonora had anticipated, Chiki died at the age of ninety-six. When she told me, on the phone, I could hear the shock in her voice: because now, she truly was the only one left of her generation.

During the time I knew her in Mexico City, the focus of Leonora's life was her sons, Gabriel and Pablo. Gabriel is married to Paty, and they have a son called Daniel. Gabriel also has two older children by his first wife, and they live in the US. Pablo and his wife Wendy have two sons, and are also grandparents.

There were two highlights to Leonora's life: her weekly lunches with Gabriel, and her frequent phone calls from Pablo. One day, when the phone rang at its usual time, she was so desperate to answer it and hear Pablo's voice that she tripped and ended up sprawled on the floor. I got down to help her up, but she shrugged me off saying, 'Answer the phone! Answer the phone, before he rings off . . .'

Lunch with Gaby was every Tuesday at 1pm, and usually involved a trip to a restaurant through the grinding traffic of Mexico City in Gaby's car. If I was in town I usually went along – it was an honour to be asked – and Paty was sometimes there too. But whoever else was round the table, the main conversation was always between Leonora and Gaby. Sometimes they discussed family news, sometimes an issue to do with a gallery or a painting; other times they would talk about a book they had both read, or some aspect of life or art. One of their favourite topics, described by Gaby in a booklet of his poems, concerned 'the visual domain . . . we agree that our contemporary visual world suffers from a disease, a disease of excess and the comfortable availability of images. We have lost the meaning of an internal vision because most visuality is processed by machines. The loss of visual meaning is becoming more severe.' Nothing made Leonora happier than a philosophical chat with one of her sons on a subject on which they were agreed; these were her best moments in the time when I knew her.

Apart from family there were occasional callers from the younger generation at the house in Colonia Roma, mostly wealthy Mexicans who bought her paintings and sculpture. Journalists were kept at bay; from time to time someone would get through the net and be politely rebuffed when they tried to question her about her life, her art and what it all meant. Leonora always steadfastly refused to enter into any discussion about what her work meant or might mean, either to herself or to anyone else. She believed it was up to the viewer to interpret it, and she did not believe there was a 'superior' way to interpret a painting. This refusal to talk about her work was part of the reason why, over the years, she garnered a reputation for being unco-operative. Of course, Leonora had always been unco-operative, all her life – the schoolgirl who would 'co-operate with neither work nor play' according to those nuns. But the art world cognoscenti had her wrong on this count: her failure to explain what she meant in her paintings was not down to contrariness, it was due to a genuine inability to verbalise what had emerged from her soul as a visual force. She told me it wasn't that she didn't want to talk about her paintings, it was that she *couldn't* talk about them: when she painted she was a conduit for the complex strands of her own history and everyone's history, for her own spirituality and everyone's spirituality, for the truths, half-truths and legends of the human story, and everything in between. It was an optical stream of consciousness, and the strands were so complicated, tangled and intertwined – a kind of artistic DNA – that they simply defied articulation. Leonora's work was what it was. Metaphorically it hung alone on the wall: no labels, no explanations. 'You're trying to intellectualise something, desperately, and you're wasting your time,' she warned me on one occasion. 'To make it into mini-logic ... you never understand by that road.' How then should one respond to art? 'By your own feelings,' she told me. In other words, you stand in front of a painting or a piece of art and you listen to what it says to you emotionally. There's no other way, no better way, no *alternative* way to assess what you make of a piece of art.

Hidden away in her cave, she seemed not quite to believe that there were people out there who were fans of her work, people who raved about her and who loved not only her paintings, her books and her sculpture, but also her story, her attitude to life, her tenacity, her rebellion.

She had always been closeted away in Mexico with the European set, but in the last decade of her life she was almost invisible on the arts scene and, almost inevitably, a kind of mythical status grew up around her. She was the eccentric English artist who dressed from head to toe in black, who lived a reclusive and solitary life, and with whom it was almost impossible to get an audience. She became increasingly nervous of strangers, which was unfortunate because, given the aura around her, they were almost always nervous of her too; this sometimes led to uncomfortable meetings around the table in her house. Her sometimes impenetrable (to Mexicans) wit seemed to isolate her further; because she made jokes without any hint of laughter or amusement, many people were unsure whether what she was saying was in jest or serious (usually it was a joke). Her anger was legendary, and for good reason: many fall-outs were never patched up, and once she made her mind up about someone it was almost impossible to get her to change it. Artist Pedro Friedeberg, famed for his *Hand Chair*, and for his saying that 'Art has died, after Surrealism there is nothing new', was part of Leonora's inner circle for many years until the day he made the mistake of telling her, not altogether seriously, that there were no great women artists because women could not produce great art. 'I threw him out of the house,' Leonora told me, 'and I never had him back.' Some years later I met Friedeberg myself, and he confirmed the story.

Occasionally, when she was feeling tired or unwell, I sat with Leonora beside her bed while she rested. Just recently I have come to realise that what I was doing, through all these hours and days we spent together, was simply being alongside her while she waited. A great deal of her life, she said to me, had been spent waiting, and she was not even sure now what she had actually been waiting for. This time, though, there was no doubt.

Death makes pioneers of us all, whether we like it or whether we don't. Leonora had been a lifelong pioneer, but she had also been a lifelong rebel: and this was the one stage of her journey when rebellion was futile. And so, almost inevitably, she struggled. Sometimes she was terrified at the prospect of dying; at other times, she seemed resigned to its inevitability. What she never did was hide behind platitudes or euphemisms. Death was close, and she did not flinch from that uncomfortable truth. What lay beyond death was a question we often talked about: in what form, if any, would she go on? Boundaries had been her lifelong fascination: this was the final boundary – perhaps – and she puzzled over it, wondered about it and mused on it.

So much about Leonora's life in the time I saw her often was to do with the final transition she was preparing to make. One afternoon we spoke about it for hours, and the next day she was waiting at the door to tell me something very important. 'I had the most extraordinary dream – I dreamt I was dead. Can you imagine it, to dream you are dead? I was dead, and I was swimming through this water, I was under the water. And I suddenly realised that it felt all right. It felt safe . . . it felt free. I wasn't frightened.'

She paused a moment.

'In fact, to my surprise I found I was rather enjoying it.'

She was happy then; and that day was one of the best we ever spent together.

She had always been good at keeping the balance between the big stories of the world outside and the mundane events around her. Most of the time we talked, not about art, but about the present: about Mexican politics, Mexican drug cartels, American presidents and the Mayor of Mexico City, and the extraordinary phenomenon of bird flu, which in 2008 transformed the country overnight into what felt like a field hospital with a vast face mask-wearing personnel. We talked about Britain too: about Tony Blair and the Labour party, about Princess Diana and the Royals. One time she talked about 'the new Queen' and I laughed, thinking how extraordinary it was that there was anyone alive who still thought of our elderly monarch as 'new'... but then I realised, with a jolt, that she was actually referring to the *Queen Mother*, who ascended to the throne with her husband King George VI a few months before Leonora left England in 1937. Her life experiences reached so far back that it was hard to grasp she had actually been around so long; in a tribute after her death, the novelist Sam Leith called Leonora 'a living fossil from the early twentieth century, swimming quietly in a distant sea'. He was right, with the proviso that what made her even more remarkable was that she was still swimming with such energy and elegance. And it was a testament to her determination to always live in the present moment that, despite being someone who had lived through so many genuinely fascinating experiences, with a personal history peppered with some of the twentieth century's biggest names, she preferred to talk about contemporary politics, or global warming, or the latest novel she'd read.

Leonora was remarkably resilient in old age, which made

it feel as though she would go on for ever. One time I arrived in Mexico City to find she had suffered a fall and was in Chiki's old wheelchair; she was spending all her time on the first floor, where her bedroom was, and I wondered whether she would ever make it downstairs again. But a few months later, when I visited again, things were exactly as they had been before the fall: despite being in her nineties, she had mustered the energy to get back on track. She had every intention of living to be a hundred: she looked forward to it, spoke about it and was planning for it. Sometimes she liked to exaggerate how close she was to it.

'I'm almost a hundred, you know that?'

'No you're not – you're barely into your nineties.'

'Well, I'm going to get there anyway. Remind me how old my mother was when she died?'

'She was in her early nineties … I think she was ninety-two … '

'Well. I'm certainly going to be older than that when I go. I'd like to be a hundred.'

So when she got pneumonia, at the beginning of May 2011, I knew it was serious, but I thought: *Leonora will survive, she's not a hundred yet.* Hearing she had been moved to hospital made it more worrying; but she would bounce back, she always did. She'd be back at home soon with her beloved Maltese terrier, Yeti, and there to meet me when I next visited.

But when I spoke to her daughter-in-law, Gaby's wife, Paty, the news was bad. Leonora was fading, she told me. Needless to say, she wasn't going to die without a struggle; she had never gone anywhere quietly, she wasn't the kind of person who would slip away. Also, both her sons were now with her.

They were the great loves of her life, and I knew she would do everything in her power to stall having to leave them.

I thought of her often over the next few days. She was facing the culmination of the battle we had spoken about so much over the last five years; she was in the eye of the storm now. Rebellion was useless, but she couldn't help hanging on. Tenacity, or bloody-mindedness, call it what you will, had always been one of her greatest strengths.

But on 25 May I found a text on my phone. 'They're saying on the news that Leonora is dead,' said a friend in Mexico City. 'Can it be true?' And I knew straight away that it was.

It isn't tragic to die aged ninety-four; but her loss was deeply painful. Like Marian Leatherby in *The Hearing Trumpet*, she had never managed to make the journey back to her roots. She had visited England, of course, occasionally; but not, by the time I knew her, for many years. And returning home had never brought forgiveness, or reconciliation, or closure. The wound Leonora opened on the day in 1937 when she set off to Paris to join Max Ernst was still an open wound on the day in 2011 when she died.

She had chosen, with her eyes wide open, a difficult life. I suspect she would entirely concur with her fellow artist Georgia O'Keeffe, who said she had been absolutely terrified every moment along the way, but that fear had never stopped her doing a single thing she wanted to do. I once told Leonora she was the bravest person I had ever known: she told me that she was not brave because she had so often been frightened. But that *is* bravery, I said, to carry on even when you're scared. She put her head on one side like a bird, the way she sometimes did, and she pondered it.

And then, in that acutely honest way of hers, she seemed to agree. 'You might be right,' she said.

It seemed desperately sad, though, that the stirrings of appreciation of her art had come so late in her long life. She had never created art with the expectation that it would be advantageous to her, either financially or in terms of critical acclaim: but all the same, it seemed hard that, by the end of her life, paintings that she had sold for a few hundred dollars in the 1940s and 50s were changing hands for hundreds of thousands of US dollars. By the time I knew her Leonora was not poor, though she had known poverty in earlier decades of her life; but she was certainly not wealthy either, and she still worried about money.

And then there was the fame, and the appreciation. Like any great artist, Leonora knew that there should be nothing people-pleasing about creating art; but like every human being, she was flattered to hear she had created something that someone admired, or that meant something to someone. Art is all about communication, as she once told me: so if an artist succeeds in communicating, that's success. Therefore she was always pleased to hear when people were moved by or interested in her paintings and her other work; but by the time it was thousands of people all over the world, she had begun to retreat into her lair, her cave, and she seemed not quite to believe it when I told her how many fans she had out there, or how much her work meant to them. And that was a shame; and it seemed particularly a shame now she was gone, and there was so much she would never know.

Because Leonora was dead. She had done one more brave thing, the brave thing we all have to one day do. She had broken another boundary. She had moved on to another universe, one of those connected yet unseen universes that her art was all about.

She was buried the following day, and I watched some TV footage on the internet of her funeral. Leonora was a tiny woman, but her coffin looked huge. It was transported through the city in a sleek, silver hearse; it seemed at times to be careering speedily through Mexico City, with photographers and outriders swooping in at every traffic light. If we had watched it together in her house we would have laughed for ages, and she would have said (as she so often did), 'Only in Mexico!'

But she wasn't there. I would never have Leonora to laugh with again.

When the cortège reached the cemetery gates Leonora's two sons, Gabriel and Pablo, got out of their car and walked, with their arms around one another's shoulders, behind the hearse as it made its way to the plot where their mother was to be buried. That would have meant so much to her: her boys, and their support for one another, were everything to her.

Leonora was an unstoppable adventurer, and I like to think that when the time finally came she embraced death with the same gusto and enthusiasm that she embraced all her other adventures. In my favourite of all her paintings, *The House Opposite* (1946) there's a tiny figure in the bottom right-hand corner, almost invisible, swimming out of the frame. Whenever I look at that painting, I think not of the Leonora of the past, but of the Leonora of today. Because that's surely where she is now. Swimming in another universe; swimming strongly and resolutely; and swimming against the tide, just as she always did.

Postscript

The Giantess

The Airbus banks steadily left, and the big brown eyes of the little Mayan girl sitting next to me open wide, before her face relaxes into a smile as she looks down at the vast city below. We are flying into Benito Juarez Airport in Mexico City from Cancún. It will be a few minutes until we land, but we've already been flying over an urban landscape for some time. When Leonora arrived three quarters of a century ago, this was a conurbation of around two million. Today, more than 21.2 million people live here; and its vastness sprawls out below us as we descend. At first the buildings and roads are tiny shattered pieces of mosaic; then they become recognisable as houses and factories, sports grounds and skyscrapers; and then, for the last minute or so before touchdown, there's a flash of bright Frida Kahlo Technicolor: pinks and blues, greens and turquoises, the signature colours of this city.

'Have you been to Mexico Sid-ee before?' asks the Mayan mom, as we wait for the plane to reach the gate; and I give an answer I couldn't possibly have anticipated ten years ago. 'Oh yes,' I say. 'Many, many times.'

Because between 2006 and 2011, when Leonora died, I returned here twice each year. I had found an excuse to keep returning, which was an exhibition of her work – the first in the UK for two decades – that I helped organise. The show, *Surreal Friends*, included not only Leonora's work but also that of Kati and Remedios: three women whose work deserved much wider attention. It ran at Pallant House Gallery in Chichester in the summer of 2010, before moving to the Sainsbury Centre for Visual Arts in Norwich that autumn. Many of the works in the exhibition were borrowed from private collectors in her adopted country and it seemed fitting that Leonora, who had carved out her career in Mexico, was now being loaned back to us from there. The truth about her was that she didn't belong to anyone or any country; but Mexico gave her a home when she needed one, and she was always grateful for that. She was pleased with the idea that her work would be seen again in the country of her birth, and she was delighted when the Tate admitted they had neglected her.

Whenever I was in Mexico, I spent every day with Leonora. It never felt like a chore, and she never felt like an elderly relative: even in her nineties, she managed to be ageless. Some days we took Yeti for a walk round the block; often, we ventured out for lunch to her favourite restaurant, Sanborns. It's a ubiquitous mid-market chain eaterie where the waitresses wear kitsch multicoloured skirts, and the food is uninspiring and frequently inedible; Leonora loved it, because unlike the more chi-chi restaurants that were springing up in her neighbourhood, where she would inevitably attract attention as the mysterious reclusive artist, in Sanborns she would always be safe. The other diners were not from the arty, intellectual middle-classes who knew who Leonora was; they were working-class Mexicans on family days out, or office workers grabbing a quick lunch. They neither knew nor cared who the black-clad Englishwoman was; she could sit in the middle of the room, and she would never be bothered by anyone. Sanborns was like so many other places she had sought out in her life: an unlikely backdrop that allowed her the space to be the person she wanted to be.

Other days we stayed in the house, sitting at the kitchen table where she had spent so many hours with Chiki and their sons, and with Remedios Varo and Kati Horna, and with Edward James. Or we sat upstairs on the sofas, in the room where she once held parties with friends like Octavio Paz and Maria Felix. Sometimes we didn't speak much; other times, we chatted for hours. On occasions she took me on expeditions to other parts of her kingdom. Her studio, which had filled Edward with such hope all those years ago. The roof garden, where the inscrutable, Spanish-speaking Yolanda hung out the washing. A locked bedroom, where Leonora kept the only three of her paintings that still belonged to her.

Leonora was great fun to be with, even in her nineties.

She had a brilliantly wicked sense of humour; she could run rings round unsuspecting Mexicans, and often did. She had never stopped being mischievous; she couldn't help herself, and she didn't want to try. One afternoon we spent a long time discussing the Surrealist manifestos; there were two of these, in 1924 and 1929. We had quite a serious chat about their content and their significance; and at some point, Leonora asked me if I had a notebook in my bag, and asked to borrow it. Later, when I got home, I remembered her writing in it, and looked to see what she had written. She often liked to write in mirror writing – it was one of her trademarks, an affectation the nuns had regarded, apparently, as a sign of her devilishness. I wasn't surprised to see that she had written me a message in mirror writing, but when I held it up to the mirror to see what she'd written, I laughed out loud at what she'd said: 'I never read the Surrealist manifesto.' I have it still, in my notebook.

Another afternoon it rained solidly (it was in August, when it's often rainy in Mexico City); we sat in a room on the first floor at the front of the house, on the wall of which curled a series of magnificent serpents, the subject of a series of tapestries she had designed in the 1960s. I told her how much I liked them; despite never wanting to discuss it, Leonora always enjoyed hearing that her work brought others pleasure. 'Do you know what the gold leaves behind the snakes are?' she asked. I confessed I did not. 'Marijuana,' she flashed, wickedly. 'They're marijuana plants.'

Leonora always made me feel at home in her house; she

understood what I was doing in Mexico, because she knew that, like her, I was following my heart and embracing the adventure. She knew that I wanted one day to write a book about her; but at some point along the journey, that ceased to be a very important part of why I was there. Her only stipulation was that no book should be published until after her death; that suited me fine, I told her, because it meant I had an excuse to go on visiting her. One day she said told me that there weren't many people she trusted, but that she trusted me. It wasn't something she had ever expected to say to a relative from her birth family; it meant, and still means, a great deal to me.

In her last couple of years her memory was fading, and as older people sometimes do, she took refuge in the poetry she remembered from her childhood and youth. Reciting it was like a safe port in a storm: she could speak confidently, and she could enjoy holding the floor and being a performer. Lewis Carroll had always been a favourite; one of the rhymes she often recited was from *The Walrus and the Carpenter*.

> *The time has come, the Walrus said,*
> *To talk of many things:*
> *Of shoes — and ships — and sealing wax —*
> *Of cabbages — and kings*
> *And why the sea is boiling hot*
> *And whether pigs have wings.*

We discussed many things, through those long, dark afternoons and evenings in her house: but one subject we returned to, time and again, was the condition of being a woman. Why had women found it so difficult to achieve what they could, and should, have achieved in their lives? Why had it been comparatively easy for women to become great writers, but so hard for them to be great painters? Leonora defied categorisation, and refused to allow herself to be called anything with an 'ism' as its ending; but it was hard not to see her as a feminist. Why women didn't achieve more with their lives, she maintained, was because too often the men in their lives – fathers, lovers, husbands, colleagues, friends – undermined them. Chiki, she said, had never undermined her: he respected her throughout their long marriage. That, she agreed, was worth a great deal.

More than anything else, what we mused on was simply the business of being human, and what it all meant. This, she told me, was the purpose of being an artist: it was to think about what life meant, although she didn't know if thinking about it more meant artists came up with any answers. 'Does anyone understand what it's all about?' she asked me one day. 'We never do. I suppose it's about relationships. It's about loving people. It's about having our children. It's about humour ... '

Friends in England sometimes asked if I was sorry I hadn't found Leonora sooner, so I could have had more time with her. That would have been good in some ways; but really, we met at the perfect time. It seemed like the right moment in her life to revisit her distant past as a member of our family; the past that had, more than anything else, made her the person and the artist she became.

Intrigued and thrilled as I was by her story, and touched as I was by her willingness to share it with me, I was also pleased that I could give something back. Because she was interested, even after all those years, perhaps especially after all those years, in how things had panned out in our family. 'What happened to so-and-so?' she would occasionally ask; and then, when I told her whom he or she had married, or what work he or she had done, she would chuckle and say: 'Really? I'd never have expected things would work out like that.'

I was forty-three when I travelled to Mexico for the first time; my middle years were beckoning, and with Leonora I was up close to someone who had revolutionised what that could mean, and would inspire me to do the same. What I learned from Leonora was that the passing of years need not mean making compromises: life can, should and will, if you allow it, be just as exciting, eventful and fun as your earlier years. The trick was to do as she had always done: to reject any notion of an easy life. This was a woman who got herself a puppy in her nineties, and who would hardly ever hold my arm when we walked along the uneven pavements of Colonia Roma. 'If I hold on to you today, I'll need someone to hold on to tomorrow and you won't be here,' she would say.

Greater fame was beckoning for Leonora in the years when I knew her, but she was still doing her best to fend it off. One day we were due to go to a glitzy lunch in the Centro Histórico in Mexico City; all the big names in the arts scene would be there, and I was going to look after Leonora. I was excited; I bought a new outfit and arrived at her house early that day – only to find her smoking a ciga-rette at the kitchen table and smiling broadly. 'Great news,' she said. 'I just had a telephone call to say I don't have to go after all. Shall we go to Sanborns instead?'

And while her house was never really part of Mexico, Mexico was constantly straining on the doorstep to get in. Rarely did a day pass by without the arrival, sometimes in a stream, of gifts from well-wishers and friends. One wealthy Mexican sent a loaf of artisan bread from one of the city's finest bakeries once a week; others sent cakes, or flowers, or tequila.

Understandably enough, Leonora enjoyed being remem-bered, enjoyed the attention. Sometimes she enjoyed the visitors, but often she didn't: she felt as though people wanted to take from her, that she was a commodity, a spec-tacle, a curiosity. She wasn't bored by her story, but she wasn't prepared to keep trotting it out for well-wishers; and there were some elements of it that it upset her to remem-ber, especially her time in Santander. She wanted to live in the present, but people (me included, on occasions) kept dragging her back into the past. And it *was* a fascinating past, and she was the last link to a spectacular moment in art history; and that came with responsibilities of which Leonora was aware.

Wider recognition came when, in February 2008, an exhibition of Leonora's sculpture opened on the main thor-oughfare in Mexico City, the Paseo de la Reforma. The wide central reservation of this busy street was festooned with pieces of her work: here, a tall figure holding aloft a fish; there, a tree-like creature with a diamond-shaped face;

a little further along, a chilling trio of hooded figures, their faces unseen. The exhibition continued for eight months; millions of Mexicans and tourists went to see it. One day I went there with Leonora, on our way to Sanborns. We were just another couple of visitors walking down the road, stopping from time to time to look at the art. At one place there was a series of huge billboards celebrating Leonora's life, with photographs of her from her youth and blown-up images of her most famous paintings; and reading the biographical notes about her early life, I was suddenly struck by the irony of it all.

'Can you imagine what your parents would have said if they had seen all this?'

She stopped for a minute and nodded her head. 'I think,' she said, 'they would have been a bit surprised.'

And then we laughed so much we had to sit down on a bench to recover. Because here was Leonora's answer to the words her father Harold had said that day back in 1937, when she told him she was leaving and he said that if she went off to be an artist she would die penniless and in a garret. Seventy years on, the people of a city Harold never visited, on the other side of the world, were paying his daughter homage. She had defied his expectations, and our family's expectations, that she would not be able to survive without them. Instead, she had flourished; and the hard road she travelled had brought her success not only on her own terms, but on the world's terms too – an unexpected side bonus.

Leonora was never wealthy, but she did not die penniless; and her paintings are now among a tiny minority of pieces by women artists that sell for millions of pounds or dollars. Much of her work remains locked in private collections, and she is woefully under-represented in the great galleries of London, Paris and New York. But an artist's life does not end with death, and her reputation may still be in its infancy. And although Leonora is nothing like as well known as she should be, she has a band of very dedicated followers: once people fall for her, they are usually smitten. Over the last few years she has garnered some important and influential followers whose own work has in turn been influenced by her. Madonna's high-art video *Bedtime Story* (1995), a copy of which is in the collection of New York's Museum of Modern Art, was inspired by work by Leonora and Remedios, and Madonna has acknowledged the debt she owes them. Björk, who wrote that song for Madonna, is another avowed fan of Leonora's work; so too is the English singer-songwriter Laura Marling, who has said Leonora's appeal lay in her refusal to be anyone's muse. Writers who have spoken of Leonora as an inspiration include the Scottish novelist Ali Smith, the novelist Chloe Aridjis, who knew her in Mexico, and the comedian Jenny Éclair, who pointed out that if Leonora had been a man, we'd probably all have heard of her. A younger generation of artists whose work links to Leonora's includes Lucy Skaer, a Turner Prize finalist in 2009, and Cathy Wilkes, whose work was exhibited alongside Leonora's at Tate Liverpool in 2015.

So, here I am, back in Mexico City. No Leonora to visit any more; but there is one place I have to go, the place where she is buried, the Panteón Británico, the British cemetery, in an area of the city called Tacuba. I catch a taxi in the street near her house. 'Never do this yourself,' she once told me, standing in the middle of the busy road with cars hurtling past, as she held up her umbrella to summon a cab, 'it's too dangerous.' But I do; and we lurch off into the usual appalling traffic, past her favourite Sanborns and out along a car-clogged three-lane road. It's a dry, hot day, and the sun is shining hazily, battling against the pollution, its rays weakened by the smog. The taxi is airless, and there's a faint smell, as there often is in Mexico City, of sewage.

The taxi driver doesn't seem to have a clue where the cemetery is, so the journey is another plunge into the unknown. As we pass graffiti-covered walls and the usual hotch-potch of Mexican architecture – here, a slum-like fifties apartment block, there, a handsome colonial-style, balconied house, next door to it, a sleek, glass office block – I'm struck again by how far Leonora came; how far she had to come, to live the life that was inside her.

Just as I'm giving up on us ever finding the cemetery, the driver announces, to his own surprise as much as mine: '*Estaban aqui!*', and we swing off the busy road and through heavy wrought-iron gates. I pay the driver, get out of the car and walk past the graves of people with suspiciously Spanish-sounding names – Juan Hernández Rivero, Rafael Ramínez, Cristina Silva Lopez. But no, it really is the British cemetery; and towards the end of the avenue of graves, here at last is Leonora's. Her stone is small and white, which feels right: she always liked small things. Nearby there's a crematorium; that means people are often milling about, and she liked being in the midst of people, so that feels right too.

Tributes from her sons are chiselled into the stone: 'I will always look into your eyes' from Gaby; and this from Pablo: 'Like a strong blinding light of imagination you came and you left us'. There are flowers too on the plot, to which I add my own bunch of white lilies. Leonora died in Mexico as she lived here, quietly and without fuss. But she is not forgotten.

Those five years I knew her have changed my life: every day is different because of her. I miss her, but I carry her spirit in my heart, and I try to be true to it.

When I think of Leonora now, I think of her as I knew her, sitting in her woollen jumper at the kitchen table in her chilly kitchen; the kitchen that should have been in Lancashire but was somehow in Mexico. I think of the fun and the conversations we had; I think of the laughter, and the adventure of knowing her. I think of the magic that swirled around her, and that swirls around all of us; Leonora was closer to that magic than most of us, and she pulled me into her magical orbit.

I think too of the question I occasionally asked her, because it fascinated me. Leonora had turned her back on a fortune and a comfortable life; she had run away from people who loved her; she had broken many hearts, both within our family and outside it. Had it all been worth it? If she could live her life over, would she make the same choices? Did she have any regrets? I thought there might be some.

But she was unequivocal. Given her time again, Leonora

said, she would do things the same. She had never taken the easy option; she had never compromised. Even when she was terrified, she was tough. The decisions she took had repercussions that were deeper, more seismic and more painful than she anticipated; but they were the decisions that reflected honestly what was in her heart. For her, there really was no other way.

Acknowledgements

Knowing Leonora and researching her story brought many new people into my life, directly and indirectly, and to many of them I owe a huge debt of gratitude for their friendship and support over the last ten years. Chief among them are Leonora's sons and their wives: Gaby and Paty, and Pablo and Wendy, all of whom have extended the same kindness and friendship to me as Leonora did.

Around Leonora's kitchen table I made new friends including Norah Horna (named after Leonora), daughter of Kati and José; French Canadian artist Alan Glass; Miguel Cervantes; Salomon Grimberg, Eva Marcovich, Miguel Escobedo and his late sister, Helen Escobedo, all of whom helped me piece together her life in Mexico. And then there was the wider circle, who extended friendship and advice: Teresa Arcq, Damian Fraser and Paloma Porraz in Mexico City, Mia Kim and Carmen Melia in New York, and Mat Holmes, Zaira Linan and the Gastalum family, especially Kako, in Xilitla. To all of them, I owe a huge debt.

In the UK I want to thank especially Adam Hogg, son of Leonora's great friend Joan Powell, who has become a great friend of mine; Tony Penrose, son of Lee Miller and Roland Penrose, who has always been supportive; Steven Reynolds, who showed me round his flat in Highpoint where Leonora and Max met for the first time; and Paul Martin at Crookhey Hall and Mark Fleuriot at Hazelwood Hall, who showed me around Leonora's former homes. In France I am indebted to Albert Neyron for his great kindness in showing me around Les Alliberts, the house Leonora and Max shared, and to Julotte Roche for talking to me about her research into their time in Saint-Martin-d'Ardèche. My thanks also to Seán Kissane of the Irish Museum of Modern Art in Dublin.

Many of our relatives have been supportive and helpful: in particular I want to thank Rupert and Helen Carrington, and Roger Carrington and his late wife Veronica, their daughter Fiona Carrington, Joe Carrington and Andrew Carrington. However, I want to make clear – and this applies to Leonora's family in Mexico, as well as to her family in the UK, that the story I am telling is Leonora's story, told in the way I believe she wanted it to be told. It is my interpretation of her story, and the input of others does not equate to their endorsement of it.

On one of my trips to Mexico in 2007 I was accompanied by Bob Pulley, then principal of West Dean College; Stefan van Raay, then director of Pallant House Gallery in Chichester, and Antonio Rodriguez. They shared an important part of this journey with me, and I am grateful for their friendship and the fun times we had, as well as for their professional support.

Acknowledgements

When it came to the idea of writing a book, I was extremely fortunate to have the support of Lennie Goodings at Virago even before she became my editor. Clever and wise, she guided me kindly and thoughtfully through the process of writing this book, and it would not have been the work it is without her input. I am also extremely grateful for the generous support of my agent, Clare Alexander.

My relationship with Leonora led me into a friendship with the community of West Dean College, the former home of her friend and patron Edward James, and I want to thank especially the chief executive Alex Barron and the trustees, who very kindly allowed me to stay in Edward's beautiful old house in the South Downs to write part of this book, and also Francine Norris, Sarah Hughes and Teresa Shergold.

My friends have learned a lot more about 1940s surrealism than they ever intended, and I cannot thank enough those who have always encouraged me in my journey towards and with Leonora, especially Peter Stanford, Brendan Walsh, Emma Burstall and Kathy Wittet. Many colleagues have been supportive too, in particular: Harriet Green, Mike Conway, Rosalind Lowe and Chris Lamb.

My late father, Michael Moorhead, had never really known Prim, as we all called her, and was bemused by my friendship with her, but also intrigued and helpful (maybe he thought there might be more to her story than he had been told). My mother, Doris Moorhead, has been, as she always is, unfailingly generous in her support, and always remembered to ask the most important question when I returned from Mexico: How is Leonora?

One friendship born of this project stands out for me: that with Catherine Petitgas. I have sometimes thought that if I had been able to make up a fairy godsister to guide me through this journey, she would look just like Catherine. When I needed an art historian, she was there; when I needed a French speaker, she was there; when I needed a companion for a fact-finding trip, she was there; when I needed help with funding, she was there. Catherine has been unfailingly generous to me and we have had many adventures together. I cannot thank her enough.

For my immediate family, my obsession (as they would say) with Leonora has an upside and a downside. On the upside: family trips to Mexico. On the downside: 'Mum, if you mention Leonora one more time I'm moving out' (they never did, of course). My husband Gary Smith held the fort on many occasions while I was away, and has always been generous in his support of what for him has often been a huge inconvenience; my daughters Rosie, Ellie, Miranda and Treenie have understood that a mother cannot always be at home. More than anything, I hope this book and its story illustrates for my daughters and girls like them the difference it makes to a woman's life to be bold, and brave, and to push ourselves way beyond our comfort zones.

And then there is the person this story is all about: Leonora Carrington, who I am so proud and so fortunate to be able to say was my cousin. She welcomed me into her life; she gave me a place at her table. She inspired and encouraged me; she shared her story, and she listened to mine. I hope our friendship changed her life, just a bit; and I know that for me it changed everything, and forever.

Additional Credits

Extracts from Leonora Carrington's *Down Below* and *Little Francis* reproduced by kind permission of The New York Review of Books.

Extracts from Leonora Carrington's letters to Pierre Matisse reproduced by kind permission of The Morgan Library & Museum, MA 5020, United States.

Extract from the Erno Goldfinger letter reproduced by kind permission of The Erno Goldfinger Papers, RIBA Collections.

Extracts from Edward James' letters reproduced by kind permission of West Dean College, part of the Edward James Foundation.

Extract from p.220 reproduced from *The Times*, October 1960.

Plate section 1
Leonora Carrington and Max Ernst, Lambe Creek, Cornwall, England, 1937, by Lee Miller © Lee Miller Archives, England 2016. All rights reserved. www.leemiller.co.uk

Four Women Asleep: Lee Miller, Ady Fidelin, Nusch Éluard and Leonora Carrington, Cornwall, England, 1937, by Roland Penrose © Roland Penrose Estate, England 2016. The Penrose Collection. All rights reserved. www. rolandpenrose.co.uk

E. L. T. Mesens, Max Ernst, Leonora Carrington and Paul Éluard, Lambe Creek, Cornwall, England, 1937, by Lee Miller © Lee Miller Archives, England 2016. All rights reserved. www.leemiller.co.uk

Lee Miller, Leonora Carrington and Max Ernst, Lambe Creek, Cornwall, England, 1937, by Roland Penrose © Roland Penrose Estate, England 2016. The Penrose Collection. All rights reserved. www.rolandpenrose.co.uk

Leonora Carrington and Max Ernst, Saint-Martin-d'Ardèche, France, 1939, by Lee Miller © Lee Miller Archives, England 2016. All rights reserved. www.leemiller.co.uk

The artists in exile, New York, 1942, in a photograph taken at Peggy Guggenheim's home. (From left to right) Front row: Stanley William Hayter, Leonora Carrington, Frederick Kiesler, Kurt Seligmann. Second Row: Max Ernst, Amédée Ozenfant, André Breton, Fernand Léger, Berenice Abbott. Third Row: Jimmy Ernst, Peggy Guggenheim, John Ferren, Marcel Duchamp, Piet Mondrian. © bpk/Münchner Stadtmuseum, Sammlung Fotografie/Archiv Landshoff

José Horna, Untitled [wedding of Leonora Carrington and Chiki Weisz at the home of Kati and José Horna, Mexico City], 1946. Seated from left to right: Kati Horna, Chiki Weisz, Leonora Carrington and Gunther Gerzso; standing by the window: Benjamin Péret and Marianne Frenkel. Gelatin silver print, 19.3 × 18.2 cm. Private collection, Mexico City. © 2005 Ana María Norah Horna y Fernández

Kati Horna, Untitled [from the series *Ode to Necrophilia*], 1962. Gelatin silver print, 20.3 × 20.3 cm. Private collection, Mexico City. © 2005 Ana María Norah Horna y Fernández

Leonora with her two sons, Gabriel and Pablo, by her husband, Chiki Weisz. Copyright © Estate of Emerick Weisz

Leonora in her home in Mexico City with the author, next to a maquette of *How Doth the Little Crocodile* and Yeti's tail. Copyright © Gloria Orenstein

Leonora in her studio in Mexico City in 2010, the year before her death. Copyright © Adriana Zehbrauskas

Plate section 2

The Giantess (The Guardian of the Egg), c. 1947, by Leonora Carrington (tempera on wood panel). Copyright © Estate of Leonora Carrington/ARS/Carrington, Leonora (1917–2011)/Private Collection/Bridgeman Images

Green Tea, 1942, by Leonora Carrington (oil on canvas). Copyright © Estate of Leonora Carrington/ARS

Leonora in the Morning Light, 1940, by Max Ernst (oil on canvas). Image courtesy of Sotheby's/© ADAGP, Paris and DACS, London 2016

Portrait of Max Ernst, 1939, by Leonora Carrington (oil on canvas). Copyright © Estate of Leonora Carrington/ARS

The House Opposite, 1945, by Leonora Carrington (tempera on panel). Copyright © Estate of Leonora Carrington/ARS

Crookhey Hall, 1947, by Leonora Carrington (casein on masonite). Private collection. (Also features on end papers.) Copyright © Estate of Leonora Carrington/ARS

The Robing of the Bride, 1940, by Max Ernst (oil on canvas). Ernst, Max (1891–1976)/Peggy Guggenheim Foundation, Venice, Italy/Bridgeman Images/© ADAGP, Paris and DACS, London 2016

Chiki, Ton Pays, 1947, by Leonora Carrington (oil on canvas). Copyright © Estate of Leonora Carrington/ARS

Grandmother Moorhead's Aromatic Kitchen, 1975, by Leonora Carrington (oil on canvas). Copyright © Estate of Leonora Carrington/ARS

Where to find the art of Leonora Carrington and her circle

Leonora painted hundred of works – every chapter in this book is named after a painting or a piece of writing by her – but they are scattered around the world, and many are in private collections, which is one of the reasons why she is not better known. However, there are galleries where you can see the paintings of Leonora and of other artists mentioned in this book.

In the UK and Europe

Tate Modern in London has Leonora's painting *Eluhim* (oil on canvas, 1960) on long-term loan. The word *Eluhim* is Hebrew for 'God', and the work features a horse-like creature and other fantastical creatures which are so often her hallmark. The Tate also has two drawings by Leonora. *Do You Know My Aunt Eliza* (ink on paper, 1941) is reminiscent of a ditty sung by Francis in Leonora's story *Little Francis*; *I am an Amateur of Velocipedes* (ink on paper, 1941), which dates from the same moment in her life, shows two figures on a one-wheeled bicycle, and may relate to a love of children's stories shared by Leonora and Max Ernst.

The Sainsbury Centre for Visual Arts in Norwich has two paintings by Leonora: *The Old Maids* (oil on board, 1947) and *The Pomps of the Subsoil* (oil on canvas, 1947).

The palazzo beside the Grand Canal in Venice where Peggy Guggenheim lived for the last decades of her life now houses her collection, including *Leonora's Oink* (1959). The two paintings by Max that relate to the love triangle of Leonora, Max and Peggy are also here: *The Robing of the Bride* (1940) and *The Antipope* (1941–2).

In the US

Leonora's *Self-Portrait*, or *The Inn of the Dawn Horse* (oil on canvas, 1937–8) is in the Metropolitan Museum in New York, in the Pierre Matisse Collection in Gallery 901. The museum also owns a costume design made by Leonora for her play *Penelope*, entitled *Fantastic Figure with Leaves* (gouache on board, 1959).

Max Ernst's *Two Children Are Threatened by a Nightingale* (oil on wood with painted wood elements, 1924) hangs in the Museum of Modern Art in New York. An image of this work in a book by Herbert Read was Leonora's introduction to Max. Ernst himself described this piece as the last example of his early collages, and 'a kind of farewell to a technique'; he said there were two possible autobiographical references for the nightingale, the death of his sister in 1897, and a hallucination in which a panel in his bedroom seemed to resemble the menacing nightingale, and a spinning top.

Grandmother Moorhead's *Aromatic Kitchen* (oil on canvas, 1975), inspired by her grandmother's kitchen in Moate in

County Westmeath, Ireland, and incorporating elements of Mexican cusine, is on show at the Charles B. Goddard Center for Visual Performing Arts in Ardmore, Oklahoma, USA.

Max's *Europe After the Rain* (oil on canvas, 1940–42) can be seen at the Wadsworth Atheneum Museum of Art in Hartford, and was painted during and after his break-up with Leonora. In the very centre of the landscape is a dark-haired young woman wearing a hat, who has turned her back on a bird-like figure with a spear, and is walking away from him.

The National Museum of Women in the Arts has one piece by Leonora: *Samhain Skin* (gouache on vellum, 1975). It relates to the ancient Celtic festival of Samhain, held on 31 October to celebrate the end of the summer.

In Mexico

Leonora's vast mural *El Mundo Mágico de los Mayas* (1963) is in the Anthropological Museum in Mexico City.

Her sculpture *How Doth the Little Crocodile* is on Paseo de Reforma in the centre of Mexico City.

Leonora's writing

The Hearing Trumpet, with an introduction by Ali Smith, is published by Penguin Modern Classics.

A new edition of *Down Below*, with an introduction by Marina Warner, is published by The New York Review of Books, as is a book of stories for children by Leonora, *The Milk of Dreams*.

Bibliography

Leonora Carrington: Surrealism, Alchemy and Art by Susan L. Aberth (Lund Humphries, 2004)

Angels of Anarchy: Women Artists and Surrealism, edited by Patricia Allmer (Prestel, 2009)

Max Ernst by Ulrich Bischoff (Taschen, 2005)

Surreal Lives: The Surrealists 1917–1945 by Ruth Brandon (Macmillan, 1999)

Lee Miller: On Both Sides of the Camera by Carolyn Burke (Bloomsbury, 2006)

Down Below by Leonora Carrington (The New York Review of Books, 2017)

The Hearing Trumpet by Leonora Carrington (Penguin Classics, 2005)

The House of Fear: Notes from Down Below by Leonora Carrington (Virago, 1989)

The Seventh Horse and Other Tales by Leonora Carrington (Virago, 1989)

Women Artists and the Surrealist Movement by Whitney Chadwick (Thames and Hudson, 1985)

Leonora Carrington: What She Might Be by the Dallas
    Museum of Art (Dallas Museum of Art, 2008)
Notes from A Not-So-Still Life by Jimmy Ernst (St Martin's, 1984)
*In Wonderland: The Surrealist Adventures of Women Artists in
    Mexico and the United States*, edited by Ilene Susan Fort
    and Tere Arcq with Terri Geis (Los Angeles County
    Museum of Art and DelMonico Books, 2012)
Leonora Carrington: The Talismanic Lens by the Frey Norris
    Gallery (Frey Norris Gallery, 2008)
The White Goddess by Robert Graves (Faber and Faber, 1961)
The Travel Books of Graham Greene: Journey Without Maps
    (Mercury Books, 1963)
Confessions of an Art Addict by Peggy Guggenheim (Andre
    Deutsch, 1960)
Frida: A Biography of Frida Kahlo by Hayden Herrera
    (Harper Perennial, 2002)
Grove Mill, Canal Mill & Botany Bay by Arthur C. Howell
    (The History Press, 2008)
Leonora Carrington: The Celtic Surrealist by the Irish Museum
    of Modern Art (Irish Museum of Modern Art and DAP,
    New York, 2013)
The Mexican Revolution 1910–20 by Philip Jowett &
    Alejandro de Quesada (Osprey Publishing, 2006)
Remedios Varo: Unexpected Journeys by Janet A. Kaplan
    (Abbeville Press, 2000)
Roland Penrose: The Life of a Surrealist by James King
    (Edinburgh University Press, 2016)
Surreal People: Surrealism and Collaboration by Alexander Klar
    (V&A Publications, 2007)
Kati Horna: Recuento de una obra by Emma Cecilia Garcia
    Krinsky (Fondo Kati Horna, 1995)

Leonora Carrington: The Mexican Years by The Mexican Museum (The Mexican Museum, San Francisco, 1991)

The Reflowering of the Goddess by Gloria Feman Orenstein (Pergamon Press, 1990)

Surreal Friends: Leonora Carrington, Remedios Varo and Kati Horna by Pallant House Gallery (Lund Humphries/ Pallant House Gallery, 2010)

The Surrealists in Cornwall by Antony Penrose (Falmouth Art Gallery, 2004)

Magnifying Mirrors: Women, Surrealism and Partnership by Renée Riese Hubert (University of Nebraska Press, 1994)

Max Ernst by John Russell (Thames and Hudson, 1967)

Surrealism in Exile and the Beginning of the New York School by Martica Sawin (MIT Press, 1995)

Leonora Carrington: Paintings, Drawings and Sculptures 1940–1990, edited by Andrea Schlieker (Serpentine Gallery, 1991)

The Essential Max Ernst by Uwe M. Schneede (Thames and Hudson, 1972)

Max Ernst: Frottages by Werner Spies (Thames and Hudson, 1969)

Max Ernst: Life and Work by Werner Spies (Thames and Hudson, 2006)

Ernst by Ian Turpin (Phaidon, 1993)

Leonora Carrington: Dibujo, pintura y grabado by Gabriel Weisz (Taller Grafica Bordes, 2007)

Leonora Carrington: A Mural in the Jungle by Gabriel Weisz (Xul Servicios SA de CV, 2008)

Index